THE ILLUSTRATED PRACTICAL BOOK OF
COUNTRY COOKING

THE ILLUSTRATED PRACTICAL BOOK OF
COUNTRY
COOKING

A CELEBRATION OF TRADITIONAL FOOD, WITH 170 TIMELESS RECIPES

SARAH BANBERY

LORENZ BOOKS

This edition is published by Lorenz Books, an imprint of
Anness Publishing Ltd, Hermes House, 88–89 Blackfriars Road,
London SE1 8HA; tel. 020 7401 2077; fax 020 7633 9499
www.lorenzbooks.com; www.annesspublishing.com

If you like the images in this book and would like to investigate
using them for publishing, promotions or advertising, please visit
our website www.practicalpictures.com for more information.

UK agent: The Manning Partnership Ltd; tel. 01225 478444;
fax 01225 478440; sales@manning-partnership.co.uk
UK distributor: Book Trade Services; tel. 0116 2759086;
fax 0116 2759090; uksales@booktradeservices.com;
exportsales@booktradeservices.com
North American agent/distributor: National Book Network;
tel. 301 459 3366; fax 301 429 5746; www.nbnbooks.com
Australian agent/distributor: Pan Macmillan Australia;
tel. 1300 135 113; fax 1300 135 103; customer.service@macmillan.com.au
New Zealand agent/distributor: David Bateman Ltd;
tel. (09) 415 7664; fax (09) 415 8892

Publisher: Joanna Lorenz
Project Editors: Amy Christian and Felicity Forster
Copy Editor: Catherine Best
Designer: Design Principals
Recipes: Pepita Aris, Catherine Atkinson, Alex Barker, Ghillie Başan,
    Georgina Campbell, Carla Capalbo, Miguel de Castro e Silva,
    Lesley Chamberlain, Carole Clements, Matthew Drennan,
    Jenni Fleetwood, Brian Glover, Christine Ingram, Bridget Jones,
    Lucy Knox, Janet Laurence, Sally Mansfield, Maggie Mayhew,
    Anna Mosesson, Keith Richmond, Rena Salaman, Jennie Shapter,
    Christopher Trotter, Suzanne Vandyck, Laura Washburn,
    Biddy White Lennon, Carol Wilson, Annette Yates
Photographers: Nicki Dowey, Ian Garlick, Amanda Heywood, Janine
    Hosegood, Dave Jordan, William Lingwood, Steve Moss, Craig Robertson
Proofreading Manager: Lindsay Zamponi
Production Controller: Wendy Lawson

ETHICAL TRADING POLICY

At Anness Publishing we believe that business should be conducted
in an ethical and ecologically sustainable way, with respect for the
environment and a proper regard to the replacement of the natural
resources we employ.

    As a publisher, we use a lot of wood pulp to make high-quality
paper for printing, and that wood commonly comes from spruce
trees. We are therefore currently growing more than 750,000 trees
in three Scottish forest plantations: Berrymoss (130 hectares/
320 acres), West Touxhill (125 hectares/305 acres) and Deveron
Forest (75 hectares/185 acres). The forests we manage contain more
than 3.5 times the number of trees employed each year in making
paper for the books we manufacture.

Because of this ongoing ecological investment programme, you,
as our customer, can have the pleasure and reassurance of knowing
that a tree is being cultivated on your behalf to naturally replace the
materials used to make the book you are holding.

    Our forestry programme is run in accordance with the UK
Woodland Assurance Scheme (UKWAS) and will be certified by
the internationally recognized Forest Stewardship Council (FSC).
The FSC is a non-government organization dedicated to promoting
responsible management of the world's forests. Certification ensures
forests are managed in an environmentally sustainable and socially
responsible way. For further information about this scheme, go to
www.annesspublishing.com/trees.

NOTES

Bracketed terms are intended for American readers. For all recipes,
quantities are given in both metric and imperial measures and,
where appropriate, in standard cups and spoons. Follow one set of
measures, but not a mixture, because they are not interchangeable.
Standard spoon and cup measures are level.
1 tsp = 5ml, 1 tbsp = 15ml, 1 cup = 250ml/8fl oz.
Australian standard tablespoons are 20ml. Australian readers
should use 3 tsp in place of 1 tbsp for measuring small quantities.
American pints are 16fl oz/2 cups. American readers should
use 20fl oz/2.5 cups in place of 1 pint when measuring liquids.
Electric oven temperatures in this book are for conventional ovens.
When using a fan oven, the temperature will probably need to be
reduced by about 10–20°C/20–40°F. Since ovens vary, you should
check with your manufacturer's instruction book for guidance.
The nutritional analysis given for each recipe is calculated per portion
(i.e. serving or item), unless otherwise stated. If the recipe gives a
range, such as Serves 4–6, then the nutritional analysis will be for
the smaller portion size, i.e. 6 servings. Measurements for sodium
do not include salt added to taste.
Medium (US large) eggs are used unless otherwise stated.

Although the advice and information in this book are believed to
be accurate and true at the time of going to press, neither the
authors nor the publisher can accept any legal responsibility or
liability for any errors or omissions that may be made nor for any
inaccuracies nor for any harm or injury that comes about from
following instructions or advice in this book.

Main front cover image shows Puff Pastry Chicken Pies – for recipe,
see pages 104–5.

CONTENTS

Introduction

Country cooking is essentially based on traditional peasant food that has evolved over the centuries. The authentic recipes of the countryside naturally rely on good ingredients and fresh seasonal produce, making use of all the fantastic richness of locally produced food throughout the year. Peasant and country dishes also include many more esoteric foods such as oysters and game which are today regarded as luxury items, but in the past would actually have been classified as poor man's food.

The hard-won knowledge and frugal habits of the country cook, developed with patience and skill over time, are reflected in our 21st-century concerns with the origin and provenance of ingredients. We are beginning to understand that local, fresh, seasonal produce has a better flavour and is far more nutritionally rich than food that is imported from far-flung countries out of season, and this is an area where country recipes shine.

The age-old custom of passing down tried-and-tested traditional family recipes from generation to generation, along with cherished cooking skills, equipment and utensils, means that country food has survived to be appreciated and enjoyed by each new generation of cooks.

The contemporary country kitchen

With a growing interest in cooking seasonally, in using organic produce and the simplest, freshest ingredients, the contemporary country kitchen retains much of what is best about traditional cooking, but with the added blessing of modern equipment, time-saving gadgets and appliances. Innovations such as pressure cookers and bread machines mean that the busy home cook can now recreate many of the more time-consuming recipes of the past in a fraction of the time, without losing any authentic taste. In modern kitchens, it is easier than ever to make the most of all the fresh, high-quality ingredients on which country cooking is based.

Home-made food

Country cooking is simply delicious home-made food using traditional raw materials, without any unnecessary waste. For example, many meat dishes involve long, slow cooking, making use of every possible part of an animal such as the trotters, the head and the offal. This thrifty custom has played a key role in developing some of the best-loved country meat recipes.

An integral part of this style of cooking was preserving food, which was an absolute necessity rather than an indulgence. Home baking and home smoking, along with pickling and salting, and making cheese and butter, were a natural part of living in the country and a matter of pride. Many a country larder contained neat rows of preserved fruit and vegetables in jars, with maybe a ham or some game hanging on a hook and a crock of salted fish ready to be eaten in the cold

Left *Summer in the country means rich grazing for farm animals and an abundance of produce from the woods, fields and vegetable plot.*

months of winter. Techniques such as making a rich stock from meat bones or vibrant crab apple jelly from windfall fruits illustrate the inventiveness that characterizes much country cooking.

The seasons

Culinary creativity was very important to the country cook, whose life revolved around the seasons. Traditional recipes tended to be structured around one central ingredient which was in season – spring vegetables tasting wonderful in a delicious soup, or pork as the main ingredient of a raised pie, for example. If there was an abundance of one crop, it was either used fresh in different ways or stored for the cold weather.

Spring could still be a time of year when the cook was largely reliant on preserved foods to support the few early vegetables, while the summer months provided plenty of fresh fruits, vegetables and salads from an overflowing kitchen garden. In the autumn, the country cook has traditionally relied heavily on wild foods to support the larder and pantry. Game from the fields and woods, as well as hedgerow fruits and nuts, complemented the last of the

summer crops. Winter recipes reflect the thriftiness of country cooking, with hearty stews making the most of the root vegetables, brassicas and dried beans and peas, and using bottled and pickled vegetables from the store cupboard to bulk up meagre winter crops.

Country traditions

The simple act of baking a certain loaf of bread or a special cake for a specific celebration or festival evolved over time to become an indelible part of country tradition. These rituals, treasured and passed down within families, connected people both to the rhythms of the countryside and to the traditions of their local community, marking the passing of the year. Harvest suppers, spiced Christmas drinks, festival sweetmeats and Easter cakes are all concocted from ancient recipes in the country kitchen.

Today, spending time in the kitchen baking a fruit cake, chopping home-grown vegetables to make soup or cooking wonderfully nutritious food

Above Home-grown local fruits such as these beautiful apples are used in many country recipes, such as a sweet pie or a savoury roast joint of meat.

from a few simple ingredients reconnects us to the countryside. Even growing a few herbs in pots on the window sill or making your own preserves can give a satisfying feeling of keeping up time-honoured culinary customs.

About the book

This book begins with a description of country cooking, its history, methods and ingredients, including some fascinating facts about the practical cooking techniques of our rural ancestors. There is also plenty of inspiration for growing your own produce, using it wisely when fresh, and preserving the inevitable glut to enjoy in the colder months.

There are eight chapters of recipes, ranging from simple, rustic soups and pot roasts to some best-loved regional specialities, puddings, breads and preserves. Many dishes can be prepared ahead of time or slow-cooked all day in traditional fashion, bringing the real taste of the country to your table.

Left Country cooking techniques often rely on a few well-loved utensils, such as this traditional rolling pin, pastry cutters, mixing bowl and jug.

Country traditions

Throughout the centuries, cooks have prepared food for the family using whatever ingredients were available. Peasant cooking relied entirely on goods from the local area, fresh and in season, plus whatever could be preserved by bottling, pickling, salting or drying to eat when the kitchen garden was covered with snow and the wheat fields were bare. Today we can be inspired by the thrifty methods of the past to make delicious meals that everyone will enjoy.

The history of country cooking

The development of our traditional cooking has its roots in pre-history. The earliest cooking would probably have been limited to roasting meat and game on a spit, toasting and grinding grain and using simple hollowed-out stones and bones to heat liquids over an open fire.

Early cooking techniques

Not until the development of settled agriculture and the introduction of pottery would cooking develop beyond the most basic methods. By the Middle Ages the resourceful country cook, restricted by the limitations of one-pot cooking on an open fire, relied on tasty dishes such as soups, stews and casseroles, spit-roasted meat and preserved fruit and vegetables for many months of the year. Bread dough was baked in a central public oven, since most of the rural populace would not have access to an oven at home.

Tools, equipment and utensils

From mankind's earliest days, much effort was put into developing tools for gathering, killing and cooking food. Clay, iron and bronze materials were

Left Fruits such as cranberries, together with spices and herbs, were important ingredients for preserves.

Above Cherished kitchen utensils and equipment were often passed from one generation of cooks down to the next.

fashioned into pots used for cooking over the fire and also for preserving food. Utensils made of wood and metal, such as ladles and knives, became stronger and more reliable.

Well-tested techniques for preserving food were vital. As well as preserving fruit and vegetables in glass jars or earthenware crocks, many rural homes would smoke fish and meat in the chimney or in a home-built smokery.

The cook now had access to a broader range of cooking equipment, as well as specialist dairy tools for making butter and cheese. The Victorian era saw the introduction of a huge number of new cooking utensils and mass-produced kitchen gadgets such as fancy pastry cutters, cheese graters and potato peelers.

Fires and ovens

Cooking food over an open fire is the basis upon which all subsequent cooking has developed. The earliest pot ovens, domed iron pots placed over hot hearth stones, gave way to clay or brick-lined ovens similar to today's

pizza ovens, but until the end of the 18th century, much cooking was still done over an open fire. Iron stoves began to appear in the late 18th century, but it was not until the 'cooking machines' or closed stoves appeared in Victorian kitchens that home cooking was really revolutionized.

By the 19th century the typical farmhouse kitchen had a fireplace with a chimney and a rudimentary range with its own ovens. The Aga stove or range cooker and other coal- or wood-fired ovens used today are still associated with a more traditional cooking style; they have certain limitations, but these stoves are often much loved by their owners, who have become experts in slow-cooking skills.

Larders and pantries

Keeping food fresh was a constant concern for the country cook. Storing vegetables and fruits in a cool place on stone floors with a good circulation of air meant they lasted longer. Eventually a larder cupboard or walk-in pantry was

Left The American plantation kitchen had an open hearth for cooking, a hand-cranked meat mincer and copper pots.

constructed in every rural kitchen, as well as in many town basement kitchens. This was the ideal place to keep dairy products and meat in the best condition before the advent of refrigeration. It was also a good place for keeping dry stores of beans, peas and grains, and preserved foods and vegetables in glass or earthenware jars. Many farmhouses in dairy farming areas

developed their own clean, cool dairies where the scrubbed stone floors and shelves gave the best conditions for making and storing butter and cheese.

Local markets

Markets were integral to country life and the rural economy. They developed from the basic need to barter or

exchange an excess of produce. These markets became the focus of many rural communities, with people travelling long distances, often on foot, to buy and sell the essentials of life. Many towns and settlements grew up around the site of a regular market, and in some countries the right to hold a market was a highly valued privilege enshrined in writing. Although both regular markets and seasonal fairs were essentially trading institutions, they became a treasured part of the life of the country. In recent eras, when many countries have seen an increase in trade and movements of population, markets played an integral role both in the dissemination of new foods and cooking styles and in the preservation of ancient local customs.

Below Fruit, vegetables and preserves are kept cool and dry in a pantry, along with dried herbs and garlic.

Frugal food

For the earliest farmers, the earth needed to be coaxed into fertility, and their hard-won skills gradually developed over many years as a response to the challenges of living off the land. The popular image of the countryside as a bucolic and tranquil place belies the reality for rural communities all over the world; the poverty and hardship of country living has always demanded an inventive and frugal way of life. Almost all country cooking relies on good sense, forward planning, a talent for improvisation when times are hard and shared skills rooted in long experience.

Making the most of the countryside

Country economy is symbolized in the use of absolutely all parts of an animal. One or two pigs were often kept in country yards to be killed and eaten in the winter – an essential source of protein for the peasant farmer and his family. Virtually no part of the pig was thrown away: once the major cuts had been eaten as roasted joints and the lesser ones as stews, fat was rendered for lard, intestines were used for sausage cases, and hearts were stuffed and braised. In many countries of the world, pig's feet and ears are a delicacy.

Recipes using ingredients collected from the wild also bear witness to the country cook's frugal outlook. These delicious dishes include soups made from wild greens, herbs and even nettles. Game, fish, nuts and seeds were all hunted or collected to enrich and diversify the country diet. Foraging for food was considered not just a source of free ingredients, but also a positive pleasure when the day could be spent hunting or fishing, picking blackberries along a field edge or searching for mushrooms in the woods.

Above Good economy means taking advantage of what the fields, woods and hedgerows have to offer.

Scarcity of ingredients has led to great culinary invention in many countries, with the creation of new dishes and exciting ways to present familiar ingredients. In Turkey, for example, there are countless recipes based on the simple aubergine (eggplant), examples of which can be found in glistening deep purple piles in every market. These include the famous aubergine and tomato dish, Imam Bayildi.

Economical food around the world

Around the world, peasant cuisines show a great regard for frugal economy. Since peasant food traditionally uses whatever ingredients the local land has to offer, it is always both accessible and inexpensive, and often based around a limited number of staple, hearty ingredients cooked in a single pot.

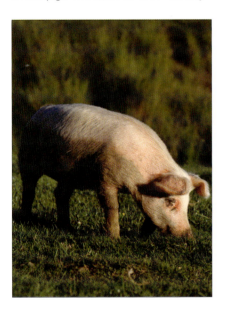

Left To make the most of a pig, the meat was salted, smoked or preserved, and also made into sausages.
Right Home-grown tomatoes are perfect for cooking if you can resist eating them as soon as they are picked.

In many countries, traditional meals vary only slightly across the borders, where the climate and ingredients are similar. The peasant dishes of Germany, such as Himmel und Erde, puréed potato and apple with blood sausage, and Sauerbrauten, a sweet and sour pot roast served with dumplings and cabbage, both remain distinctively German but share a common culinary heritage with other 'peasant' foods such as Irish Stew or French Cassoulet. The technique of marinating and slow cooking the less tender cuts of meat such as the shoulder, shanks and ribs resulted in mouth-watering casseroles, pot roasts and stews.

Waste not, want not

Leftovers feature prominently in country cooking. In Italy, rice left over from a risotto would be added to soups or made into Arancini – balls of cooked rice stuffed with cheese and deep-fried. Spanish Gazpacho, Italian Pappa al Pomodoro and English Queen of Puddings were all made to use up stale bread. Pizza is the ultimate peasant dish, a flour and olive oil dough base topped with tomato sauce and whichever vegetables and cheese are available.

Sourcing ingredients today

With the rise of the grass-roots movement that promotes traditionally raised food, today's resourceful cook can take advantage of the best their country has to offer. Financial imperatives paired with an increased desire to buy good, natural food means that many people are more educated about where their food comes from and what they should pay for it. Awareness of the amount of pesticides used in commercially grown crops and the less welcome effects of agro-chemicals and antibiotics used to rear livestock intensively means that many people are beginning to buy

organic and bio-dynamic foods instead. In particular, the furore over the advent of genetically modified crops has starkly illustrated the number of artificial processes associated with modern food production. In contrast, vegetable and fruit varieties grown organically may take longer to grow and have lower yields of uneven-sized crops, but they have time to develop more flavour and are nutritionally richer.

The reintroduction of traditional and rare-breed animals and an increased concern for animal welfare means that

Left A thick slice of home-baked bread, such as this cheese and onion loaf, is a delicious and filling country snack.

many more livestock and poultry are raised free-range and slaughtered in more humane conditions. Meat can often be sourced from farmers as many rural producers now sell direct to the consumer. Buying a whole or half animal from a farmer, butchered into convenient portions and ready for the freezer, means fantastic meat at a reasonable price.

Growing your own is the best way of ensuring freshness, but there are also increased opportunities for sourcing frugal ingredients. Farmers' markets, farm shops, co-operatives and box schemes offer locally grown and organic supplies which are, by definition, in season and fresh. Buying food from the person who grew or raised it has the added benefit of the exchange of knowledge, ideas and perhaps even recipes. In this way, the city-dwelling cook with an interest in traditional food can bridge the gap between urban and rural life.

Below Free-range meat from animals such as these sheep can be sourced direct from farmers and markets.

The kitchen garden

Growing fruits, vegetables and herbs has always been an integral part of the self-sufficiency of the country cook. A well-planned kitchen garden will provide an ongoing supply of fruit and vegetables throughout the year – just as one crop is coming to an end, a new one will take over – and as long as the cook has enough skill and imagination to make the most of a glut, to preserve everything that cannot be eaten immediately, and to plan ahead so that best use is made of the available space, the kitchen garden can be an inspiring place.

The renewed interest in 'growing your own' means that planting a kitchen garden is no longer solely the privilege of the rural population. Allotments, land shares, community gardens and urban plots, or even a pot or two in a small yard or on a windowsill, make home-grown fruits and vegetables available to all.

Nowadays, there are plenty of dwarf varieties available that crop well but take up limited space. Even vegetables such as runner (green) beans or aubergines (eggplants) – which would usually need a large area to grow in – can now be grown in containers on patios.

Grow your own

One of the major advantages of home-grown food is that it encourages the country cook to make recipes that are prepared from scratch. Having a handy selection of your favourite fruits, vegetables and herbs flourishing just outside the kitchen window is a huge help – and also an attractive addition to any back garden.

In order to avoid making expensive mistakes, it is a good idea to check the gardening catalogues for ideas and maybe borrow some books from the library before you start. There is plenty of practical advice to be had on the best varieties to grow, whatever the size and shape of your plot. The traditional varieties of many vegetables, including 'heirloom' varieties, often

Left Damsons are ideal for jam-making, and the trees look very pretty in spring with their snow-white blossom.

Above This neat kitchen garden has a recently harvested crop of onions drying on the ground before being stored.

taste fantastic, and you will have the additional pleasure of knowing that you are preserving our culinary heritage.

Containers and window boxes are a great way to start growing vegetables because they are manageable and can be very productive. Some climbing varieties of fruit and vegetables do not need deep soil and can be grown in grow bags or containers in a small space. A small herb garden or pots of herbs on a windowsill will offer an easy introduction to growing at home, with the attraction of fresh ingredients to hand for cooking. There is nothing quite like the aroma of a dish of new potatoes with home-grown mint or parsley sprinkled on top.

Another big incentive to start cultivating a small plot or vegetable garden is that it is an easy way to

While many crops can be harvested gradually over a long growing season, other fruits and vegetables will have a short but extravagantly abundant burst of activity, providing a big yield in just a few weeks.

For this reason, preserving has long been an integral part of getting the most from a home harvest, helping to avoid groans from the family as they face yet another courgette (zucchini) or tomato dish for supper. While many crops will freeze well, some fruits and vegetables do not respond favourably to this treatment, becoming soggy or tasteless, and so the old traditional methods of making jams, jellies, relishes and chutneys, and bottling, drying, salting and pickling come into their own.

The great value of home-made preserves is in capturing the colours, textures, smells and tastes of summer at any time of the year. There is also the undeniably warm glow that comes from eating your own produce, preserved in your own kitchen, all year round.

Above *A space for potting seeds is useful when growing fruits and vegetables at home or in an allotment.*

introduce children to new fruits and vegetables which they might otherwise be reluctant to try. Windowsill gardening is ideal for children, as they can inspect the crop regularly.

Vegetable gardens can also be much more than a working part of the garden. Certain fruits and vegetables, such as potatoes, onions, lettuce and the dwarf varieties of beans, can be integrated into an ornamental garden, although this is not an easy option – both vegetables and flowers are going to need constant attention to keep them pest-free and avoid one variety swamping the others. Even if there is no room in the flower garden for vegetables, many fruit trees flourish against a sunny wall and also look extremely decorative, with their spring blossom and autumn fruits.

Plot to pantry

Growing fruit and vegetables can very easily result in over-production of certain varieties at particular times of the year.

Below *Home-grown thyme, asparagus, onions, figs, radishes and carrots can go straight from the garden to the kitchen.*

Seasonal food

Eating seasonally is as relevant today as it was centuries ago. Cooking and eating within the year's natural rhythm means that fruit and vegetable varieties are eaten when they are at their best in terms of flavour and ripeness, as well as nutritional qualities.

But it is not only the taste and goodness of traditional fresh food that should focus everyone's minds on buying seasonal produce. An increasing concern about the impact of fossil fuels used to transport foods from far-flung countries has added to the renewed interest in cooking and eating local produce. Awareness of food miles and reluctance to pay a premium price for tasteless out-of-season foods are now coupled with a desire to support local economies and reconnect with the seasons.

Seasonal recipes

In many regions of the world, shopping every day naturally means having the choice of produce restricted seasonally – but often this is no hardship as long as the cook is prepared to settle into a pattern of traditional cooking dictated by the harvests. This is where growing your own or buying local fresh produce

Above *Spring carrots are best when lightly cooked and simply served with butter and some chopped parsley.*

really pays dividends. Newly harvested fruits and vegetables that are cooked on the same day they are picked retain their natural goodness and will be eaten before their natural sugars turn to starch, thus making them sweeter and more flavoursome; they often have a better texture and cook more quickly.

Everyone can tell the difference between a bowl of fragrant, firm strawberries eaten at the height of the harvesting season in early summer, and the tired, soggy, tasteless examples bought in midwinter. But this also applies to other ingredients such as tomatoes, courgettes (zucchini), new potatoes, peaches, spring lamb and many more. Why not make good use of all these wonderful flavours when they are at their absolute peak?

Left *Succulent summer fruits such as strawberries are delicious in fruit fools, with ice cream or in a sweet pudding.* **Right** *Orchard apples are perfect for autumn puddings such as crumbles, or baked with dried fruits and honey.*

Spring

As the first spring produce appears, it is time to move on from the casseroles and stews of the winter months and enjoy the vibrant new flavours of spring vegetables and early fruits. The best way to cook these fantastically fresh ingredients changes from long, slow cooking to quick stir-fries and grilling (broiling), or even serving raw in a salad.

Early spring is the ideal time to use up the last of the winter staple crops and pair them with new herbs and dressings, perhaps using the first wild greens in a casserole or simmering the new pink shoots of rhubarb and blending them with cream to make a tasty dessert. Later, spring shoots and tender young vegetables such as broad (fava) beans and new potatoes make interesting salads, and this is also the time of year when luxuries such as asparagus start to appear.

Summer

The sunshine brings the opportunity to make plain but exquisite dishes focusing on the best-quality ingredients. Early summer offers young, sweet vegetables

Left Many fruits and vegetables are at their best in the autumn, such as these pumpkins and squashes.

Winter

The colder months may be restricted in the variety of seasonal foods available, but winter is the time to bring out the preserved and stored foods hoarded in the summer and preserved in the autumn. There are still some fresh vegetables available, such as cabbages and Brussels sprouts, which do not reach their peak of flavour until the first frosts.

Late autumn cooking apples and berries can be stewed or baked in a pie. Beans and peas are a good store cupboard stand-by at this time of year and can be made into warming dinners for winter evenings; they taste great paired with root vegetables. Steamed puddings are essential winter warmers, and a home-baked fruit cake bursting with dried fruits is a tempting treat for the winter store cupboard.

Below Winter is the season for root vegetables, citrus fruits and dried fruit, which can be stored until needed.

such as new potatoes, lettuce, peas and beans; later, the focus moves to sun-ripened tomatoes and bell peppers, courgettes, marrows and main-crop potatoes. The soft fruits in the kitchen garden – raspberries, strawberries, peaches and apricots – are perfect for desserts such as fruit fools and tarts.

Cooking with warm weather in mind means making simple, light food – delicious fresh dishes such as chilled soups, salads, grilled (broiled) meat and fish, for example – to allow the flavour and texture of the produce to shine. Summer is also a good time to turn a glut of soft fruit and summer berries into cordials and cooling drinks, which are very welcome on a hot day.

Autumn

As summer draws to a close, the thrifty country cook begins to preserve the abundant harvest of fruits and vegetables and to make jams, pickles and other preserves. The autumn season is blessed with an overlap between the last of the summer produce and the first of the root vegetables and brassicas,

with the opportunity to start making hearty soups and roasting pumpkins, squashes, potatoes and parsnips.

Autumn is also the season for game, wild mushrooms and nuts, as well as being the perfect time to start making treats for Christmas such as fruit cake, pudding and presents of bottled fruit or spicy chutney.

Preserving and storing

Smoking, drying, bottling or making jams and chutneys are all major activities in the country kitchen. These techniques are really worth learning, even in an era when all kinds of foodstuffs are available the whole year round in the supermarket. Eating your own preserves, made with best-quality, tasty fruits and vegetables, is a reminder of summer in the depths of winter. There is no comparison between a cheap shop-bought strawberry jam with its high sugar content and red colouring, for example, and the darker colour and richer, purer flavour of home-made strawberry jam, bursting with fruit.

Jams, jellies and marmalades

Making delicious jams and jellies is the most common way to enjoy the summer's harvest all year round. Jams and jellies are particularly versatile preserves, with many uses in the country kitchen – they can be spread between the layers of a sponge cake, used as a dessert topping, or simply served with freshly made bread for tea.

Jam is made by simmering prepared fruits, either whole or chopped, with sugar. Fruits that are low in pectin, such as strawberries, make a soft-set jam, whereas those that are naturally full of

pectin, such as plums or gooseberries, make a firmer preserve. Compôtes are simply soft-set jams made with a little less sugar, served fresh, as they will not keep for long. Many traditional jellies are made from hedgerow crops such as crab apple, mint and elderflower, and these delicately flavoured preserves are usually served with meats or cheese.

Old-fashioned fruit butters and cheeses are preserves made with the fruit pulp left in a jelly bag after the juice has dripped. Making fruit butter requires less sugar than jam and the texture is softer – perfect for spreading.

Fruit cheeses have a firmer texture and are made from well-sieved (strained) thick fruit purées, often from fruits with lots of pips or stones such as damsons or quince. In contrast, fruit curds are made with the addition of butter and eggs, gently cooking the fruit to create a thick, sweet conserve which has a shorter shelf-life than other preserves because of the dairy content. Piquant lemon curd is the best known, but other fruits such as gooseberries, apricots and quince also lend themselves well to this treatment.

Marmalade is made in a similar way to jam, using citrus fruits. The fruit rind in marmalade needs longer cooking than the usual jam fruits, so water is

Above Home-made jams and jellies look very attractive when finished with pretty tops, to give as gifts.

added to the fruit and sugar while it is cooked. The marmalade can be flavoured with alcohol or fragrant spices such as ginger.

Pickles, chutneys and relishes

Both fruits and vegetables can be made into mouth-watering pickles and chutneys. Chutney is made with chopped fruit and/or vegetables simmered with varying amounts of spices, sugar and vinegar to a thick pulp and then stored in jars. As it improves with age, chutney stores very well and has a long shelf-life. It is particularly useful for using up end-of-season fruits such as windfall apples and green tomatoes, mixed with dried vine fruits such as sultanas (golden raisins) and currants.

In contrast, pickles are more often made with whole vegetables, such

Far left Stone fruits such as these ripe plums can be bottled, or made into jam, chutney or a rich fruit cheese.
Left Some autumn fruits, if carefully wrapped and properly stored, can last for many weeks or months into winter.

as baby onions, cauliflower florets or beetroot (beet). The vegetables are first salted or soaked to remove excess moisture, then packed into jars and covered in vinegar, with the addition of strong herbs and spices to add a really zingy taste to the mixture. Pickles do not require the long cooking of chutney, and benefit from being kept for a few weeks for the flavours to develop.

Both pickles and chutneys are usually served straight from the jar with cold meats, terrines, pies or cheese, but they can also be regarded as an instant ingredient to add zest to many winter dishes. Pickled onions can be rinsed and added to a robust casserole or stew, for example.

Relish is halfway between chutneys and pickles. It consists of coarsely chopped fruit or vegetables, spices and vinegar cooked together for a shorter time than chutney, so the vegetables tend to keep their shape. There are even traditional recipes for uncooked relishes that make the best of a summer glut – vegetables or fruits such as tomatoes, courgettes (zucchini), bell peppers or plums can be chopped and mixed

Right *Pretty bottles can be re-used for pickling if they are sterilized and have new, air-tight tops.*

with chillies, herbs and seasoning and served cold. These should be kept in the refrigerator and used within a few days.

Bottling

The technique of bottling is most often used for preserving best-quality whole fruits and vegetables. Fruit is usually bottled in syrup or alcohol to keep the colour and flavour of these pristine ingredients; vegetables are more often bottled in brine. Fruit and vegetables for

bottling must be fresh and not too ripe. Stone (pit) fruits such as apricots and plums are particularly suitable for this method and look glorious with their beautiful colours shining through the glass jar.

Drying

Home-drying fruit and vegetables was long regarded as an important part of preserving. Dried vegetables are oven-, sun- or air-dried, and then often packed in oil, while dried fruits are kept in boxes. Fruit, vegetables and herbs will keep for many months when properly dried, and most characteristically have a particular intensity of flavour. Sun-drying crops such as tomatoes, aubergines (eggplants) and bell peppers is popular in the Mediterranean, India and the Middle East, where these vegetables grow easily and the sun is strong enough to preserve all the goodness quickly.

The country kitchen

Country recipes rely on traditional cooking techniques combined with the quality and freshness of good produce. Focusing on natural, seasonal ingredients will enable any cook to produce wholesome food which is both healthy and delicious. This chapter gives an overview of all the basic ingredients used in country cooking, from the familiar fruits and vegetables of the kitchen garden to autumn berries and nuts, and from meat and dairy products to fish and shellfish.

Garden, field and orchard

In the past, most country gardens contained a few vegetables, a fruit tree or two and maybe a beehive or some chickens – all with one aim in mind, to put food on the table. Nowadays, many rural and city gardeners are turning at least part of their flower beds over to food production, and expressing an interest in traditional methods of harvesting, cooking and preserving. Even city-dwellers with no garden usually have access to the most wonderful fresh, seasonal produce in their local shops and markets.

Vegetables

The vegetable garden was always the basis of country cooking. Gardeners knew how to prepare the ground, rotate their crops to get the best from the nutrients in the soil and raise as many excellent vegetables as they could cram into their plot.

Bulb vegetables, including onions and shallots, garlic, leeks and salad onions, have always been a favourite in the country kitchen. They provide a quick and easy way of adding depth of flavour to many dishes.

Leafy greens and brassicas include broccoli, Brussels sprouts, cauliflower, cabbage, spinach, endive and salad leaves – all of which are best eaten very soon after picking.

Root vegetables such as potatoes, carrots, squash and parsnips are amazingly versatile winter vegetables. Often used as thickening agents in casseroles or stews, they can also be mashed, roasted, puréed or made into delicious velvety soups.

Peas, broad (fava) beans, French (green) beans, borlotti beans and corn grow prolifically but need lots of space, and should be harvested while young.

Asparagus is slow to establish in the garden and has a very short season, but should not be missed. Other summer vegetables that need the full warmth of the sun to ripen include tomatoes, bell peppers, avocados and aubergines (eggplants) – these grow well in hot countries or under glass in cooler areas.

Dried beans, peas and lentils

The number of varieties of the dried seeds of plant legumes runs into thousands. As they are inexpensive,

Above Courgettes are part of the squash family, which also includes pumpkins, marrows and gourds.

easy to grow and have a good storage life, dried beans, peas and lentils have long been an integral part of the country diet. They are high in protein and complex carbohydrates, low in fat and nutritionally rich.

Bean stews, salads, soups and casseroles, re-interpreted for each culture, appear in recipes from all over the world, such as Tuscan Ribollito or Southern Succotash Chicken Soup from the United States. Beans, peas and lentils can also be puréed and mashed into delicious dips and pâtés or included in curries and highly spiced meat dishes.

Fruits

An enormous number of fruit varieties are now available. Among the best-known are tree fruits such as apples, pears and quinces, which appear in the late summer and autumn, while stone (pit) fruits such as apricots, cherries,

Left A variety of healthy vegetables and fruits has always been part of the rural diet, especially in the summer.

damsons, greengages, nectarines, peaches and plums tend to ripen earlier in the year.

Soft fruits and berries include bilberries, blackberries, black, white and red currants, blueberries, gooseberries, raspberries and strawberries, and are mainly summer and autumn crops, some of which can be found growing wild in the countryside.

Grapefruit, oranges, lemons, limes, mandarins and kumquats need consistent warmth and sunlight to flourish; in northern parts of the world they can only be grown indoors. Bananas, dates, figs, mangoes, pomegranates, melons

and pineapples are some of the best-known 'exotic' fruits that can only be grown in hot, humid climates or in a heated greenhouse.

Central to the country larder is a good supply of preserved fruits, which keep well and can therefore be imported from warmer countries to the cooler parts of the world: dried vine fruits such as currants and sultanas (golden raisins) appear in numerous traditional European cakes and biscuits, and dried dates, figs and apricots are used extensively in Mediterranean and Middle Eastern savoury dishes.

Nuts

In country cooking, nut butters are often used to thicken soups and stews or added to stuffings and sauces, and nut oils are made into fragrant dressings. French cooks use walnuts and chestnuts extensively, and in Italy almonds are a staple ingredient, with

Left Each variety of nut has its own distinctive taste. Nuts can either be added to dishes or eaten as a snack. Right Fresh herbs add essential flavour to country meals, and are very easy to grow on a sunny windowsill.

fragrant almond paste central to many seasonal celebration dishes and sweetmeats. Sweet chestnuts are also made into chestnut flour, which used to be a substitute for the more expensive wheat flour in peasant kitchens.

Seeds

Pumpkin seeds are delicious roasted and tossed with a little sea salt and eaten as a snack. Pine nuts, sesame seeds and sunflower seeds are all important, nutritionally rich elements in peasant cooking throughout Europe, North Africa and the Middle East, and form the basis of many traditional dishes.

Herbs

Easy to grow and versatile, herbs can be used fresh or dried, cooked or raw in both savoury and sweet dishes, and each has its own distinct flavour and texture. In slow-cooked recipes, a bouquet garni added at the beginning of cooking allows the flavour to permeate throughout the dish, while a sprinkling of chopped parsley or coriander (cilantro) on a bowl of cooked rice or vegetables adds freshness and colour.

Wild foods

In the past, foraging for wild roots and fruits was a vital part of country life, providing nutritious, succulent treats to supplement the kitchen garden and store cupboard. Wild food can also add variety and indeed a luxurious, unexpected flavour to some traditional dishes.

Rural cooks have always regarded the hedgerow and field as an extension to their larder, and this tradition survives today, with many families enjoying a day out with a picnic to pick the produce of the countryside. As long as care is taken to avoid poisonous varieties of fungi or polluted bushes near main roads, wild mushrooms and hedgerow fruits such as blackberries, elderberries and rosehips still present great possibilities for making delicious meals. They can occasionally be found in magnificent abundance, and the opportunity for preserving a glut of berries in the form of jam or jelly, for example, should not be missed.

Depending on your location, there is usually some sort of wild food available for gathering in every month of the year, including nuts and berries, wild greens, roots, herbs, seeds and flowers such as elderflowers and rosehips. In the early spring, there is a 'hungry gap', when the last winter vegetables are finishing, the spring vegetables have not yet appeared, and the store

cupboard is emptying fast. At such times, wild food such as watercress, nettles and mushrooms have been essential additions to the country diet.

Fruits and berries

In Europe, the autumn and early winter is a particularly rich time for foraging, with fruits such as blackberries, damsons, juniper berries, sloes, crab apples and rosehips all ready for picking.

The tradition of pickling, bottling and preserving these fruits and vegetables, storing nuts and drying fungi are all methods by which the country cook bolsters the store cupboard. In Spain, wild quince is customarily made into Membrillo, a sweet quince paste. Fruit wines, syrups and drinks made from windfall fruits feature in many cultures: cider made from apples, elderflower or damson wine and rosehip syrup are all traditional treats. Fiercely alcoholic vodka, gin and other spirits, made from

Left These tiny, bright red crab apples can be harvested in the autumn to make tasty home-made apple jelly.
Right Full of healthy vitamin C, rosehips can be used for making delicious teas, syrups and jellies.

Above Hedgerows are a great source of wild berries, such as these blackberries which make lovely bramble jam.

bland grains or root vegetables, are often flavoured with herbs and berries such as juniper or sloes that were gathered in the autumn.

Green leaves

Since most cultivated vegetables are descended from native ancestors, there are many greens and leaves growing wild which make good additions to the cooking pot – spinach, nettles, rocket

Left Many different kinds of wild mushrooms can be found in the woods and fields, especially in the autumn.

(arugula) and sorrel all grow abundantly and are delicious. Italian family recipes for Minestrone soup often include wild greens, such as dandelion leaves. English cooks often use horseradish root and mint made into piquant sauces to accompany a roast joint of meat.

Mushrooms and fungi

Wild mushrooms grow throughout the year, but autumn is often the most rewarding time for harvesting fungi because this season offers such an abundant and varied selection. They are delicious, but there are some varieties that are extremely poisonous. It is essential to take a good guidebook with you to identify edible varieties, or find an expert to check your collection. Bear in mind that many highly poisonous varieties look remarkably similar to edible ones.

Like many uncultivated foods, wild mushrooms tend to have a superior flavour to cultivated varieties, and they also have their own distinct texture and taste. Some fungi are found in large abundant groups, while others are less easy to spot. Many wild mushrooms dry very well, and highly prized varieties such as morels and ceps are an important winter ingredient in Italy and Spain.

Unlike most other foraging, mushroom collecting requires focus, knowledge and commitment, and especially so if it is truffles that are being hunted. In France and Italy, these are the most highly prized fungi, requiring great skill and commitment to find – preferably with the help of a truffle hound or pig to sniff out these delicacies.

Herbs and edible flowers

When collected from the wild, herbs generally have a stronger flavour than commercially cultivated varieties. They may grow in great profusion, and

armfuls of some herbs can be gathered and dried for use in winter cooking. Native herbs tend to have an affinity with local foods. Hardy, woody-stemmed herbs such as rosemary, thyme and oregano grow prolifically in hot climates, and their pungent aroma works best when cooked with strong-tasting meat and fish, but they can also be used for infusing oils for cooking. More delicate herbs such as basil, sorrel or chervil are better used raw with vegetable, fish or chicken dishes.

Edible flowers such as nasturtiums and dandelions have been used for centuries, not just for their visual appeal but also for their delicate flavour in salads or preserves.

Folklore often credits these foods with beneficial properties – many herbs, flowers and wild foods are still used as remedies, such as feverfew for headaches and peppermint to aid digestion.

Below left Wild green plants from the countryside, such as these nettles, often feature in traditional recipes. *Below* Edible flowers, such as pansies, nasturtiums and rose petals, look pretty in salads and as cake decorations.

Fish and shellfish

Saltwater fish, freshwater fish and shellfish have long been recognized as a vital source of protein and minerals, supplementing the country diet of vegetables, cereals, dairy and meat. The earliest hunter-gatherers foraged the coastline for shellfish, and tidal zones of the seashore provided valuable sea vegetables, including seaweed.

Fish

There are countless classic fish recipes, and shellfish such as crab and prawns (shrimp) also appear in local dishes all over the world. Freshwater crayfish and eels, long considered peasant food, have been re-invented for the modern cook, and appear on menus alongside more glamorous companions such as scallops and oysters.

As many of our oceans are now over-fished, dishes once made to use up unwanted leftover fish from the catch – such as Bouillabaisse from southern France – are now regarded as rather a luxury. Smaller fish such as sardines, mackerel and herring, once the staple diet of Portuguese, Spanish and northern European fishermen,

are replacing fish such as cod, whose stocks are diminished through pollution and over-fishing.

Drying, salting, pickling and smoking were all traditional methods of preserving before canning and freezing procedures became available, and many countries have their own techniques depending on the variety of fish – for instance, tasty pickled or soused herring from Scandinavia, strong-flavoured smoked

Above left Large whole fish such as sea bream or this sea bass are perfect for poaching or oven-roasting in foil. *Above* Wild salmon is delicious poached and served warm or cold with home-made herb mayonnaise.

mackerel and salmon from Scotland and the acquired taste of salt cod from Spain and Portugal.

The seasons affect fish, just as they do the fruit and vegetable crop. It is worth investigating when native varieties are at their best, in terms of abundance and availability. Seasonality as the foundation of traditional cooking means that locally caught fish will give a really authentic flavour and texture.

When buying fresh fish, look out for unclouded, bright eyes, firm flesh and pink gills, and a pleasantly fresh aroma of the sea rather than a strong 'fishy' smell. Delicate white fish responds best to simple baking, steaming or grilling (broiling), perhaps with a few herbs and butter, while more substantial, meatier fish can take bolder handling and richer sauces.

Left Fast-flowing inland rivers and streams are good sources of freshwater fish such as salmon and trout.

Each country has its own native species and plenty of traditional dishes to match; it is worth experimenting with whatever fish is available locally, as many recipes are transferable, but you should keep to the right kind of fish – white fish, flat fish or the nutritionally rich oily fish species.

Shellfish

The term 'shellfish' covers crustaceans such as prawns and shrimp, langoustines, lobster and crab, as well as molluscs and cephalopods such as clams, oysters, scallops, mussels, cockles, winkles, cuttlefish and squid.

Traditionally harvested from the sea shallows and caught in inland waters, shellfish proved a useful part of the diet of early mankind. Oyster and clam shells have been found in the archaeological remains of many of the earliest peoples, from the Aborigines of Australia to the Celts of the Scottish Outer Hebrides. Most shellfish recipes make the most of the delicate, salty flavour of these tasty morsels by cooking them when they are really fresh; some, such as oysters, are generally eaten raw.

Cured and preserved fish

Fish has been preserved in many different ways since ancient times. Drying, smoking, salting or preserving in vinegar or oil was once essential if the fish was to be enjoyed out of season. Freezing and canning have largely supplanted older methods of preservation, but smoking is still popular – less for its preservative qualities than for the texture and flavour it imparts.

In the pre-refrigeration days, salting fish was a necessity to preserve it on the long sea journey from the fishing grounds to port, but nowadays the salting process is more commonly used to create luxuries such as smoked salmon. The salting process draws moisture out of the fish, and as it dries, the flesh firms up, making it easier to carve and changing both its flavour and its texture.

Salt cod, or bacalao, as it is known in Spain, is still very popular in many European countries, and is used in dishes such as Brandade and Salt Cod

Right *Coastal communities have the advantage of choosing from the catch of the day as it lands on the quayside.*

Far left *There are many varieties of clam. They are quick to cook and taste great in pasta or risotto dishes.* ***Left*** *Oysters, once 'poor man's' food, are now a luxury, served fresh or deep-fried with tartare sauce.*

Fritters. Salted and preserved anchovies were traded as long ago as Roman times, and salted, cured fish roe – Bottarga – remains a favourite food of the Portuguese.

Smoking preserves fish by a hot or cold smoking process. In cold smoking, the fish is first cured and then smoked at low temperatures for anything between 24 hours and 3 weeks. In contrast, hot smoking effectively 'cooks' the fish, as it is smoked at a higher temperature for between 6 and 12 hours.

Smoke houses have evolved slightly differently around the world, but generally the principle is the same: fish are salted, rinsed and then strung up to air dry, and finally smoked over smouldering woodchips or peat. The strength of the cure and length of smoking affects the colour and flavour of the fish, and adding sugar, juniper berries or other flavouring to the flesh will change its character. Oily fish such as eel respond particularly well to smoking.

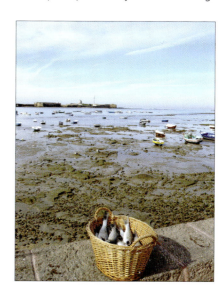

Poultry and feathered game

Many a country garden, from the most prosperous farm to the tiniest cottage, once had a group of hens happily pecking in the dirt, jealously guarded by the resident cockerel, or a few ducks swimming on a tiny pond. These creatures were a fantastic source of eggs and meat and would be carefully protected from marauding foxes. Out in the woods and pastures, country people also had access to feathered game such as partridge, pheasant and grouse, which would be hunted and then cooked to make a tasty autumn or winter casserole, with their rich, dark flesh.

Chicken

The most popular and widely available poultry, chicken is a staple in most kitchens around the world, even though these days they are often bought in markets or shops. Traditional recipes use the whole bird; once the flesh of the chicken has been eaten, there is still the liver to make into pâté and the carcass to boil with a few vegetables for a rich jellied stock.

As with all country cooking, recipes have developed over the years to make the most of the kind of chicken available, whether it is a young spring chicken, at its best simply roasted with fresh herbs, or a laying hen past its

productive years, which is ideal for casseroles with plenty of vegetables and a full-flavoured gravy.

Traditional country chickens would have been raised in conditions now defined as 'free range' – they would have lived mainly in the open, foraging and feeding outside, eating a varied diet of grains and scraps from the kitchen, with plenty of space to establish their pecking order. The free-range and organic chickens now available in many shops and markets are likely to have a similar flavour and texture to those found in the traditional farmyard.

Above Organic free-range chickens are reared in the open air with plenty of space and opportunities to forage.

Turkey

Once only appearing at Thanksgiving or Christmas, the large, domesticated descendant of the North American wild turkey is now available all year round, as a whole bird, leg pieces or breast pieces. It makes a splendid roast dinner for a special occasion, accompanied by lots of vegetables and a light stuffing packed with fresh herbs.

Guinea fowl

Until recently regarded as game birds, guinea fowl are slightly smaller than chickens and have a more pronounced, stronger flavour; the hen birds are considered to be more tender. Sold as squabs, chicks or fowl, they can weigh

Far left A traditional roast turkey with all the trimmings is central to Christmas and Thanksgiving celebrations.
Left Guinea fowl are perfect for a casserole or a pot roast slow-cooked with fresh seasonal vegetables.

up to 2kg/4½lb, and are cooked in similar ways to chicken – they can be either roasted whole or sliced into pieces to make a delicious dish with a creamy sauce.

Duck and goose

These were traditionally wild game birds, but both duck and goose are now more widely available as they are bred and raised commercially. The rich flesh of duck and goose blends particularly well with orchard fruits such as apples, pears and quince, whose tartness cuts through the strong flavour of the meat. In France goose is often eaten with prunes. Goose was the proud centrepiece of many traditional English feasts and celebration meals, especially at Christmas.

Feathered game

Wild birds hunted for the table have long been a staple country food, being readily available in the woods and fields of many rural areas, mostly during the autumn and winter months. Wild birds tend to have a stronger flavour and denser texture than domestic poultry. Young game birds are usually roasted, and older birds are braised or stewed in much the same way as domestic chicken.

While the countryman would shoot his own, birds such as pheasant and quail are now reared commercially, and are widely available in shops and markets. Rarer birds such as grouse and woodcock are usually found only at specialist game dealers.

Perhaps the most widely available game bird is the pheasant, which originated in China and is related to the chicken. They are usually sold as a 'brace' – a hen and a cock bird – and the two birds are cooked together, roasted or braised in a large casserole dish with vegetables, herbs and spices such as juniper berries. As with most game birds, pheasant are low in fat and lean, with a strong, distinctive flavour, which develops according to how long they have been hung.

Grouse are truly wild game birds. They include the sage and red grouse, and the capercaillie, particularly prized for its distinctive flavour and lean flesh. The smaller birds are highly prized for their rich flavour; a single bird such as

Left Goose has a rich, fatty meat that is delicious when served with berry sauces or fruit jellies.
Right The classic way to prepare partridge is to roast it whole with strips of bacon, and serve with cabbage.

Above left A male or 'cock' pheasant, with its colourful head feathers, is a common sight in the autumn woods.
Above Grouse are a wild game bird hunted only for a limited season, and much prized for their flavour.

partridge, pigeon or quail will serve only one person. Quail are pink-fleshed and succulent, quick to cook and often available part-boned. Their attractive speckled eggs are often used in canapés.

The rarest and most prized wild birds are woodcock and snipe. Both have dark, intensely flavoured meat, and are usually roasted whole (including their intestines and head) and served one per person.

Meat and furred game

Central to the country diet, both domestically raised meat and wild game have always been a prime source of protein. While there are plenty of traditional recipes for roast meat as the centrepiece of a special meal, many country recipes call for the cheaper cuts of meat or offal, which work so well in rich, tasty stews and casseroles cooked gently and slowly in the oven.

Beef, lamb, pork and offal

The meat from domestic cattle is one of the most prized sources of protein, used in both everyday and celebration meals around the world. Generally 'prime' or 'rare' beef comes from a pedigree herd, while 'dairy cross' comes from a dairy cow, and veal is the paler, tender meat of a young calf up to the age of six months. Traditional methods of cooking beef vary hugely, depending on the cut, including everything from a standing rib roast of the best, most succulent meat to a homely shepherd's pie made of beef mince (ground meat).

Good-quality lamb should have light red, moist flesh with a good layer of firm, creamy fat. The leg and shoulder are usually roasted, but again there are plenty of lesser cuts that melt into tenderness when simmered slowly in stock with some vegetables and mint from the garden. In past centuries,

mutton was preferred to lamb because of its richer flavour; it has been unfashionable and difficult to obtain but is undergoing something of a comeback with the revival of interest in our culinary heritage.

Domesticated pork was regarded traditionally as a seasonal meat, much of which was processed, preserved and salted to provide ham, bacon and sausages throughout the winter. Good pork should be pale pink with creamy white fat and a pliable rind.

As 'rare breed' pork is now becoming fashionable again, many excellent and diverse traditional breeds have made a comeback.

Above There are many different kinds of beef cattle. Hand-fed animals will produce the most tender meat.

Offal was a natural part of the diet in the days when nothing was wasted from a precious carcass. It can be really delicious, and there are many traditional recipes from around the world for sausages, fricassees and casseroles made with these strong-tasting ingredients. Pig's blood is also used to make black pudding, known as Boudin Noir in France and blood sausage in Germany and the USA.

Preserved and processed meats

Age-old techniques of preserving meat include curing methods such as salting, pickling, air- or wind-drying and smoking. One of the best meats for preserving is pork, which makes delicious joints such as ham and bacon. These were once the mainstay of a farmhouse pantry.

Far left Young prime lamb chops are best simply cooked quickly on a griddle, barbecue or grill, with rosemary.
Left A stuffed tenderloin of pork wrapped in bacon to keep the meat moist makes an impressive lunch dish.

Far left Good sausages have a high meat content. Pan-fry them and serve with pickles and home-made bread. *Left* Young rabbit and hare can be roasted, but are also good slowly casseroled with wine and vegetables.

Pâtés and terrines are a good way of using up leftover meat. The difference between the two is that a terrine usually contains layers of meat that are immediately visible once the dish is sliced up, whereas a pâté is a smoother, more blended mixture. Cold raised pies are simply a variation on the terrine, where pastry replaces the dish in which terrines are cooked. Traditional raised pies with lard-rich, hot-water pastry can last up to a month, and make perfect picnic fare.

Sausages are another important staple of country cooking, whether they are fresh, smoked or dried. Fresh sausages are made by blending chopped meat – usually pork – with fat, seasonings and spices, fresh or dried herbs, cereal or rusk stuffed into cleaned intestines. Sausages can be made from virtually any blend of meat, game or poultry, and some varieties contain no meat at all – the French country sausage andouillette, for instance, is made from tripe.

Dried sausages, such as salamis and chorizo, have been air-dried to extend the amount of time they will keep and, like North African merguez sausage, might have chilli and other dried herbs or spices added to them.

Furred game

Game animals, like game birds, are a vital part of the country kitchen. These days, venison is more likely to come from farmed deer than to be caught wild. The meat is dark and lean, and can be cooked in similar ways to beef, with the saddle, haunch and loin best suited to roasting and the fillet or boned loin providing a juicy, well-flavoured steak. Lesser cuts of venison can be slow-cooked or made into sausages or minced

(ground) meat. Venison is often marinated in red wine with tart juniper berries to tenderize the meat, and has a great affinity with other astringent fruits such as blackberries and redcurrants.

The smaller furred game such as rabbit and hare, which populate the countryside, naturally feature in many country recipes, and lend themselves to a wide variety of cooking methods, from casseroles to pies. Hare is larger and less common than rabbit, and is considered a delicacy, with its moist, rich flesh and distinctive flavour.

Wild boar meat is more widely available in recent years. Traditionally a game animal, this sturdy wild pig is hunted across Europe and prized for its rich, dark meat. It makes a wonderful stew with a full-bodied flavour.

Below Sheep which have grazed on particular ground, such as salt marshes, provide meat with a distinctive flavour.

Dairy produce and eggs

The country cook has always had access to the freshest milk, cream and eggs, and dairy produce is a very important part of rural cooking. Before the advent of the centralized dairy, many homes had their own cow for providing milk and a few chickens for fresh eggs. Making butter, cream and cheese was a regular ritual and a delicate skill often handed down among the women of the family. Any excess produce was useful for trading, and always found a market.

Milk, cream and yogurt

Domesticated cows, sheep and goats provide milk for the country kitchen, and this can be processed into wonderful thick cream and sour cream, butter, yogurt and cheeses of all kinds and flavours. Buffalo and camels also produce milk, providing a staple food for many cultures.

A rich source of calcium and vitamins, and infinitely versatile, milk can vary in fat content, with the richest full-fat (whole) milk being the best type for cooking.

Traditionally, buttermilk was the liquid left over after churning milk into butter, but today it is more likely to be formed by the addition of lactic acid bacteria to milk, creating a liquid with a thickish texture between milk and yogurt. With its piquant flavour,

buttermilk is used for pancakes, scones and bread, and for tenderizing meat or poultry before cooking.

Double (heavy) cream has a high butterfat content, and is therefore the most frequently used cream for cooking. Whipping cream and single or light cream have much less butterfat and are not so suitable for cooking, but they add richness to a sweet pudding or a white sauce.

Crème fraîche and sour cream are both manufactured products that can add creaminess and bite to a dish. Before the introduction of pasteurization, crème fraîche was created when the bacteria naturally present in cream fermented and thickened. Sour cream

Above Old-fashioned dairy containers like these were often made from pottery to keep the contents cool.

was made by letting fresh cream sour naturally, the acids and bacteria occurring in the cream producing a thick textured cream with a slightly acidic taste, ideal for stirring into savoury soups and casseroles or for adding a twist to a rich, sweet dessert.

Below left Dairy cows provide milk for a range of products, including butter, cream, yogurt and cheese. *Below* Enamel bowls were used for separating curds from whey, and enamel pint pots for measuring milk.

Above Dairy butter, made into blocks or 'pats', was used fresh or salted down to preserve it for longer.

Above This farmhouse goat's cheese has a thick rind, showing it has been aged and has a well-developed flavour.

such as Greek halloumi and feta. The final flavour and texture of the cheese depends on many factors: the type of milk used, what other ingredients are added and how long the cheese is aged or matured.

Eggs

Fresh eggs are an integral part of country cooking, and are a hugely versatile ingredient. Hen's eggs are the most readily available, but duck, goose and quail eggs are also useful additions to the country kitchen – there are numerous traditional recipes which make the most of them in omelettes, cakes and savoury tarts.

Eggs should be kept cool in a pantry or refrigerator, but always brought up to room temperature before use. Always choose the freshest eggs available, especially for recipes such as mayonnaise or chocolate mousse, which use uncooked eggs. Vulnerable groups such as babies and the elderly should avoid eating raw egg.

Yogurt is the bacterial fermentation of milk, to create curds. The most common is made from cow's milk, but sheep and goat's milk also makes good yogurt with a more tangy taste. Probably originating from India, Asia and southern Europe, yogurt may well have been introduced to the rest of the world by travelling nomads. As it has been made for thousands of years, there are many regional varieties. Greek (US strained plain) yogurt is strained to reduce the water content and produce a richer, thicker variety that can easily stand in for cream as a dessert topping. Middle Eastern yogurt – labneh – is thicker still, and used in many savoury dishes.

Butter and cheese

New butter was an everyday luxury in the country for those with access to fresh cream. It was churned from cream and then formed into butter 'pats' or 'rolls', and wrapped in linen or vine leaves to keep it cool and clean. Butter was used fresh and unsalted in the spring and summer, with any surplus salted down to help preserve it for autumn and winter. It is essential in

many cake and biscuit (cookie) recipes, lending flavour to a plain sponge cake or light pastry. It is also used in savoury sauces, or mixed with herbs and seasoning to melt over a simple fish dish or a grilled (broiled) steak. In India, ghee is made by heating butter and straining out the impurities, and this clarified butter is used widely in traditional country cooking.

Cheese, the most versatile and portable of all milk products, can be made from almost any type of milk. Some cheeses are produced with a mixture of two or three types of milk,

Below left Free-range and organic chickens lay eggs that have a bright yolk colour and are nutritionally rich. *Below* The freshest eggs should always be used for recipes that are made with raw egg, such as mayonnaise.

Baking ingredients

Some of the best-loved breads, cakes and biscuits (cookies) that we enjoy today are based on ancient traditional recipes. Early civilizations cooked flat, unleavened bread made simply from ground grains and water, and subsequently baking developed through the centuries with the addition of yeast to make leavened loaves. The first cakes were simply bread dough with added eggs or butter; many country cakes also contained fruit, nuts and seeds gathered wild from the hedgerows. Before commercially refined sugar was available, honey was used to sweeten baked goods. Many recipes for substantial country fruit cakes make the most of rather meagre ingredients, using very little flour, sugar and eggs with plenty of fruit and nuts, which gives a dark, moist cake that has a long storage life.

Unlike much country cooking, baking is based on careful attention to the amounts of each ingredient, and most recipes for cakes and bread rely on measuring by weight or by cup and spoon measures. Most baking also requires specific types of key basic ingredients such as flour. Strong bread flour, for instance, should only be used for baking bread, never cakes.

Like much that is best in country cooking, many rural baking recipes can be time-consuming to prepare, but the flavour and texture of a light home-made sponge cake or a tasty wholemeal (whole-wheat) loaf is well worth the effort.

Bread and cakes

Using only a few ingredients and with very simple equipment, bread-making was a skill which every traditional country cook needed to acquire. Although bread at its simplest is just flour, water, yeast and a little salt and sugar, many country breads are made with numerous other additions, including wholemeal flour, grains such as rye and barley, and oats or seeds added for extra texture and flavour.

Above There are many types of flour and they are not interchangeable – use the correct one to suit the recipe.

Through necessity, many peasant breads dispense with the need for yeast altogether. These include Irish soda bread, Turkish simit, American cornbread and unleaved breads such as Indian chapatis and Mexican tortillas. The need for bread which would keep well throughout the dark winter months led to the flat crisp breads of Scandinavia, while German and Polish peasants baked dark rye bread with added treacle or molasses to give a dense, sustaining texture.

Most of the best-loved, so-called 'fancy breads' were made from the dough left over from a weekly bread baking, with the addition of eggs, sugar, fruit or nuts to make sweetened loaves. Speciality breads with added spices and fruit were often made for celebrations or festivals: many had symbolic relevance, such as English hot cross buns to mark the Easter holiday.

Country cakes tend to be rather substantial, and based on simple but delicious ingredients rather than the elaborate cream-filled confections typical of pâtisserie. Many traditional cakes have their origins rooted in rituals and

Left Bread comes in a variety of shapes and colours, from dark fruity sweet loaves to the classic farmhouse plait.

Left *Baking day was a regular country tradition, providing home-made cakes and muffins for the coming week.*

worship. The Chinese offered up round cakes at harvest time to honour a moon goddess, while the ancient Celts used cakes in rituals on the first day of spring.

All cultures developed their own versions of basic recipes, with home-made cakes in Eastern Europe tending to be darker, spicier and containing more fruit, while in the USA muffins are the ultimate portable breakfast. Plain, nutritious mixtures such as

oatcakes were peasant standbys eaten in place of bread during lean times when wheat was scarce or expensive.

Biscuits, pastry and puddings

From tray-baked flapjacks to crumbly shortbread, biscuits and cookies offered a variety of sweet treats to supplement a basic diet. Many traditional country cooks had a weekly baking day when they made enough cakes and biscuits (as well as bread) to last throughout the rest of the week.

From the simplest plain biscuits made from flour, sugar and a little fat, to rich, chocolate and nut-studded American cookies, the inventive cook has always made use of whatever was available in order to enliven plain dough mixtures. Tray bakes or bar cakes, such as brownies and flapjacks, are easy to

make and transport, and make a good addition to a lunch box or picnic.

Tarts, pies and puddings are emblematic of the country kitchen, and sum up the sort of comfort food that traditional cooking does best. Pastry is a simple mixture of flour and fat, and is the basis of many of the best-known savoury country recipes, such as quiches, pasties, flans and pies. Its sweet form comes in many variations, such as doughnuts or fried churros from Spain. Sweet pastry made with almonds is widely used in Italian, Spanish and Middle Eastern cooking, and the almond-stuffed Gateau de Roi is still the traditional Christmas pastry of Provence.

Steamed puddings were popular in the country because they do not require an oven. A sponge or suet (US chilled, grated shortening) mixture is gently steamed in a covered bowl on the hob for an hour or two. These substantial puddings, often containing fruit inside the pastry crust, only need the addition of a jug (pitcher) of creamy custard to make a delicious sweet treat.

Left *A home-made harvest loaf, shaped like a wheatsheaf to celebrate the end of the harvest, symbolizes the importance of our 'daily bread'.*
Right *Baked desserts and cakes make the most of the fruits and other ingredients available in each season.*

Soups and appetizers

A warming bowl of home-made soup with some crusty bread and a chunk of cheese is a staple lunch or supper, relying, like most country cooking, on good seasonal ingredients. Using a home-made stock makes all the difference. Country pâtés and terrines make the most of off-cuts and can be made with a wide variety of meat and game. They are irresistible when served with home-made pickles.

Rustic mushroom soup

Using a mixture of mushrooms gives real depth of flavour to this soup – if you have some wild mushrooms include them for extra character. Serve with cream and chopped parsley.

**Serves 4–6 as a light meal or
6–8 as a soup course**

20g/¾oz/1½ tbsp butter

15ml/1 tbsp oil

1 onion, roughly chopped

4 potatoes, about 250–350g/
9–12oz, roughly chopped

350g/12oz mixed mushrooms,
such as Paris Browns,
field (portabello) and
button (white)

1 or 2 garlic cloves, crushed

150ml/¼ pint/⅔ cup white
wine or dry (hard) cider

1.2 litres/2 pints/5 cups
good chicken stock

bunch of fresh parsley, chopped

salt and ground black pepper

whipped or sour cream, to garnish

◀ **1** Heat the butter and oil in a large pan, over medium heat. Add the onion and potatoes. Cover and sweat over a low heat for 5–10 minutes until softened but not browned. Chop the mushrooms.

2 Add the mushrooms, garlic and white wine or cider and stock. Season, bring to the boil and cook for 15 minutes, until all the ingredients are tender.

3 Put the mixture through a mouli-légumes (food mill), using the coarse blade, or liquidize (blend). Return the soup to the rinsed pan, and add three-quarters of the parsley. Bring back to the boil, season, and garnish with cream and the remaining parsley.

Per portion Energy 155kcal/648kJ; Protein 3.3g; Carbohydrate 13.6g, of which sugars 3.4g; Fat 7.6g, of which saturates 3.1g; Cholesterol 11mg; Calcium 23mg; Fibre 2.1g; Sodium 117mg.

Garlic soup

This subtly flavoured, aromatic soup is best made with plenty of fresh garlic and good stock – a French traditional soup that is not only delicious but very healthy too.

Serves 8

12 large garlic cloves, peeled

15ml/1 tbsp olive oil

15ml/1 tbsp melted butter

1 small onion, finely chopped

15g/½oz/2 tbsp plain
(all-purpose) flour

15ml/1 tbsp white wine vinegar

1 litre/1¾ pints/4 cups
chicken stock

2 egg yolks, lightly beaten

bread croûtons, fried in
butter, to serve

1 Crush the garlic. Put the oil and butter into a pan, add the garlic and onion, and cook them gently for 20 minutes.

2 Add the flour and stir to make a roux. Cook for a few minutes, then stir in the wine vinegar, stock and 1 litre/1¾ pints/ 4 cups water. Simmer for 30 minutes.

3 When ready to serve, whisk in the egg yolks and do not allow the soup to boil again. Put the croûtons into soup bowls and pour the hot soup over.

Cook's tip This garlic soup brings a great sense of well-being and is a real treat for garlic-lovers.

Per portion Energy 55kcal/229kJ; Protein 1.3g; Carbohydrate 3g, of which sugars 0.5g; Fat 4.4g, of which saturates 1.6g; Cholesterol 54mg; Calcium 12mg; Fibre 0.3g; Sodium 50mg.

French onion soup with Gruyère croûtes

Traditionally served to the working market porters at Les Halles produce market in Paris, this is perhaps the most famous of all French country soups. With the delicious melting Gruyère cheese croûtes floating in the warm bowl, it is a hearty meal in itself.

Serves 6

50g/2oz/¼ cup butter

15ml/1 tbsp olive or groundnut (peanut) oil

2kg/4½lb yellow onions, peeled and sliced

5ml/1 tsp chopped fresh thyme

5ml/1 tsp caster (superfine) sugar

15ml/1 tbsp sherry vinegar

1.5 litres/2½ pints/6¼ cups good beef, chicken or duck stock

25ml/1½ tbsp plain (all-purpose) flour

150ml/¼ pint/⅔ cup dry white wine

45ml/3 tbsp brandy

salt and ground black pepper

For the croûtes

6–12 thick slices day-old French stick or baguette, about 2.5cm/1in thick

1 garlic clove, halved

15ml/1 tbsp French mustard

115g/4oz/1 cup coarsely grated Gruyère cheese

1 Melt the butter with the oil in a large pan. Add the onions and stir to coat them in the fat.

2 Cook over a medium heat for 5–8 minutes, stirring once or twice, until the onions begin to soften. Stir in the thyme.

3 Reduce the heat to very low, cover the pan and cook the onions for about 20–30 minutes, stirring frequently, until they are very soft and golden yellow.

4 Uncover the pan and increase the heat slightly. Stir in the sugar and cook for 5–10 minutes, until the onions start to brown.

5 Add the sherry vinegar and increase the heat again, then continue cooking, stirring frequently, until the onions turn a deep, golden brown – this could take up to 20 minutes. Meanwhile, bring the stock to the boil in another pan.

6 Stir the flour into the onions and cook for about 2 minutes, then gradually pour in the hot stock. Add the wine and brandy and season the soup to taste with salt and pepper. Simmer for 10–15 minutes.

7 For the croûtes, preheat the oven to 150°C/300°F/Gas 2. Place the slices of bread on a greased baking tray and bake for 15–20 minutes, until dry and lightly browned. Rub the bread with the cut surface of the garlic.

8 Spread the croûtes with the mustard, then sprinkle the grated Gruyère cheese over the slices.

9 Preheat the grill (broiler) on the hottest setting. Ladle the soup into a large flameproof pan or six flameproof bowls. Float the croûtes on the soup, then grill (broil) until the cheese melts, bubbles and browns. Serve the soup immediately.

Per portion Energy 484kcal/2030kJ; Protein 15.3g; Carbohydrate 67.2g, of which sugars 21.5g; Fat 15.1g, of which saturates 8.7g; Cholesterol 36mg; Calcium 314mg; Fibre 6.4g; Sodium 611mg.

Parsnip soup

This is a spicy winter country soup. It can also be made with other root vegetables, such as carrots or celeriac. It is delicious garnished with parsnip crisps or fried garlic croûtons.

Serves 6

900g/2lb parsnips

50g/2oz/¼ cup butter

1 onion, chopped

2 garlic cloves, crushed

10ml/2 tsp ground cumin

5ml/1 tsp ground coriander

about 1.2 litres/2 pints/5 cups hot chicken stock

150ml/¼ pint/⅔ cup single (light) cream

salt and ground black pepper

chopped fresh chives or parsley and/or croûtons, to garnish

1 Peel and thinly slice the parsnips. Heat the butter in a large heavy pan and add the peeled parsnips and chopped onion with the crushed garlic. Cook until softened, stirring occasionally.

2 Add the cumin and coriander to the vegetable mixture and cook, stirring, for 1–2 minutes, then gradually blend in the hot chicken stock and mix well.

3 Cover and simmer for about 20 minutes, or until the parsnip is soft. Purée the soup, adjust the texture with extra stock or water if it seems too thick, and check the seasoning. Add the cream and reheat without boiling.

4 Serve immediately, sprinkled with chopped chives or parsley and/or croûtons, to garnish.

Per portion Energy 215kcal/899kJ; Protein 3.9g; Carbohydrate 21.3g, of which sugars 10.6g; Fat 13.3g, of which saturates 7.7g; Cholesterol 32mg; Calcium 92mg; Fibre 7.3g; Sodium 74mg.

Leek and potato soup

A hearty winter classic, this soup is full of chunky vegetables. If you prefer a smooth version, press the soup through a sieve and finish with crème fraîche and sliced fried leeks.

Serves 4

50g/2oz/¼ cup butter

2 leeks, washed and chopped

1 small onion, peeled and finely chopped

350g/12oz potatoes, peeled and chopped

900ml/1½ pints/3¾ cups chicken or vegetable stock

salt and ground black pepper

chopped fresh parsley, to garnish

1 Heat 25g/1oz/2 tbsp of the butter in a large pan over a medium heat. Add the leeks and onion and cook gently, stirring occasionally, for about 7 minutes, until they are softened but not browned.

Cook's tips
• Don't use a food processor to purée this soup as it can give the potatoes a gluey consistency. The potatoes should be left to crumble and disintegrate naturally as they boil, making the consistency of the soup thicker the longer you leave them.
• If you can, make your own chicken or vegetable stock by simmering bones and vegetables in water for 2 hours and straining the liquid.

2 Add the potatoes to the pan and cook for about 2–3 minutes, then add the stock and bring to the boil. Cover and simmer for 30–35 minutes.

3 Season to taste and remove the pan from the heat. Dice and stir in the remaining butter. Garnish with the chopped parsley and serve hot.

Per portion Energy 179kcal/747kJ; Protein 3.2g; Carbohydrate 17.9g, of which sugars 4g; Fat 11g, of which saturates 6.7g; Cholesterol 27mg; Calcium 32mg; Fibre 3g; Sodium 88mg.

Tuscan ribollita

'Ribollita' literally means 're-boiled', and this is a typical dish to make the most of leftovers, including bread and vegetables. Use dark-leaved cavolo nero for an authentic taste.

Serves 4

115g/4oz/generous ½ cup cannellini beans, soaked overnight and drained

8 garlic cloves, unpeeled

30ml/2 tbsp olive oil

6 celery sticks, chopped

3 carrots, chopped

2 onions, chopped

400g/14oz can plum tomatoes, drained

30ml/2 tbsp chopped fresh flat leaf parsley

grated rind and juice of 1 lemon

800g/1¾lb cavolo nero cabbage, sliced

1 day-old ciabatta loaf

salt and ground black pepper

olive oil, to serve

1 Put the beans in a pan and cover with fresh water. Bring to the boil and boil for 10 minutes. Drain again. Cover generously with fresh cold water and add six garlic cloves. Bring to the boil, cover and simmer for 45–60 minutes, until the beans are tender. (The cooking time varies according to how old the beans are.) Set the beans aside in their cooking liquid.

2 Heat the oil in a pan. Peel and chop the remaining garlic and add it to the pan with the celery, carrots and onions. Cook gently for 10 minutes, until beginning to soften.

3 Stir in the tomatoes, parsley, lemon rind and juice. Cover and simmer for 25 minutes.

4 Add the sliced cavolo nero cabbage and half the cannellini beans with enough of their cooking liquid to cover all of the ingredients. Simmer for 30 minutes.

5 Meanwhile, process the remaining beans with a little of their cooking liquid in a food processor until just smooth. Add to the pan and pour in boiling water to thin the mixture to the consistency of a thick soup.

6 Remove the crust from the ciabatta loaf and tear the bread into rough pieces. Stir the torn chunks into the soup. Season well. This soup should be very thick, but you may need to add a little more boiling water because the consistency varies depending on the bread.

7 Ladle the soup into four serving bowls and drizzle a little olive oil over each. Serve immediately.

Per portion Energy 104kcal/436kJ; Protein 5.7g; Carbohydrate 14.5g, of which sugars 6.9g; Fat 3g, of which saturates 0.5g; Cholesterol 0mg; Calcium 78mg; Fibre 5.9g; Sodium 218mg.

Provençal bean and pistou soup

This substantial soup makes the most of nourishing dried beans and fresh vegetables with fresh pistou, the Provençal garlic and basil sauce. Top with a drizzle of olive oil to serve.

Serves 4–6

150g/5oz/scant 1 cup dried haricot (navy) beans, soaked overnight

150g/5oz/scant 1 cup dried flageolet or cannellini beans, soaked overnight

1 onion, chopped

1.2 litres/2 pints/5 cups hot vegetable stock

2 carrots, roughly chopped

225g/8oz Savoy cabbage, shredded

1 large potato, about 225g/8oz, roughly chopped

225g/8oz French (green) beans, chopped

salt and ground black pepper

basil leaves, to garnish

For the pistou

4 garlic cloves

8 large sprigs basil leaves

90ml/6 tbsp olive oil

60ml/4 tbsp freshly grated Parmesan cheese

2 Add the chopped onion and pour over sufficient cold water to come 5cm/2in above the beans. Cover and place the pot in an unheated oven. Set the oven to 200°C/400°F/Gas 6 and cook for about 1½ hours, or until the beans are tender.

3 Drain the beans and onions. Place half the beans and onions in a food processor or blender and process to a paste. Return the beans and paste to the bean pot. Add the vegetable stock.

4 Add the chopped carrots, shredded cabbage, chopped potato and French beans to the pot. Season, cover and return the pot to the oven. Reduce the oven temperature to 180°C/350°F/Gas 4 and cook for 1 hour, or until all the vegetables are cooked.

5 Meanwhile place the garlic and basil in a mortar and pound with a pestle, then gradually beat in the oil. Stir in the grated Parmesan.

6 Stir half of the pistou into the soup and then ladle into warmed bowls. Top each bowl of soup with a spoonful of the remaining pistou and serve immediately, garnished with basil.

1 Soak a bean pot in cold water for 20 minutes, then drain. Drain the soaked haricot and flageolet or cannellini beans and place in the bean pot.

Per portion Energy 286kcal/1214kJ; Protein 19.8g; Carbohydrate 50.9g, of which sugars 11.1g; Fat 1.8g, of which saturates 0.3g; Cholesterol 0mg; Calcium 142mg; Fibre 16.1g; Sodium 36mg.

Country minestrone

The famous Italian country soup from Lombardy is made with small pasta, beans and vegetables, which can include whatever ingredients are at hand from the store cupboard.

Serves 4

45ml/3 tbsp olive oil

115g/4oz pancetta, any rinds removed, roughly chopped

2–3 celery sticks, finely chopped

3 medium carrots, finely chopped

1 medium onion, finely chopped

1–2 garlic cloves, crushed

2 x 400g/14oz cans chopped tomatoes

about 1 litre/1¾ pints/4 cups chicken stock

400g/14oz can cannellini beans, drained and rinsed

50g/2oz/½ cup short–cut macaroni

30–60ml/2–4 tbsp chopped flat leaf parsley, to taste

salt and ground black pepper

shaved Parmesan cheese, to serve

1 Heat the oil in a large pan. Add the pancetta, celery, carrots and onion and cook over a low heat for 5 minutes, stirring constantly, until the vegetables are softened.

2 Add the garlic and tomatoes, breaking them up with a wooden spoon. Pour in the stock. Season to taste and bring to the boil. Half cover the pan, lower the heat and simmer gently for 20 minutes, until the vegetables are soft.

3 Drain the beans and add to the pan with the macaroni. Bring to the boil again. Cover, lower the heat and continue to simmer for about 20 minutes more. Check the consistency and add more stock if necessary. Stir in the parsley and taste for seasoning.

4 Serve hot, sprinkled with plenty of Parmesan cheese.

Per portion Energy 198kcal/833kJ; Protein 15.6g; Carbohydrate 23.3g, of which sugars 3.9g; Fat 5.4g, of which saturates 1.4g; Cholesterol 30mg; Calcium 31mg; Fibre 3.2g; Sodium 224mg.

Summer minestrone

For the warmer months, this colourful and delicious light version of the classic soup is full of summer vegetables and herbs, with new potatoes replacing the pasta.

Serves 4

45ml/3 tbsp olive oil

1 large onion, finely chopped

15ml/1 tbsp sun-dried tomato paste

450g/1lb ripe Italian plum tomatoes, peeled and finely chopped

450g/1lb green and yellow courgettes (zucchini), trimmed and chopped

3 waxy new potatoes, diced

2 garlic cloves, crushed

1.2 litres/2 pints/5 cups chicken stock

60ml/4 tbsp shredded fresh basil

50g/2oz/⅔ cup grated Parmesan cheese

salt and ground black pepper

1 Heat the oil in a large pan, then add the chopped onion and cook gently for about 5 minutes, stirring constantly.

2 Stir in the sun-dried tomato paste, chopped tomatoes, chopped green and yellow courgettes, diced new potatoes and crushed garlic.

3 Mix together well and cook gently for 10 minutes, uncovered, shaking the pan frequently to stop the vegetables sticking to the base.

4 Carefully pour in the chicken stock. Bring to the boil, lower the heat, half cover the pan and simmer gently for 15 minutes or until the vegetables are just tender. Add more stock if necessary.

5 Remove the pan from the heat and stir in the basil and half the cheese. Taste for seasoning. Serve hot, sprinkled with the remaining cheese.

Per portion Energy 201kcal/839kJ; Protein 8.1g; Carbohydrate 18.1g, of which sugars 7.8g; Fat 11.2g, of which saturates 3.4g; Cholesterol 10mg; Calcium 170mg; Fibre 3g; Sodium 138mg.

Autumn pumpkin soup with yogurt

This smooth puréed soup is delicious topped with strained yogurt and melted butter drizzled over the top, but a scattering of crunchy toasted pumpkin seeds make a good garnish too. If pumpkins are not in season, you can use butternut squash instead.

Serves 3–4

1kg/2¼lb prepared pumpkin flesh, cut into cubes

1 litre/1¾ pints/4 cups chicken stock

10ml/2 tsp sugar

25g/1oz/2 tbsp butter, or ghee

60–75ml/4–5 tbsp thick and creamy natural (plain) yogurt

salt and ground black pepper

1 Put the pumpkin cubes into a pan with the stock, and bring the liquid to the boil. Reduce the heat, cover the pan, and simmer for about 20 minutes, or until the pumpkin is tender.

2 Liquidize (blend) the soup in a blender, or use a potato masher to mash the pumpkin flesh. Return the soup to the pan and bring it to the boil again.

3 Add the sugar to the pan and season to taste with salt and pepper. Keep the pan over a low heat while you gently melt the butter or ghee in a small pan over a low heat.

4 Pour the soup into a tureen, or carefully ladle it into individual serving bowls. Swirl a little yogurt on to the surface of the soup and drizzle the melted butter over the top.

5 Serve immediately, offering extra yogurt so that you can enjoy the contrasting burst of sweet and tart in each mouthful.

Per portion Energy 97kcal/406kJ; Protein 2.6g; Carbohydrate 9.3g, of which sugars 8g; Fat 5.8g, of which saturates 3.6g; Cholesterol 14mg; Calcium 104mg; Fibre 2.5g; Sodium 51mg.

Creamy garden pea and mint soup

New peas combined with freshly picked mint from the garden produce a velvety, fresh-tasting soup with a wonderful taste of summer. When peas are out of season, frozen peas will work just as well for this wonderfully green dish.

Serves 6

25g/1oz/2 tbsp butter

1 medium onion,
finely chopped

675g/1½lb shelled fresh peas

1.5ml/¼ tsp sugar

1.2 litres/2 pints/5 cups chicken
or vegetable stock

handful of fresh mint leaves

150ml/¼ pint/⅔ cup double
(heavy) cream

salt and ground black pepper

chopped fresh chives, to serve

1 Melt the butter in a large pan and add the onion. Cook over a low heat for about 10 minutes, stirring occasionally, until soft and just brown.

2 Add the peas, sugar, stock and half the mint. Cover and simmer gently for 10–15 minutes until the peas are tender.

3 Leave to cool slightly. Add the remaining mint and process or blend until smooth. Return the soup to the pan and season to taste.

4 Stir in the cream and reheat gently without boiling. Serve garnished with chopped chives.

Per portion Energy 121kcal/506kJ; Protein 6.1g; Carbohydrate 9.2g, of which sugars 5.2g; Fat 7g, of which saturates 4.2g; Cholesterol 18mg; Calcium 113mg; Fibre 3g; Sodium 123mg.

Country tomato soup

This creamy soup owes its great flavour to a generous mix of fresh and canned tomatoes, but in the summer it can be made with all ripe sweet and fragrant fresh tomatoes from the vine and garnished with a few fresh basil leaves from the kitchen garden.

Serves 4–6

25g/1oz/2 tbsp butter

1 medium onion, finely chopped

1 small carrot, finely chopped

1 celery stick, finely chopped

1 garlic clove, crushed

450g/1lb ripe tomatoes, roughly chopped

400g/14oz can chopped tomatoes

30ml/2 tbsp tomato purée (paste)

30ml/2 tbsp sugar

15ml/1 tbsp chopped fresh thyme or oregano leaves

600ml/1 pint/2½ cups chicken or vegetable stock

600ml/1 pint/2½ cups milk

salt and ground black pepper

1 Melt the butter in a large pan. Add the onion, carrot, celery and garlic. Cook over a medium heat for about 5 minutes, stirring occasionally, until soft and just beginning to brown. Add the tomatoes, purée, sugar, stock and herbs, retaining some to garnish.

2 Bring to the boil, then cover and simmer gently for about 20 minutes until all the vegetables are very soft. Process or blend the mixture until smooth, then press it through a sieve (strainer) to remove the skins and seeds, which can be discarded.

3 Return the sieved (strained) soup to the cleaned pan and stir in the milk. Reheat gently.

4 Stir, without allowing it to boil. Season with salt and pepper. Garnish with the remaining herbs and serve.

Per portion Energy 107kcal/447kJ; Protein 2.3g; Carbohydrate 11.4g, of which sugars 10.9g; Fat 6.1g, of which saturates 3.5g; Cholesterol 13mg; Calcium 50mg; Fibre 3.9g; Sodium 71mg.

Chunky country vegetable soup

Soup-making is an excellent way of making the most of fresh seasonal vegetables just harvested from the garden. This substantial soup makes a hearty appetizer or a satisfying light meal, and goes well with chunks of crusty bread and wedges of cheese.

Serves 6

15ml/1 tbsp oil

25g/1oz/2 tbsp butter

2 medium onions, finely chopped

4 medium carrots, sliced

2 celery sticks, sliced

2 leeks, sliced

1 potato, cut into small cubes

1 small parsnip, cut into small cubes

1 garlic clove, crushed

900ml/1½ pints/3¾ cups vegetable stock

300ml/½ pint/1¼ cups milk

25g/1oz/4 tbsp cornflour (cornstarch)

handful of frozen peas

30ml/2 tbsp chopped fresh parsley

salt and ground black pepper

2 Add the stock to the pan and stir into the vegetables. Bring the mixture slowly to the boil, cover and simmer gently for 20–30 minutes until all the vegetables are tender but not too soft.

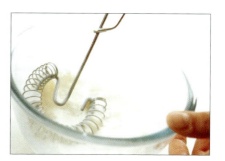

3 Whisk the milk into the cornflour, making a paste. Stir into the vegetables. Add the frozen peas. Bring to the boil and simmer for 5 minutes. Adjust the seasoning, stir in the parsley and serve.

1 Heat the oil and butter in a large pan and add the onions, carrots and celery. Cook over a medium heat for 5–10 minutes, stirring occasionally, until soft and just beginning to turn golden brown. Add the leeks, potato, parsnip and garlic and stir well together.

Per portion Energy 160kcal/665kJ; Protein 3.6g; Carbohydrate 11.5g, of which sugars 10g; Fat 11.4g, of which saturates 6.8g; Cholesterol 27mg; Calcium 72mg; Fibre 5.4g; Sodium 106mg.

Clam, mushroom and potato chowder

This one-pot dish is hearty and substantial enough for supper. The chowder includes sweet, delicately flavoured clams and the earthy flavours of wild and cultivated mushrooms.

Serves 4

48 clams, scrubbed

50g/2oz/¼ cup unsalted (sweet) butter

1 large onion, chopped

1 celery stick, sliced

1 carrot, sliced

225g/8oz assorted wild and cultivated mushrooms

225g/8oz floury potatoes, sliced

1.2 litres/2 pints/5 cups boiling light chicken or vegetable stock

1 thyme sprig

4 parsley stalks

salt and ground black pepper

thyme sprigs, to garnish

1 Place the clams in a large, heavy pan, discarding any that are open. Add 1cm/½in of water to the pan, then cover and bring to the boil.

2 Cook over a medium heat for 6–8 minutes, shaking the pan occasionally, until the clams open (discard any clams that do not open).

3 Drain the clams over a bowl and remove most of the shells, leaving some in the shells as a garnish.

4 Strain the cooking juices into the bowl, add all the cooked clams and set aside.

5 Add the butter, onion, celery and carrot to the pan and cook gently until softened but not coloured.

6 Add the assorted mushrooms and cook for 3–4 minutes until their juices begin to appear. Add the potato slices, the clams and their juices, the chicken or vegetable stock, thyme sprig and parsley stalks.

7 Bring the chowder to the boil, then reduce the heat, cover and simmer for about 25 minutes.

8 Season to taste with salt and pepper, ladle into individual soup bowls, and serve immediately, garnished with thyme sprigs.

Per portion Energy 203kcal/848kJ; Protein 10.8g; Carbohydrate 15.8g, of which sugars 5.2g; Fat 11.2g, of which saturates 6.8g; Cholesterol 60mg; Calcium 66mg; Fibre 2.4g; Sodium 696mg.

Fisherman's soup

Use whichever fish and shellfish you prefer for this tasty main-course soup, which is almost as substantial as a stew. Serve with slices of home-made crusty brown or soda bread.

Serves 6

25g/1oz/2 tbsp butter

1 onion, finely chopped

1 garlic clove, crushed or chopped

1 small red (bell) pepper, seeded and chopped

2.5ml/½ tsp sugar

a dash of Tabasco sauce

25g/1oz/¼ cup plain (all-purpose) flour

about 600ml/1 pint/2½ cups fish stock

450g/1lb ripe tomatoes, skinned and chopped, or 400g/14oz can chopped tomatoes

115g/4oz/1½ cups mushrooms, chopped

about 300ml/½ pint/1¼ cups milk

225g/8oz white fish, such as haddock or whiting, filleted and skinned, and cut into bitesize cubes

115g/4oz smoked haddock or cod, skinned, and cut into bitesize cubes

12–18 mussels, cleaned (optional)

salt and ground black pepper

chopped fresh parsley or chives, to garnish

1 Melt the butter in a large heavy pan and cook the chopped onion and crushed garlic gently in it until softened but not browned. Add the chopped red pepper. Season with salt and pepper, the sugar and Tabasco sauce. Sprinkle the flour over and cook gently for 2 minutes, stirring. Gradually stir in the stock and add the tomatoes, with their juices and the mushrooms.

2 Bring to the boil over medium heat, stir well, then reduce the heat and simmer until the vegetables are soft. Add the milk and bring back to the boil.

3 Add the fish to the pan and simmer for 3 minutes, then add the mussels, if using, and cook for another 3–4 minutes, or until the fish is just tender but not breaking up. Discard any mussels that remain closed. Adjust the consistency with a little extra fish stock or milk, if necessary. Check the seasoning and serve immediately, garnished with parsley or chives.

Per portion Energy 142kcal/597kJ; Protein 13.9g; Carbohydrate 10.7g, of which sugars 7.1g; Fat 5.2g, of which saturates 2.9g; Cholesterol 36mg; Calcium 84mg; Fibre 1.7g; Sodium 91mg.

Southern succotash chicken soup

This home-style soup from the Deep South of America includes fresh corn kernels, butter beans and chicken for a satisfying lunch or supper. Serve with crackers or crisp tortillas.

Serves 4

750ml/1¼ pints/3 cups chicken stock

4 skinless chicken breast fillets

50g/2oz/¼ cup butter

2 onions, chopped

115g/4oz piece rindless smoked streaky (fatty) bacon, chopped

25g/1oz/¼ cup plain (all-purpose) flour

4 cobs of corn

300ml/½ pint/1¼ cups milk

400g/14oz can butter (lima) beans, drained

45ml/3 tbsp chopped fresh parsley

salt and ground black pepper

5 Using a sharp knife, remove the kernels from the corn cobs. Stir the kernels into the pan with half the milk. Return the pan to the heat and cook, stirring occasionally, for about 12–15 minutes, until the corn is tender.

6 Cut the chicken into bitesize pieces and stir into the soup. Stir in the butter beans and the remaining milk. Bring to the boil and cook for 5 minutes, then season well and stir in the parsley.

1 Bring the chicken stock to the boil in a large pan. Add the chicken breasts and bring back to the boil. Reduce the heat and cook for 12–15 minutes, until cooked through and tender. Use a slotted spoon to remove the chicken from the pan and leave to cool. Reserve the stock.

2 Melt the butter in a pan over a low heat. Add the onions and cook for about 4–5 minutes, until softened but not brown.

3 Add the bacon to the pan and cook for 5–6 minutes, until beginning to brown. Sprinkle in the flour and cook for 1 minute, stirring constantly.

4 Gradually stir in the hot stock and bring to the boil, constantly stirring the mixture until the liquid is thickened. Remove from the heat.

Per portion Energy 539kcal/2267kJ; Protein 51.8g; Carbohydrate 37.4g, of which sugars 11.5g; Fat 21.4g, of which saturates 10.3g; Cholesterol 155mg; Calcium 155mg; Fibre 6.4g; Sodium 1120mg.

Mediterranean sausage and pesto soup

This filling soup is a wonderful and satisfying one-pot winter warmer. It is equally good when made with classic Genovese green pesto or sun-dried tomato red pesto.

Serves 4

15ml/1 tbsp olive oil, plus extra for frying

1 red onion, chopped

450g/1lb smoked pork sausages

225g/8oz/1 cup red lentils

400g/14oz can chopped tomatoes

1 litre/1¾ pints/4 cups water

oil, for deep-frying

salt and ground black pepper

60ml/4 tbsp pesto and fresh basil sprigs, to garnish

1 Heat the oil in a large pan and cook the onion until softened. Coarsely chop all the sausages except one and add them to the pan. Cook for about 5 minutes, stirring, or until the sausages are cooked.

2 Stir in the lentils, tomatoes and water, and bring to the boil. Reduce the heat, cover and simmer for about 20 minutes.

3 Cool the soup slightly before puréeing it in a blender. Return the soup to the rinsed-out pan.

4 Cook the remaining sausage in a little oil in a small frying pan for 10 minutes, turning it often, or until lightly browned and firm.

5 Transfer to a chopping board or plate and leave to cool slightly, then slice thinly.

6 Heat the oil for deep-frying to 190°C/375°F or until a cube of bread browns in about 60 seconds. Deep-fry the sausage slices and basil until the sausages are brown and the basil leaves are crisp.

7 Lift the sausages and basil leaves out of the oil using a draining spoon and allow to drain on kitchen paper.

8 Reheat the soup, add seasoning to taste, then ladle into warmed individual soup bowls.

9 Sprinkle each bowl of soup with the deep-fried sausage slices and basil and swirl a little pesto through each portion. Serve with warm crusty bread.

Per portion Energy 656kcal/2741kJ; Protein 30.9g; Carbohydrate 46.7g, of which sugars 8.2g; Fat 39.7g, of which saturates 13.1g; Cholesterol 75mg; Calcium 250mg; Fibre 4.8g; Sodium 1109mg.

Bacon and barley broth

Use a good-sized bacon hock to flavour this soup, which is thick with barley and lentils.
Hearty peasant cooking makes this a nutritious and comforting soup.

Serves 6–8

1 bacon hock, about 900g/2lb

75g/3oz/⅓ cup pearl barley

75g/3oz/⅓ cup lentils

2 leeks, sliced, or onions, diced

4 carrots, diced

200g/7oz swede (rutabaga), diced

3 potatoes, diced

small bunch of herbs (thyme,
parsley, bay leaf)

1 small cabbage, trimmed,
quartered or sliced

salt and ground black pepper

chopped fresh parsley,
to garnish

brown bread, to serve

Cook's tip Traditionally, the cabbage
is simply trimmed and quartered,
although it may be thinly sliced or
shredded, if you prefer.

1 Soak the bacon in cold water
overnight. Next morning, drain it and
put it into a large pan with enough
fresh cold water to cover it. Bring to
the boil, skim off any scum that rises
to the surface, and then add the barley
and lentils. Bring back to the boil and
simmer for about 15 minutes.

2 Add the vegetables to the pan with
some black pepper and the herbs. Bring
back to the boil, reduce the heat and
simmer gently for 1½ hours, or until
the meat is tender.

3 Lift the bacon hock from the pan
with a slotted spoon. Remove the skin,
then take the meat off the bones and
break it into bitesize pieces. Return to
the pan with the cabbage. Discard the
herbs and cook for a little longer until
the cabbage is cooked to your liking.

4 Adjust the seasoning and ladle into
large serving bowls, garnish with
parsley and serve with freshly baked
brown bread.

Per portion Energy 306kcal/1284kJ; Protein 17.7g; Carbohydrate 33.5g, of which sugars 8.3g; Fat 12.1g, of which saturates 4.3g; Cholesterol 35mg; Calcium 74mg; Fibre 4.6g; Sodium 1.05g.

Lamb and vegetable broth

A contemporary version of the classic Irish mutton soup, this meaty broth includes lots of winter vegetables. It is very tasty served with chunks of Irish soda bread.

Serves 6

675g/1½lb neck of lamb (US shoulder or breast) on the bone

1 large onion

2 bay leaves

3 carrots, chopped

½ white turnip, diced

½ small white cabbage, shredded

2 large leeks, thinly sliced

15ml/1 tbsp tomato purée (paste)

30ml/2 tbsp chopped fresh parsley

salt and ground black pepper

1 Trim any excess fat from the meat. Chop the onion, and put the lamb and bay leaves in a large pan. Add 1.5 litres/2½ pints/6¼ cups water and bring to the boil. Skim the surface and then simmer for about 1½–2 hours. Remove the lamb on to a board and leave to cool until ready to handle.

2 Remove the meat from the bones and cut into small pieces. Discard the bones and return the meat to the broth. Add the vegetables, tomato purée and parsley, and season well. Simmer for another 30 minutes, until the vegetables are tender. Ladle into soup bowls and serve.

Per portion Energy 162kcal/675kJ; Protein 13.1g; Carbohydrate 8.5g, of which sugars 7g; Fat 8.6g, of which saturates 3.8g; Cholesterol 44mg; Calcium 42mg; Fibre 3g; Sodium 55mg.

Oxtail soup

Frugal country cooks utilize every part of an animal. Even the cheapest cuts respond well to slow cooking – oxtail becomes rich, dark and tender when slow cooked.

Serves 4–6

1 oxtail, cut into joints, total weight about 1.3kg/3lb

25g/1oz/2 tbsp butter

2 medium onions, chopped

2 medium carrots, chopped

2 celery sticks, sliced

1 bacon rasher (strip), chopped

2 litres/3½ pints/8 cups beef stock

1 bouquet garni

2 bay leaves

30ml/2 tbsp flour

squeeze of fresh lemon juice

60ml/4 tbsp port, sherry or Madeira

salt and ground black pepper

5 When the oxtail has cooled sufficiently to handle, pick all the meat off the bones and cut it into small pieces.

6 Skim off any fat that has risen to the surface of the stock, then transfer the stock into a large pan. Add the pieces of meat and reheat.

1 Wash and dry the pieces of oxtail, trimming off any excess fat. Melt the butter in a large pan, and when foaming, add the oxtail a few pieces at a time and brown them quickly on all sides. Lift the meat out on to a plate.

2 To the same pan, add the onions, carrots, celery and bacon. Cook over a medium heat for 5–10 minutes, stirring, until the vegetables are softened.

3 Return the oxtail to the pan and add the stock, bouquet garni, bay leaves and seasoning. Bring just to the boil and skim off any foam. Cover and simmer gently for about 3 hours or until the meat is so tender that it is falling away from the bones.

4 Strain the mixture, discarding the vegetables, bouquet garni and bay leaves, and leave to stand.

7 With a whisk, blend the flour with a little cold water to make a smooth paste. Stir in a little of the hot stock, then stir the mixture into the pan. Bring to the boil, stirring, until the soup thickens slightly. Reduce the heat and simmer gently for about 5 minutes.

8 Season with salt, pepper and lemon juice to taste. Just before serving, stir in the port, sherry or Madeira.

Per portion Energy 459kcal/1914kJ; Protein 45.4g; Carbohydrate 6.5g, of which sugars 2.6g; Fat 26.8g, of which saturates 11.8g; Cholesterol 176mg; Calcium 36mg; Fibre 0.7g; Sodium 403mg.

Beef and split pea broth

A restorative and nutritious meaty broth that will taste even more delicious when reheated, this hearty country soup will warm and comfort on a dark winter evening.

Serves 6–8

450–675g/1–1½lb rib steak, or other stewing beef on the bone

2 large onions

50g/2oz/¼ cup pearl barley

50g/2oz/¼ cup green split peas

3 large carrots, chopped

2 white turnips, peeled and chopped into dice

3 celery stalks, chopped

1 large or 2 medium leeks, thinly sliced and washed in cold water

sea salt and ground black pepper

chopped fresh parsley, to serve

1 Bone the meat and put the bones and half an onion, roughly sliced, into a large pan. Cover with cold water, season with salt and pepper, and bring to the boil. Skim if necessary, then simmer until needed.

2 Meanwhile, trim any fat or gristle from the meat and cut into small pieces. Chop the remaining onions finely with a sharp knife.

3 Drain the stock from the bones, make it up with water to 2 litres/3½ pints/ 9 cups, and return to the rinsed pan with the meat, onions, barley and split peas.

4 Season, bring to the boil, and skim if necessary. Reduce the heat, cover and simmer for about 30 minutes.

5 Add the carrots, turnip, celery and leeks to the pan and simmer for a further 1 hour, or until the meat is tender. Check the seasoning and adjust if necessary.

6 Serve the soup immediately in large individual warmed bowls, generously sprinkled with the chopped parsley.

Per portion Energy 167kcal/705kJ; Protein 16g; Carbohydrate 21.4g, of which sugars 7.8g; Fat 2.6g, of which saturates 0.8g; Cholesterol 34mg; Calcium 54mg; Fibre 3.6g; Sodium 58mg.

Field mushrooms stuffed with hazelnuts

Meaty field mushrooms filled with an aromatic mix of garlic and parley and topped with crunchy chopped hazelnuts make a delicious vegetarian appetizer or side dish.

Serves 4

2 garlic cloves

grated rind of 1 lemon

90ml/6 tbsp olive oil

8 large field (portabello) mushrooms

50g/2oz/½ cup hazelnuts, coarsely chopped

30ml/2 tbsp chopped fresh parsley

salt and ground black pepper

1 Crush the garlic cloves with a little salt. Place in a bowl and stir in the grated lemon rind and the olive oil. If time allows, leave to infuse (steep).

2 Preheat the oven to 200°C/400°F/ Gas 6. Arrange the field mushrooms, stalk side up, in a single layer in an ovenproof earthenware dish.

3 Drizzle over about 60ml/4 tbsp of the oil mixture and bake in the oven for about 10 minutes.

4 Remove the mushrooms from the oven and baste them with the remaining oil mixture, then sprinkle the chopped hazelnuts evenly over the top.

5 Bake for a further 10–15 minutes, or until the mushrooms are tender. Season with salt and pepper and sprinkle with chopped parsley. Serve immediately.

Cook's tip Almost any unsalted nuts can be used in place of the hazelnuts in this recipe – try pine nuts, cashew nuts, almonds or walnuts. Nuts can go rancid quickly so, for the freshest flavour, either buy nuts in small quantities or buy them in shells and remove the shells just before use.

Per portion Energy 255kcal/1052kJ; Protein 5.2g; Carbohydrate 1.7g, of which sugars 1g; Fat 25.4g, of which saturates 3.1g; Cholesterol 0mg; Calcium 43mg; Fibre 3.1g; Sodium 12mg.

Wild mushroom and sun-dried tomato soufflés

Foraged wild mushrooms would be ideal for this recipe. These delightful soufflés are remarkably easy to prepare, and are perfect either as an appetizer or light lunch.

Serves 4

25g/1oz/½ cup dried
cep mushrooms

40g/1½oz/3 tbsp butter, plus extra
for greasing

20ml/4 tsp grated Parmesan cheese

40g/1½oz/⅓ cup plain
(all-purpose) flour

250ml/8fl oz/1 cup milk

50g/2oz/½ cup grated mature (sharp)
Cheddar cheese

4 eggs, separated

2 sun-dried tomatoes in oil, drained
and chopped

15ml/1 tbsp chopped fresh chives

salt and ground black pepper

Cook's tip A variety of different dried mushrooms are available – any can be used instead of the ceps.

1 Place the ceps in a bowl, pour over enough warm water to cover and leave to soak for 15 minutes. Grease four individual earthenware soufflé dishes with a little butter.

2 Sprinkle the grated Parmesan cheese into the soufflé dishes and rotate each dish to coat the sides with cheese. Preheat the oven to 190°C/375°F/Gas 5.

3 Melt the 40g/1½oz/3 tbsp of butter in a large pan, remove from the heat and stir in the flour. Cook over a low heat for 1 minute, stirring constantly. Remove the pan from the heat and gradually stir in the milk. Return to the heat and bring to the boil, stirring constantly, until the sauce has thickened.

4 Remove the sauce from the heat, then stir in the grated Cheddar cheese and plenty of seasoning. Beat in the egg yolks, one at a time, then stir in the chopped sun-dried tomatoes and the chives. Drain the soaked mushrooms, then coarsely chop them and add them to the cheese sauce.

5 Whisk the egg whites until they stand in soft peaks. Mix one spoonful into the sauce, then carefully fold in the remainder. Divide the mixture among the soufflé dishes and bake for 25 minutes, or until the soufflés are golden brown on top, well risen and just firm to the touch. Serve immediately – before they sink.

Per portion Energy 290kcal/1207kJ; Protein 14.7g; Carbohydrate 11.6g, of which sugars 3.9g; Fat 20.8g, of which saturates 11.2g; Cholesterol 232mg; Calcium 274mg; Fibre 0.6g; Sodium 305mg.

Feta and olive tartlets

Delicious for lunch or a snack, these crisp little tarts showcase the best Mediterranean flavours. They freeze well and can be stuffed with a variety of fillings.

Serves 4

25g/1oz sun-dried aubergine (eggplant) slices

300ml/½ pint/1¼ cups boiling water

45ml/3 tbsp sunflower oil

1 onion, thinly sliced

150g/5oz/2 cups button (white) mushrooms, sliced

1 garlic clove, crushed

12–16 cherry tomatoes, halved

8 black or green olives, pitted and chopped

115g/4oz/1 cup feta cheese, crumbled

350g/12oz ready-made puff pastry

salt and ground black pepper

1 Preheat the oven to 200°C/400°F/ Gas 6. Place the aubergine slices in a shallow dish. Pour over the boiling water and leave to soak for 10 minutes. Rinse in cold water, drain and dry on kitchen paper. Cut the aubergine slices in half or quarters, depending on their size.

Cook's tip Choose cherry tomatoes on the vine or some semi-dried sun blush tomatoes for the very best flavour in these tartlets.

2 Heat 30ml/2 tbsp of the sunflower oil in a frying pan and fry the onion over a medium heat for 4–5 minutes. Add the mushrooms and cook for 3–4 minutes, or until the onions are light golden. Remove and set aside.

3 Heat the remaining oil in the frying pan, add the aubergine slices and garlic and lightly fry for 1–2 minutes. Lightly oil four individual clay pots. Mix the halved tomatoes with the onions, mushrooms, aubergines, olives and feta cheese and divide among the clay pots. Season well.

4 Roll out the pastry thinly into an oblong, then cut out four rounds, each slightly larger than the diameter of the clay pots.

5 Place the pastry rounds on top of the vegetable and cheese mixture, tucking any overlapping pastry down inside the dish.

6 Bake the tarts for about 20 minutes, or until the pastry is risen and golden. Allow to cool slightly, then carefully invert on to individual warmed serving plates to serve.

Per portion Energy 506kcal/2105kJ; Protein 11.1g; Carbohydrate 35.9g, of which sugars 4.1g; Fat 37.2g, of which saturates 5.2g; Cholesterol 20mg; Calcium 175mg; Fibre 1.6g; Sodium 989mg.

Savoury leek and onion tarts

Leeks are a great winter vegetable, and when combined with sliced onion and grated Gruyére cheese, these tarts make a good addition to a picnic, buffet or a vegetarian lunch.

Serves 6

25g/1oz/2 tbsp butter, plus extra for greasing

1 onion, thinly sliced

2.5ml/½ tsp dried thyme

450g/1lb/4 cups leeks, thinly sliced

50g/2oz/½ cup Gruyère cheese, grated

3 eggs

300ml/½ pint/1¼ cups single (light) cream

pinch of freshly grated nutmeg

salt and ground black pepper

mixed salad leaves, to serve

For the pastry

175g/6oz/1½ cups plain (all-purpose) flour

75g/3oz/6 tbsp cold butter

1 egg yolk

30–45ml/2–3 tbsp cold water

2.5ml/½ tsp salt

1 To make the pastry, sift the flour into a large bowl and add the cold butter. Using your hands, gently rub the butter into the flour until the mixture resembles fine breadcrumbs.

2 Make a well in the flour mixture. Beat together the egg yolk, water and salt. Pour into the well and mix lightly to form a stiff dough. Form into a flattened ball. Wrap and chill for 30 minutes.

3 Butter six 10cm/4in tartlet tins (muffin pans). On a lightly floured surface, roll out the dough until 3mm/⅛in thick then, using a 12.5cm/5in cutter, cut as many rounds as possible. Ease the rounds into the tins, pressing the pastry firmly into the base and sides. Reroll the trimmings and line the remaining tins. Prick the bases and chill for 30 minutes.

4 Preheat the oven to 190°C/375°F/Gas 5. Line the pastry cases with foil and fill with baking beans. Place them on a baking sheet and bake for 6–8 minutes until golden at the edges.

5 Remove the foil and beans, and bake for 2 minutes until the bases appear dry. Transfer to a wire rack to cool. Reduce the oven temperature to 180°C/350°F/Gas 4.

6 In a large frying pan, melt the butter over a medium heat, then add the onion and thyme, and cook for 3–5 minutes until the onion is just softened, stirring frequently. Add the leeks and cook for 10–12 minutes until they are soft and tender. Divide the mixture among the pastry cases and sprinkle each with cheese, dividing it evenly.

7 In a medium bowl, beat the eggs, cream, nutmeg and salt and pepper. Place the pastry cases on a baking sheet and pour on the egg mixture.

8 Bake for 15–20 minutes until set and golden. Transfer the tartlets to a wire rack to cool slightly, then remove them from the tins and serve warm or at room temperature with a selection of fresh salad leaves.

Per portion Energy 422kcal/1755kJ; Protein 11.5g; Carbohydrate 26.8g, of which sugars 3.9g; Fat 30.4g, of which saturates 17.7g; Cholesterol 200mg; Calcium 189mg; Fibre 2.7g; Sodium 215mg.

Warm potato cakes with smoked salmon

Smoked wild salmon or trout are both delicious on these versatile little potato cakes.
They can also be served for breakfast with scrambled eggs and crispy bacon or pancetta.

Serves 6

450g/1lb potatoes, cooked
and mashed

75g/3oz/⅔ cup plain
(all-purpose) flour

2 eggs, beaten

2 spring onions
(scallions), chopped

a little freshly grated nutmeg

50g/2oz/¼ cup butter, melted

150ml/¼ pint/⅔ cup sour cream

12 slices of smoked salmon

salt and ground black pepper

chopped fresh chives,
to garnish

1 Put the potatoes, flour, eggs and spring onions into a large bowl. Season with salt, pepper and a little nutmeg, and add half the butter. Mix thoroughly and shape into 12 small potato cakes.

◀ **2** Heat the remaining butter in a non-stick pan and cook the potato cakes until browned on both sides.

3 To serve, mix the sour cream with some salt and pepper. Fold a piece of smoked salmon and place on top of each potato cake. Top with the cream and chives and serve immediately.

Cook's tip You can make the potato cakes in advance and keep them in the refrigerator. When required, warm them through in a hot oven 15 minutes before serving and assembling.

Variation Top the potato cakes with smoked mackerel and a squeeze of lemon juice, if you like.

Per portion Energy 326kcal/1365kJ; Protein 21.9g; Carbohydrate 22.9g, of which sugars 2.3g; Fat 17g, of which saturates 8.6g; Cholesterol 119mg; Calcium 70mg; Fibre 1.2g; Sodium 1315mg.

Potted prawns

Traditionally made with tiny brown shrimp which can be fiddly to prepare, this recipe is equally good with prawns. Serve with toasted country bread and lemon quarters.

Serves 4

225g/8oz/2 cups peeled prawns (shrimp)

225g/8oz/1 cup butter

pinch of ground mace

salt, to taste

cayenne pepper

dill sprigs, to garnish

lemon wedges and thin slices of brown bread and butter, to serve

1 Chop a quarter of the prawns. Melt 115g/4oz/½ cup of the butter slowly, carefully skimming off any foam that rises to the surface with a metal spoon.

2 Stir all the prawns, the mace, salt and cayenne into the pan and heat gently without boiling. Pour the prawns and butter mixture into four individual pots and leave to cool.

3 Heat the remaining butter in a clean small pan, then carefully spoon the clear butter over the prawns, leaving behind the sediment.

4 Leave until the butter is almost set, then place a dill sprig in the centre of each pot. Leave to set completely, then cover and chill.

5 Transfer the prawns to room temperature 30 minutes before serving with lemon wedges for squeezing over and thin slices of brown bread and butter.

Variation Other fish can be prepared in the same way. Try cooked salmon or trout fillet, skinned and flaked, or try a mixture of prawns and salmon.

Per portion Energy 461kcal/1901kJ; Protein 10.3g; Carbohydrate 0.4g, of which sugars 0.4g; Fat 46.6g, of which saturates 29.4g; Cholesterol 230mg; Calcium 55mg; Fibre 0g; Sodium 448mg.

Country duck pâté with redcurrants

Depending on availability, chicken or duck livers can be used interchangeably to make this lovely country appetizer. The tart flavours and pretty colour and texture of the tiny red berries complement the rich pâté perfectly. This recipe is easy to prepare and the pâté keeps for about a week in the refrigerator if the butter seal is not broken.

Serves 4–6

1 onion, finely chopped

1 large garlic clove, crushed

115g/4oz/½ cup butter

225g/8oz duck livers

10–15ml/2–3 tsp chopped fresh mixed herbs, such as parsley, thyme or rosemary

15–30ml/1–2 tbsp brandy

bay leaf (optional)

50–115g/2–4oz/¼ –½ cup clarified butter, or melted unsalted (sweet) butter

salt and ground black pepper

a sprig of flat leaf parsley, to garnish

For the redcurrant sauce

30ml/2 tbsp redcurrant jelly

15–30ml/1–2 tbsp port

30ml/2 tbsp redcurrants

For the Melba toast

8 slices white bread, crusts removed

1 Cook the onion and garlic in 25g/1oz/2 tbsp of the butter in a pan over gentle heat, until just turning colour.

2 Trim the duck livers. Add to the pan with the herbs and cook together for about 3 minutes, or until the livers have browned on the outside but are still pink in the centre. Allow to cool.

3 Dice the remaining butter, then process the liver mixture in a food processor, gradually working in the cubes of butter by dropping them down the chute on to the moving blades, to make a smooth purée.

4 Add the brandy, then check the seasoning and transfer to a 450–600ml/½–1 pint/scant 2 cups dish. Lay a bay leaf on top if you wish, then seal the pâté with clarified or unsalted butter. Cool, and then chill in the refrigerator until required.

5 To make the redcurrant sauce, put the redcurrant jelly, port and redcurrants into a small pan and bring gently to boiling point. Simmer for about 10 minutes to make a rich consistency. Leave to cool.

6 To make the Melba toast, toast the bread on both sides, then carefully slice each piece of toast vertically to make 16 very thin slices.

7 Place each piece of toast, with the untoasted side up, on a grill (broiler) rack and grill (broil) until browned. (The toast can then be stored in an airtight container for a few days, then warmed through to crisp up again just before serving.)

8 Serve the chilled pâté garnished with parsley and accompanied by Melba toast or toasted slices of brioche and the redcurrant sauce.

Per portion Energy 794kcal/3312kJ; Protein 101.3g; Carbohydrate 11.3g, of which sugars 9.9g; Fat 36.8g, of which saturates 19g; Cholesterol 2213mg; Calcium 73mg; Fibre 1.3g; Sodium 608mg.

Gamekeeper's terrine

Hare and other furred game are popular in country cooking, having been hunted as food for centuries. For tender meat and a good flavour, use young hare that has been hung for at least a week. Rabbit would also be delicious in this terrine, or a mixture of minced pork and rabbit meat. Make sure you have plenty of hot toast to serve with it.

Serves 4–6

5 dried mushrooms, rinsed and soaked in warm water for 30 minutes

saddle, thighs, liver, heart and lungs of 1 hare

2 onions, cut into wedges

1 carrot, chopped

1 parsnip, chopped

4 bay leaves

10 allspice berries

300g/11oz calf's liver

165g/5½oz unsmoked streaky (fatty) bacon rashers (strips)

75g/3oz/1½ cups soft white breadcrumbs

4 eggs

105ml/7 tbsp 95 per cent proof Polish spirit or vodka

5ml/1 tsp freshly grated nutmeg

10ml/2 tsp dried marjoram

10g/¼oz juniper berries

4 garlic cloves, crushed

150g/5oz smoked streaky (fatty) bacon rashers (strips)

salt and ground black pepper, to taste

redcurrant jelly and salad, to serve

Cook's tip To make sure the bacon doesn't shrink during cooking, stretch each rasher (strip) out thinly on a board with the back of a knife.

1 Drain the mushrooms and slice into strips. Put the pieces of hare in a large pan and pour in enough water to just cover. Add the onions, carrot, parsnip, mushrooms, bay leaves and allspice.

2 Bring to the boil, then cover and simmer gently for 1 hour. Add a pinch of salt and allow the meat to cool in the stock.

3 Slice the liver and 50g/2oz unsmoked bacon into small pieces and put in a medium pan. Add a ladleful of the stock and simmer for 15 minutes.

4 Preheat the oven to 180°C/350°F/Gas 4. Put two ladlefuls of the stock in a small bowl, add the breadcrumbs and leave to soak.

5 Remove the hare pieces, liver and bacon from the stock and chop finely with a large knife.

6 Transfer to a large bowl, then add the soaked breadcrumbs, eggs, Polish spirit or vodka, nutmeg, marjoram, juniper berries and crushed garlic. Season to taste and mix well to combine thoroughly.

7 Line a 1.2 litre/2 pint/5 cup ovenproof dish with the smoked and remaining unsmoked bacon rashers, making sure they overhang the edges. Spoon in the meat mixture and bring the overhanging bacon over the top. Cover with buttered baking parchment, then cover with a lid or foil.

8 Place the dish in a roasting pan containing boiling water, then put in the oven and bake for 1½ hours, or until a skewer pushed into the centre comes out clean and the juices run clear. Remove the baking parchment and lid or foil about 15 minutes before the end of cooking to allow the terrine to brown.

9 Remove from the oven, and take the dish out of the roasting pan. Cover the terrine with baking parchment and a board and weight down with a 900g/2lb weight (such as two cans). Leave to cool, then turn out on to a serving dish. Serve in slices with redcurrant jelly and a green salad.

Per portion Energy 266kcal/1112kJ; Protein 27.1g; Carbohydrate 6.4g, of which sugars 1.4g; Fat 14g, of which saturates 5g; Cholesterol 182mg; Calcium 25mg; Fibre 0.3g; Sodium 432mg.

Fish and shellfish

Steamed, grilled or barbecued, fish and shellfish are the ultimate fast food. More elaborate dishes, such as Bouillabaisse, originate from the practical needs of fisher folk – after selling the prime catch, the leftover small or ugly fish would be included in tasty and filling stews, transforming them into delicious and nutritious meals. Many cultures share the same basic fish recipes, which can be adapted to include whichever fish are available.

Kedgeree

A popular breakfast dish in Victorian England, Kedgeree can be made with a variety of smoked fish, and is equally good when served for brunch or at lunchtime.

Serves 4–6

450g/1lb smoked haddock

300ml/½ pint/1¼ cups milk

175g/6oz/scant 1 cup long grain rice

pinch of grated nutmeg and cayenne pepper

50g/2oz/¼ cup butter

1 onion, peeled and finely chopped

2 hard-boiled eggs

salt and ground black pepper

chopped fresh parsley, to garnish

lemon wedges and wholemeal (whole-wheat) toast, to serve

1 Poach the haddock in the milk, made up with just enough water to cover the fish, for about 8 minutes, or until just cooked. Skin the haddock, remove all the bones and flake the flesh with a fork. Set aside.

2 Bring 600ml/1 pint/2½ cups water to the boil in a large pan. Add the rice, cover closely with a lid and cook over a low heat for about 25 minutes, or until all the water has been absorbed by the rice. Season with salt and a grinding of black pepper, and the nutmeg and cayenne pepper.

3 Meanwhile, heat 15g/½oz/1 tbsp butter in a pan and fry the onion until soft and transparent. Set aside. Roughly chop one of the hard-boiled eggs and slice the other into neat wedges.

4 Stir the remaining butter into the rice and add the flaked haddock, onion and the chopped egg. Season to taste and heat the mixture through gently (this can be done on a serving dish in a low oven if more convenient).

5 To serve, pile up the kedgeree on a warmed dish, sprinkle generously with parsley and arrange the wedges of egg on top. Put the lemon wedges around the base and serve hot with the toast.

Variation Instead of the haddock, try leftover cooked salmon.

Per portion Energy 399kcal/1668kJ; Protein 28.9g; Carbohydrate 38g, of which sugars 2.2g; Fat 14.6g, of which saturates 7.6g; Cholesterol 181mg; Calcium 62mg; Fibre 0.5g; Sodium 974mg.

Plaice with sorrel and lemon butter sauce

Sorrel is a delicate wild herb that is perfect in this recipe because it does not overwhelm the flavour of the fish. The lemon butter sauce would be good with turbot or brill.

Serves 4

200g/7oz/scant 1 cup butter

500g/1¼lb plaice fillets, skinned and patted dry

30ml/2 tbsp chopped fresh sorrel

90ml/6 tbsp dry white wine

a little lemon juice

1 Heat half the butter in a large frying pan and place the fillets skin side down. Cook briefly, just to firm up, reduce the heat and turn the fish over. The fish will be cooked in less than 5 minutes.

2 Try not to let the butter brown or allow the fish to colour. Remove the fish fillets from the pan and keep warm between two plates. Cut the remaining butter into chunks. Add the chopped sorrel to the pan and stir.

3 Add the wine, then the butter, swirling it in and not allowing the sauce to boil. Stir in a little lemon juice. Serve the fish with the sorrel and lemon butter spooned over, with some crunchy green beans and new potatoes, if you like.

Per portion Energy 494kcal/2047kJ; Protein 25.7g; Carbohydrate 0.5g, of which sugars 0.5g; Fat 43.3g, of which saturates 26.4g; Cholesterol 170mg; Calcium 98mg; Fibre 0.3g; Sodium 501mg.

Haddock in cider sauce

Both smoked and unsmoked, haddock is a popular fish that finds its way into many
traditional country dishes. It is a firm, meaty fish, so is beautifully complemented by
the well-flavoured dry cider sauce in this recipe. New potatoes, carrots and mangetouts
are perfect accompaniments, together with a garnish of sliced apple sautéed in butter.

Serves 4

675g/1½lb haddock fillet

1 medium onion, thinly sliced

1 bay leaf

2 sprigs fresh parsley

10ml/2 tsp lemon juice

450ml/¾ pint/2 cups dry (hard) cider

25g/1oz/¼ cup cornflour (cornstarch)

30ml/2 tbsp single (light) cream

salt and ground black pepper

1 Cut the haddock fillet into four equal
portions and place in a pan big enough
to hold them neatly in a single layer.
Add the onion, bay leaf, parsley and
lemon juice, and season with salt.

2 Pour in most of the cider, reserving
30ml/2 tbsp for the sauce. Cover and
bring to the boil, reduce the heat
and simmer for 10 minutes, or until
the fish is just cooked.

3 Strain 300ml/½ pint/1¼ cups of the
fish liquor into a measuring jug (cup).
In a small pan, mix the cornflour with
the reserved cider, then gradually
whisk in the fish liquor and bring to
the boil, whisking constantly for about
2 minutes, until it is smooth and
thickened. Add more of the cooking
liquor, if necessary, to make a pouring
sauce. Remove the pan from the heat,
stir in the single cream and season to
taste with salt and freshly ground
black pepper.

4 To serve, remove any skin from
the fish, arrange on individual hot
serving plates with the onion over the
vegetables and pour the sauce over.

Per portion Energy 227kcal/964kJ; Protein 32.8g; Carbohydrate 11.8g, of which sugars 5.2g; Fat 2.6g, of which saturates 1.1g; Cholesterol 65mg; Calcium 50mg; Fibre 0.5g; Sodium 128mg.

West coast fisherman's stew

The location in the title of this recipe refers to the little ports along the west coast of Scotland, places where fishermen land small catches of monkfish, haddock, prawns and crabs. This recipe uses whatever fish and shellfish appear in the catch of the day. Use your favourite fish and vary the shellfish – clams, mussels, prawns or crayfish all work well.

Serves 4

30ml/2 tbsp olive oil

1 large onion, roughly chopped

1 leek, roughly chopped

2 garlic cloves, crushed

450g/1lb ripe tomatoes, roughly chopped

5ml/1 tsp tomato purée (paste)

1.3kg/3lb fish bones

a piece of pared orange peel

a few parsley stalks and fennel fronds

1 bay leaf

250ml/8fl oz/1 cup dry white wine

whisky or pastis, such as Pernod (optional)

1kg/2¼lb mixed fish fillets, such as salmon, sole and haddock, cut into chunks, and prepared shellfish

salt and ground black pepper

chopped fresh parsley, to garnish

1 Heat the olive oil in a large pan, then sweat the onion and leek until soft. Add the garlic, tomatoes and tomato purée, and cook for 5 minutes.

2 Put in the fish bones, orange peel, herbs and wine, and add a little salt and ground black pepper. Then add enough water just to cover. Bring to a gentle boil, then reduce the heat and simmer for 30 minutes.

3 Strain the soup into a clean pan, pressing the juices out of the solid ingredients with the back of a spoon.

4 Bring the liquid back to the boil and check for seasoning and texture. If you like, add a splash of whisky or Pernod. The fish takes just minutes to cook so add the firmer, larger pieces first, such as monkfish or salmon and mussels in the shell, and end with delicate scallops or prawn (shrimp) tails. Do not allow the stew to boil once you add the fish.

5 Serve in warmed soup plates, garnished with chopped fresh parsley.

Per portion Energy 341kcal/1432kJ; Protein 47.5g; Carbohydrate 6.5g, of which sugars 5.8g; Fat 7.8g, of which saturates 1.2g; Cholesterol 115mg; Calcium 53mg; Fibre 2.3g; Sodium 165mg.

Cod and bean casserole with saffron and paprika

It's sometimes nice to dine away from the table, and this is just the no-nonsense dish to do it with. With everything cooked in one pot, this appetizing casserole with chunks of fresh, flaky cod can be served simply with hunks of crusty bread and a crisp green side salad.

Serves 6–8

1 large red (bell) pepper

45ml/3 tbsp olive oil

4 rashers (strips) streaky (fatty) bacon, roughly chopped

4 garlic cloves, finely chopped

1 onion, sliced

10ml/2 tsp paprika

5ml/1 tsp hot pimentón (smoked Spanish paprika)

large pinch of saffron threads or 1 sachet powdered saffron, soaked in 45ml/3 tbsp hot water

400g/14oz jar Spanish butter (lima) beans (judias del barco or judias blancas guisadas) or canned haricot (navy) beans, drained and rinsed

about 600ml/1 pint/2½ cups fish stock, or water and 60ml/4 tbsp Thai fish sauce

6 plum tomatoes, quartered

350g/12oz fresh skinned cod fillet, cut into large chunks

45ml/3 tbsp chopped fresh coriander (cilantro), plus a few sprigs to garnish

salt and ground black pepper

crusty bread, to serve

1 Preheat the grill (broiler) and line the pan with foil. Halve the red pepper and scoop out the seeds.

2 Place the red pepper, cut-side down, in the grill pan and grill (broil) under a hot heat for about 10–15 minutes, until the skin is black and charred.

3 Put the pepper into a plastic bag, seal and leave for 10 minutes to steam, which will make the skin easier to remove.

4 Remove the pepper from the bag, peel and chop into large pieces.

5 Heat the olive oil in a pan, then add the chopped streaky bacon and the chopped garlic. Fry for about 2 minutes, then add the sliced onion.

6 Cover the pan and cook for about another 5 minutes until the onion is soft. Stir in the paprika and pimentón, the saffron and its soaking water, and salt and pepper.

7 Stir the beans into the pan and add just enough of the stock to cover them. Bring to the boil and simmer, uncovered, for about 15 minutes, stirring occasionally to prevent it from sticking.

8 Stir in the chopped pepper and tomato quarters. Drop in the cubes of cod and bury them in the sauce.

9 Cover and simmer for 5 minutes until the fish is cooked. Stir in the chopped coriander.

10 Divide the stew equally between six to eight warmed soup plates or bowls, garnishing each one with the coriander sprigs. Serve with lots of crusty bread.

Cook's tip If you prefer to use dried beans, soak them in water for 12 hours or overnight, rinse and then boil for 40–50 minutes depending on the beans.

Per portion Energy 449kcal/1883kJ; Protein 44.5g; Carbohydrate 25.3g, of which sugars 3.9g; Fat 19.5g, of which saturates 3g; Cholesterol 84mg; Calcium 85mg; Fibre 9.8g; Sodium 403mg.

Salt cod fritters with garlic aioli

A favourite dish of Portuguese, Spanish and French fishermen, salt cod fritters are delicious when served with an aromatic garlic mayonnaise. If you have any leftover aioli, it can be stirred into a bowl of cold potatoes to make a delicious potato salad.

Serves 6

450g/1lb salt cod

500g/1¼lb floury potatoes

300ml/½ pint/1¼ cups milk

6 spring onions (scallions), finely chopped

30ml/2 tbsp extra virgin olive oil

30ml/2 tbsp chopped fresh parsley

juice of ½ lemon, to taste

2 eggs, beaten

60ml/4 tbsp plain (all-purpose) flour

90g/3½oz/1⅓ cups dry white breadcrumbs

vegetable oil, for shallow frying

salt and ground black pepper

lemon wedges and salad, to serve

For the aioli

2 large garlic cloves

2 egg yolks

300ml/½ pint/1¼ cups olive oil

lemon juice, to taste

1 Soak the salt cod in cold water for 24 hours, changing the water about 5 times. The cod should swell as it rehydrates and a tiny piece should not taste too salty when tried. Drain well.

2 Cook the potatoes, unpeeled, in a pan of boiling salted water for about 20 minutes, until tender. Drain, then peel and mash the potatoes.

3 Poach the cod very gently in the milk with half the spring onions for 10–15 minutes, or until it flakes easily. Remove the cod and flake it with a fork into a bowl, discarding bones and skin.

4 Add 60ml/4 tbsp mashed potato to the flaked cod and beat with a wooden spoon. Work in the olive oil, then gradually add the remaining potato. Beat in the remaining spring onions and parsley. Season with lemon juice and pepper to taste – it may need a little salt. Beat in 1 egg, then chill until firm.

5 Shape the mixture into 12 round cakes. Coat them in flour, then dip in the remaining egg and coat with the breadcrumbs. Chill until ready to fry.

6 Meanwhile, make the aioli. Place the garlic and a good pinch of salt in a mortar and pound to a paste with a pestle. Using a small whisk or a wooden spoon, gradually work in the egg yolks.

7 Add the olive oil, a drop at a time, until half is incorporated. When the sauce is as thick as soft butter, beat in 5–10ml/ 1–2 tsp lemon juice, then continue adding oil until the aioli is very thick. Adjust the seasoning, adding lemon juice to taste.

8 Heat 2cm/¾in depth of oil in a frying pan. Add the fritters and cook over a medium-high heat for 4 minutes. Turn over and cook for a further 4 minutes on the other side, until crisp and golden. Drain on kitchen paper, then serve with the aioli, lemon wedges and salad leaves.

Per portion Energy 653kcal/2721kJ; Protein 32.7g; Carbohydrate 28.1g, of which sugars 4.2g; Fat 46.4g, of which saturates 7.6g; Cholesterol 178mg; Calcium 123mg; Fibre 1.4g; Sodium 472mg.

Fresh mackerel with gooseberry relish

Packed with beneficial oils, fresh mackerel is not only tasty but also nutritionally rich. The tart gooseberries in this recipe are good for you too, as well as being a perfect accompaniment to any type of oily fish, including salmon and sardines.

Serves 4

4 whole mackerel

60ml/4 tbsp olive oil

For the sauce

250g/9oz gooseberries

25g/1oz/2 tbsp soft light brown sugar

5ml/1 tsp wholegrain mustard

salt and ground black pepper

1 For the sauce, wash and trim the gooseberries and then roughly chop them, so there are some pieces larger than others.

2 Cook the gooseberries in a little water with the sugar in a small pan. A thick and chunky purée will form. Add the mustard and season to taste with salt and ground black pepper.

Cook's tips
• Turn the grill (broiler) on well in advance as the fish need a fierce heat to cook quickly. If you like the fish but hate the smell, try barbecuing outside.
• The foil lining in the grill pan is to catch the smelly drips. Simply roll it up and throw it away afterwards, leaving a nice clean grill pan.

3 Preheat the grill (broiler) to high and line the grill pan with foil. Using a sharp knife, slash the fish two or three times down each side, then season and brush with the olive oil.

4 Place the fish in the grill pan and grill (broil) for about 4 minutes on each side until cooked. You may need to cook them for a few minutes longer if they are particularly large. The slashes will open up to speed cooking and the skin should be lightly browned. To check that they are cooked properly, use a small sharp knife to pierce the skin and check for uncooked flesh.

5 Place the mackerel on warmed plates and spread generous dollops of the gooseberry relish over them. Pass the remaining sauce around at the table.

Per portion Energy 576kcal/2390kJ; Protein 38.1g; Carbohydrate 8.4g, of which sugars 8.4g; Fat 43.5g, of which saturates 8.2g; Cholesterol 108mg; Calcium 43mg; Fibre 1.5g; Sodium 128mg.

Barbecued stuffed sardines

Perfect for summer barbecues, this recipe can also be made with red mullet or trout. Use plump fresh fish and a mixture of fresh herbs. Simply grill, griddle or barbecue the fish, and then serve with extra lemon wedges for squeezing over the top.

Serves 4

15ml/1 tbsp currants

4 good-sized sardines

30ml/2 tbsp olive oil

6 spring onions (scallions), finely sliced

2–3 garlic cloves, crushed

5ml/1 tsp cumin seeds, crushed

5ml/1 tsp sumac

15ml/1 tbsp pine nuts

1 small bunch flat leaf parsley, leaves finely chopped

salt and ground black pepper

For basting

45ml/3 tbsp olive oil

juice of 1 lemon

5–10ml/1–2 tsp sumac

1 Prepare the barbecue, if using. Soak four wooden skewers in cold water for 30 minutes. Soak the currants in warm water for about 15 minutes, then drain them.

2 Slit the sardines from head to tail with a sharp knife and remove the backbone by gently massaging the area around it to loosen it. Using your fingers, carefully prise out the bone, snapping it off at each end, while keeping the fish intact. Rinse the fish and pat it dry.

3 Heat the oil in a large, heavy frying pan, stir in the spring onions and cook until soft. Add the garlic, cumin and sumac.

4 Add the pine nuts and currants, stir them into the mixture and fry until they begin to turn golden.

5 Toss in the parsley, and season to taste with salt and pepper. Leave to cool.

6 Heat the grill (broiler), if using. Place each sardine on a flat surface and spread the filling inside each one. Seal by threading the skewers through the soft belly flaps.

7 Mix together the olive oil, lemon juice and sumac, and brush some of it over the sardines.

8 Place the fish on the rack over the hot coals and cook them for 2–3 minutes on each side over a medium heat, basting them with the remainder of the olive oil mixture. Alternatively, grill (broil) the sardines. Serve immediately.

Per portion Energy 265kcal/1098kJ; Protein 16.7g; Carbohydrate 4g, of which sugars 3.1g; Fat 20.3g, of which saturates 3.6g; Cholesterol 0mg; Calcium 90mg; Fibre 0.4g; Sodium 88mg.

Pan-fried trout with citrus and basil

Fillets of freshwater trout or sea trout are pan-fried and served with a fresh, citrus sauce.
This light, summer supper is very good served with new potatoes and samphire.

Serves 4

4 trout fillets, each about 200g/7oz

2 lemons

3 oranges

105ml/7 tbsp olive oil

45ml/3 tbsp plain
(all-purpose) flour

25g/1oz/2 tbsp butter

5ml/1 tsp soft light
brown sugar

15g/½oz/½ cup fresh
basil leaves

salt and ground black pepper

1 Arrange the trout fillets in the base of a non-metallic shallow dish. Grate the rind from one lemon and two of the oranges, then squeeze these fruits and pour the combined juices into a jug (pitcher). Slice the remaining fruits and reserve to use as a garnish.

2 Add 75ml/5 tbsp of the oil to the citrus juices. Beat with a fork and pour over the fish. Cover and leave to marinate in the refrigerator for at least 2 hours.

3 Preheat the oven to 150°C/300°F/ Gas 2. Using a fish slice or metal spatula, carefully remove the trout from the marinade.

4 Season the fish and coat each in flour. Heat the remaining oil in a frying pan and add the fish. Fry for 2–3 minutes on each side until cooked, then transfer to a plate and keep hot in the oven.

5 Add the butter and the marinade to the pan and heat gently, stirring until the butter has melted. Season with salt and pepper, then stir in the sugar. Continue cooking gently for 4–5 minutes until the sauce has thickened slightly.

6 Finely shred half the basil leaves and add them to the pan. Pour the sauce over the fish and garnish with the remaining basil and the orange and lemon slices.

Cook's tip Basil leaves bruise very easily, so they should always be shredded by hand or used whole rather than cut with a knife. Don't use any leaves that are shrivelled or have brown patches on them.

Per portion Energy 266kcal/1119kJ; Protein 40.5g; Carbohydrate 7.9g, of which sugars 7.7g; Fat 8.3g, of which saturates 0.2g; Cholesterol 0mg; Calcium 140mg; Fibre 1.7g; Sodium 177mg.

Flanders fish gratin

The coastal ports of Belgium are renowned for the quality of their seafood, and this dish makes the most of the catch. It is topped with bubbling hot cheese.

Serves 4

400g/14oz firm fish fillets, such as monkfish, salmon, turbot or cod

200g/7oz cooked grey shrimp and/or shelled cooked mussels, or peeled uncooked scampi (extra large shrimp)

1 litre/1¾ pints/4 cups fish stock

100g/3½oz/scant ½ cup butter

50g/2oz/½ cup plain (all-purpose) flour

100ml/3½fl oz/scant ½ cup dry white wine or dry vermouth

100ml/3½fl oz/scant ½ cup double (heavy) cream

115g/4oz/1 cup grated cheese (see Cook's tip)

45ml/3 tbsp chopped fresh parsley

salt and ground white pepper

crusty bread or potato croquettes, to serve

Cook's tip Use a mixture of cheeses. Belgians use a combination of local cheeses, but a mixture of Gruyère and Parmesan cheese also works well. A mixture of cheese and breadcrumbs also makes a good topping.

1 Preheat the oven to 200°C/400°F/ Gas 6. Grease a 1.2 litre/2 pint/5 cup baking dish or four individual dishes.

2 Cut the fish fillets into even cubes, removing any stray bones.

3 Bring the fish stock to the boil in a large pan. Add the fish cubes, reduce the heat and poach for 2 minutes. If using scampi, poach them for 1 minute, until barely pink.

4 As soon as the fish pieces are cooked, lift them out with a slotted spoon and layer in the dish or dishes. Season and cover to keep warm. Pour the fish stock into a measuring jug (cup).

5 Melt the butter in a large pan over a medium heat. When the butter begins to foam, whisk in the flour and stir for 2 minutes.

6 Stirring all the time, add 500ml/ 17fl oz/generous 2 cups of the reserved fish stock in a steady stream, saving the rest to thin the sauce later if necessary. Add the white wine or vermouth in the same way. Simmer for 3 minutes, stirring, then add the cream. Season and simmer for 1 minute more.

7 Remove from the heat and add the grated cheese, reserving 45ml/3 tbsp for the topping. Stir in the grey shrimp and/or mussels, with 15ml/1 tbsp of the parsley, and spoon evenly over the fish. Sprinkle with the reserved cheese.

8 Bake for 10–15 minutes, until the cheese melts and turns golden. Sprinkle with the remaining parsley and serve immediately with crusty bread or potato croquettes.

Per portion Energy 612kcal/2541kJ; Protein 36g; Carbohydrate 10.5g, of which sugars 1g; Fat 45.3g, of which saturates 27.9g; Cholesterol 190mg; Calcium 358mg; Fibre 0.4g; Sodium 531mg.

Whole baked salmon with watercress sauce

Served as an impressive centrepiece, this whole baked salmon would make a stunning focal point for a country dining table. Healthy and delicious, the dish is equally good served hot or cold. The peppery watercress sauce and fresh cucumber complement the salmon perfectly.

Serves 6–8

2–3kg/4$\frac{1}{2}$–6$\frac{1}{2}$lb salmon, cleaned, with head and tail left on

3–5 spring onions (scallions), thinly sliced

1 lemon, thinly sliced

1 cucumber, thinly sliced

salt and ground black pepper

sprigs of fresh dill, to garnish

lemon wedges, to serve

For the sauce

3 garlic cloves, chopped

200g/7oz watercress leaves, finely chopped

40g/1$\frac{1}{2}$oz/$\frac{3}{4}$ cup finely chopped fresh tarragon

300g/11oz/1$\frac{1}{4}$ cups mayonnaise

15–30ml/1–2 tbsp lemon juice

200g/7oz/scant 1 cup unsalted (sweet) butter

1 Preheat the oven to 180°C/350°F/ Gas 4. Rinse the salmon and lay it on a large piece of foil. Stuff the fish with the sliced spring onions and lemon. Season with salt and black pepper.

2 Loosely fold the foil around the fish and fold the edges over to seal. Bake in the preheated oven for about 1 hour.

3 Remove the fish from the oven and leave it to stand, still wrapped in the foil, for about 15 minutes. Then gently unwrap the foil parcel and set the salmon aside to cool.

4 When the fish has cooled, carefully lift it on to a large plate, still covered with lemon slices. Cover the fish tightly with clear film (plastic wrap) and chill for several hours in the refrigerator.

5 Remove the lemon slices from the top of the fish. Use a blunt knife to lift up the edge of the skin and carefully peel the skin away from the flesh, avoiding tearing the flesh. Pull out any fins at the same time. Carefully turn the salmon over and repeat on the other side. Leave the head on for serving, if you wish. Discard the skin.

Variation If you prefer to poach the fish rather than baking it, you will need to use a fish kettle. Place the salmon on the rack in the kettle. Cover the salmon completely with cold water, place the lid over to cover, and slowly bring to a simmer. Cook for 5–10 minutes per 450g/1lb until tender. The fish is cooked when pink and opaque.

6 To make the sauce, put the garlic, watercress, tarragon, mayonnaise and lemon juice in a food processor or bowl, and process or mix to combine.

7 Melt the butter, then add to the watercress mixture a little at a time, processing or stirring until the butter has been incorporated and the sauce is thick and smooth. Cover and chill.

8 Arrange the cucumber slices in overlapping rows along the length of the fish, so that they look like large fish scales. You can also slice the cucumber diagonally to produce longer slices for decoration. Trim the edges with scissors. Serve the fish, garnished with dill and lemon wedges, with the watercress sauce alongside.

Cook's tip Do not prepare the sauce hours before you need it because the watercress will discolour. Alternatively, add the watercress just before serving.

Per portion Energy 1044kcal/4323kJ; Protein 51.6g; Carbohydrate 1.4g, of which sugars 1.2g; Fat 92.4g, of which saturates 28.5g; Cholesterol 231mg; Calcium 135mg; Fibre 0.7g; Sodium 558mg.

Chunky salmon and potato fishcakes

The secret of a good fishcake is to make it with freshly prepared fish and potatoes, home-made breadcrumbs and plenty of interesting seasoning. This recipe makes a great mid-week supper, and you can serve the fishcakes with tartare sauce or garlic mayonnaise.

Serves 4

450g/1lb cooked salmon fillet

450g/1lb freshly cooked potatoes, mashed

25g/1oz/2 tbsp butter, melted

10ml/2 tsp wholegrain mustard

15ml/1 tbsp each chopped fresh dill and chopped fresh flat leaf parsley

grated rind and juice of ½ lemon

15g/½oz/1 tbsp plain (all-purpose) flour

1 egg, lightly beaten

150g/5oz/generous 1 cup dried breadcrumbs

60ml/4 tbsp sunflower oil

salt and ground white pepper

rocket (arugula) leaves and fresh chives, to garnish

lemon wedges, to serve

1 Flake the cooked salmon, watching carefully for and discarding any skin and bones. Place the flaked salmon in a bowl with the mashed potato, melted butter and wholegrain mustard. Mix well, then stir in the chopped fresh dill and parsley, lemon rind and juice. Season to taste.

2 Divide the mixture into eight portions and shape each into a ball, then flatten into a thick disc. Dip the fishcakes first in flour, then in egg and finally in breadcrumbs, making sure they are evenly coated.

3 Heat the oil in a frying pan until very hot. Fry the fishcakes in batches until golden brown and crisp all over. As each batch is ready, drain on kitchen paper and keep hot.

4 Warm some plates and place two fishcakes on to each one. Garnish with rocket leaves and chives, and serve with lemon wedges.

Variations
• Almost any fresh white or hot-smoked fish is suitable; smoked cod and haddock are particularly good.
• A mixture of smoked and unsmoked fish also works well, as does a mixture of salmon and chopped prawns (shrimp).

Per portion Energy 586kcal/2453kJ; Protein 29.8g; Carbohydrate 49.9g, of which sugars 3.2g; Fat 31g, of which saturates 7.2g; Cholesterol 117mg; Calcium 79mg; Fibre 1.3g; Sodium 266mg.

Grilled scallops with bacon

This simple recipe combines succulent scallops and crispy bacon with butter that has just begun to burn but not quite. This gives the dish a lovely nutty smell and a mouth-watering texture. It is delicious served with minted peas and sautéed potatoes.

Serves 4

12 rashers (strips) streaky (fatty) bacon

12 scallops

225g/8oz/1 cup unsalted (sweet) butter

juice of 1 lemon

30ml/2 tbsp chopped fresh flat leaf parsley

ground black pepper

1 Preheat the grill (broiler) to high. Wrap a rasher of bacon around each scallop so it goes over the top and not round the side.

2 Cut the butter into chunks and put them into a small pan over a low heat.

3 Meanwhile grill (broil) the scallops with the bacon facing up so it protects the meat. The bacon fat will help to cook the scallops. This will take only a few minutes; once they are cooked set aside and keep warm.

4 Allow the butter to turn a nutty brown colour, gently swirling it from time to time. Just as it is foaming and darkening, take off the heat and add the lemon juice. Be warned, it will bubble up quite dramatically.

5 Place the scallops on warmed plates, dress with plenty of chopped fresh parsley and pour the butter over.

Cook's tip Get the scallops on to warmed plates just as the butter is coming to the right colour, then add the lemon juice.

Per portion Energy 665kcal/2749kJ; Protein 24.4g; Carbohydrate 2.7g, of which sugars 0.6g; Fat 62g, of which saturates 34.7g; Cholesterol 189mg; Calcium 51mg; Fibre 0.5g; Sodium 1240mg.

Maryland crab cakes with tartare sauce

One of the most famous American country dishes, these crab cakes are a modern version
of Baltimore crab cakes. The tasty white crab meat is coated in breadcrumbs and fried.

Serves 4

675g/1½lb fresh crab meat

1 egg, beaten

30ml/2 tbsp mayonnaise

15ml/1 tbsp Worcestershire sauce

15ml/1 tbsp sherry

30ml/2 tbsp finely chopped
fresh parsley

15ml/1 tbsp finely chopped
fresh chives

salt and ground black pepper

45ml/3 tbsp olive oil

For the sauce

1 egg yolk

15ml/1 tbsp white wine vinegar

30ml/2 tbsp Dijon-style mustard

250ml/8fl oz/1 cup vegetable oil

30ml/2 tbsp fresh lemon juice

20g/¾oz/¼ cup finely chopped
spring onions (scallions)

30ml/2 tbsp chopped drained capers

few finely chopped sour dill pickles

60ml/4 tbsp finely chopped
fresh parsley

1 Pick over the crab meat, removing
any shell or cartilage.

2 In a mixing bowl, combine the
beaten egg with the mayonnaise,
Worcestershire sauce, sherry and herbs.
Season with salt and pepper. Gently
fold in the crab meat. Divide the
mixture into eight portions and gently
form each one into an oval cake. Place
on a baking sheet between layers of
baking parchment and chill for 1 hour.

3 Make the sauce. In a bowl, beat the
egg yolk. Add the vinegar, mustard and
salt and pepper, and whisk for 10 seconds.
Whisk in the oil in a slow, steady stream.

4 Add the lemon juice, spring onions,
capers, pickles and parsley and mix
well. Check the seasoning. Cover
and chill for at least 30 minutes.

5 Preheat the grill (broiler). Brush the
crab cakes with the olive oil. Place on
an oiled baking sheet, in one layer.

6 Grill (broil) 15cm/6in from the heat
until golden brown, about 5 minutes
on each side. Serve the crab cakes hot
with the tartare sauce.

Variation You can use defrosted
frozen or canned crab meat instead.

Per portion Energy 710kcal/2934kJ; Protein 33.8g; Carbohydrate 1.9g, of which sugars 1.7g; Fat 62.6g, of which saturates 8.1g; Cholesterol 225mg; Calcium 234mg; Fibre 0.2g; Sodium 1249mg.

Moules marinière

Serve this French country classic with a big bowl of fries and chunks of crusty bread to soak up the sauce. As an alternative, you could try cooking the mussels in Belgian beer.

Serves 2

25g/1oz/2 tbsp butter

300ml/½ pint/1¼ cups dry white wine

1kg/2¼lb mussels, cleaned

45ml/3 tbsp chopped fresh parsley

salt and ground black pepper

Cook's tip Use line-grown mussels if possible and the freshest you can find. Tip them into the sink and rinse several times in cold water before draining well.

1 Heat the butter in a large pan until foaming, then pour in the wine. Bring to the boil.

2 Discard any open mussels that do not close when sharply tapped, and add the remaining ones to the pan.

3 Cover with a tight-fitting lid and cook over a medium heat for 4–5 minutes, shaking the pan every now and then. By this time, all the mussels should have opened. Discard any that are still closed.

4 Line a large sieve (strainer) with kitchen paper and strain the mussels and their liquid through it. Transfer the mussels to warmed serving bowls.

5 Pour the liquid into a small pan and bring to the boil. Season with salt and pepper and stir in the parsley. Pour over the mussels and serve immediately.

Per portion Energy 189kcal/799kJ; Protein 26.4g; Carbohydrate 2.4g, of which sugars 1.9g; Fat 3.1g, of which saturates 0.5g; Cholesterol 60mg; Calcium 308mg; Fibre 0.4g; Sodium 319mg.

Dressed crab with asparagus

Considerably cheaper than lobster, crab meat is just as juicy and flavourful, and at its best when asparagus comes into season. Try this crab dish with a splash of Tabasco sauce.

Serves 4

24 asparagus spears

4 dressed crabs

30ml/2 tbsp mayonnaise

15ml/1 tbsp chopped fresh parsley

1 Wash the asparagus and trim off the bases. Boil in a pan of water for about 7 minutes, until you can spear a stem with the blade of a knife and the blade slips out easily. Plunge the spears into iced water to stop them from cooking further. Drain them when cold, and pat dry with kitchen paper.

2 Scoop out the white crab meat from the shells and claws and place it in a bowl. If you can't find fresh crabs, you can use the same amount of canned or frozen white crab meat. Ensure the meat is completely defrosted and place on to kitchen paper to dry.

3 Add the mayonnaise and chopped fresh parsley and combine with a fork.

4 Place the mixture into the crab shells and add six asparagus spears per serving. Serve with crusty bread and a handful of lightly dressed salad leaves.

Per portion Energy 207kcal/859kJ; Protein 19.5g; Carbohydrate 3g, of which sugars 2.8g; Fat 13g, of which saturates 1.9g; Cholesterol 72mg; Calcium 157mg; Fibre 2.6g; Sodium 540mg.

Prawn, chilli and potato stew

This quick and tasty shellfish stew makes the most of new potatoes that have plenty of flavour, such as Jersey Royals, Maris Piper or Nicola. You could add extra chilli if you prefer the dish really hot, then serve with a garden salad and crusty bread to mop up the sauce.

Serves 4

675g/1½lb small new potatoes, scrubbed

15g/½oz/½ cup fresh coriander (cilantro)

350g/12oz jar tomato and chilli sauce

300g/11oz cooked peeled prawns (shrimp), thawed and drained if frozen

1 Cook the potatoes in lightly salted, boiling water for 15 minutes, until tender. Drain and return to the pan.

2 Finely chop half the coriander and add to the pan with the tomato and chilli sauce and 90ml/6 tbsp water. Bring to the boil, reduce the heat, cover and allow to simmer gently for 5 minutes.

3 Stir in the prawns and heat until they are warmed through. Do not overheat the prawns or they will quickly shrivel, becoming tough and tasteless. Spoon into bowls and serve sprinkled with the remaining coriander, torn into pieces.

Per portion Energy 218kcal/924kJ; Protein 16.9g; Carbohydrate 30.4g, of which sugars 5.4g; Fat 4.1g, of which saturates 0.7g; Cholesterol 146mg; Calcium 84mg; Fibre 2.9g; Sodium 171mg.

Spaghetti vongole

One of Italy's most famous country recipes, this tasty dish using carpet shell clams is an effortlessly easy supper or lunch dish that can be made with any small clams. It is lovely served with a green salad of peppery rocket or watercress leaves.

Serves 4

1kg/2¼lb fresh clams

60ml/4 tbsp olive oil

45ml/3 tbsp chopped fresh flat leaf parsley

120ml/4fl oz/½ cup dry white wine

350g/12oz dried spaghetti

2 garlic cloves

salt and ground black pepper

1 Scrub the clams under cold running water, discarding any that are open or that do not close when sharply tapped against the work surface.

2 Heat half the oil in a large pan, add the clams and 15ml/1 tbsp of the parsley and cook over a high heat for a few seconds.

3 Pour in the wine, then cover tightly. Cook for 5 minutes, shaking the pan frequently, until the clams have opened. Meanwhile, cook the pasta in salted boiling water according to the instructions on the packet.

4 Using a slotted spoon, transfer the clams to a bowl, discarding any that have failed to open.

5 Strain the liquid and set it aside. Put eight clams in their shells to one side for the garnish, then remove the rest from their shells.

6 Heat the remaining oil in the clean pan. Fry the garlic cloves until golden, crushing them with the back of a spoon. Remove the garlic with a slotted spoon and discard.

7 Add the shelled clams to the oil remaining in the pan, gradually add some of the strained liquid from the clams, then add plenty of pepper.

8 Cook for about 1–2 minutes, gradually adding a little more liquid as the sauce reduces. Add the remaining parsley and cook for a further 1–2 minutes.

9 Drain the pasta, add it to the pan and toss well. Serve in individual dishes, carefully scooping the shelled clams from the bottom of the pan and placing some of them on top of each serving.

10 Garnish with the reserved clams in their shells and serve immediately.

Per portion Energy 519kcal/2187kJ; Protein 30.9g; Carbohydrate 67.7g, of which sugars 3.4g; Fat 13.5g, of which saturates 2g; Cholesterol 84mg; Calcium 142mg; Fibre 3.2g; Sodium 1508mg.

Seafood pie

A taste of the sea, a good fish pie includes both fresh and smoked fish – ideal winter fare when the fishing fleets are hampered by gales and fresh fish is in short supply. Add shellfish such as mussels, and a few capers and dill for extra piquancy.

Serves 4–5

450g/1lb haddock or cod fillet

225g/8oz smoked haddock or cod

150ml/¼ pint/⅔ cup milk

150ml/¼ pint/⅔ cup water

1 slice of lemon

1 small bay leaf

a few fresh parsley stalks

For the sauce

25g/1oz/2 tbsp butter

25g/1oz/¼ cup plain (all-purpose) flour

5ml/1 tbsp lemon juice, or to taste

45ml/3 tbsp chopped fresh parsley

ground black pepper

For the topping

450g/1lb potatoes, boiled and mashed

25g/1oz/2 tbsp butter

1 Preheat the oven to 190°C/375°F/ Gas 5. Rinse the fish, cut it into manageable pieces and put into a pan with the milk, water, lemon, bay leaf and parsley stalks.

2 Bring the fish slowly to the boil, then simmer gently for 15 minutes until tender. Strain and reserve 300ml/ ½ pint/1¼ cups of the cooking liquor. Leave the fish until cool, then flake the cooked flesh and discard the skin and bones. Set aside.

3 To make the sauce, melt the butter in a heavy pan, add the flour and cook for 1–2 minutes over low heat, stirring constantly.

4 Gradually add the reserved cooking liquor, stirring well to make a smooth sauce.

Variations
• Almost any mixture of prepared seafood can go into this fish pie. Cut all the fish into roughly the same size, and cut large scallops or prawns in half.
• Try adding other soft herbs such as chervil, dill or chives to the sauce, or a teaspoon of grain mustard.

5 Simmer the sauce gently for about 1–2 minutes, then remove the pan from the heat and stir in the flaked fish, chopped parsley and lemon juice. Season to taste with ground black pepper.

6 Turn into a buttered 1.75 litre/3 pint/ 7½ cup pie dish or shallow casserole, cover evenly with the mashed potato for the topping, smoothing with the back of a fork if necessary. Cut the butter into small pieces and dot the potato with the butter.

7 Cook the pie in the preheated oven for about 20 minutes, or until it is thoroughly heated through. The potato topping should be golden brown and crunchy.

8 Divide the pie among four or five warmed plates and serve immediately with a lightly cooked green vegetable, such as fresh broccoli florets.

Per portion Energy 336kcal/1413kJ; Protein 35.1g; Carbohydrate 24.3g, of which sugars 0.9g; Fat 11.6g, of which saturates 6.7g; Cholesterol 87mg; Calcium 45mg; Fibre 1.7g; Sodium 587mg.

Poultry and game

Chicken and other poultry are among the most popular and versatile meats, and they can be prepared in a huge variety of ways, from a simple roasted bird to delicious slow-cooked classics such as Coq au Vin. In the past, game was a seasonal meat available only at certain times of the year, but it is now possible to obtain a wide variety of game all year round. It is, however, still rewarding to cook game with traditional seasonal ingredients.

Roast chicken with herb stuffing

A staple of traditional country cooking, a simply roasted free-range chicken with herbs and home-made stuffing is hard to beat. Serve with roast potatoes, sausages, bacon rolls and seasonal vegetables, along with a fruit jelly such as cranberry sauce or elderberry jelly.

Serves 6

1 large chicken, about 1.8kg/4lb, with giblets and neck if possible

1 small onion, sliced

1 small carrot, sliced

small bunch of parsley and thyme

15g/½oz/1 tbsp butter

30ml/2 tbsp chicken fat or oil

6 rashers (strips) of streaky (fatty) bacon

salt and ground black pepper

For the stuffing

1 onion, finely chopped

50g/2oz/¼ cup butter

150g/5oz/2½ cups fresh white breadcrumbs

15ml/1 tbsp fresh chopped parsley

15ml/1 tbsp fresh chopped mixed herbs, such as thyme, marjoram and chives

finely grated rind and juice of ½ lemon

1 small egg, lightly beaten (optional)

15ml/1 tbsp plain (all-purpose) flour

1 Remove the giblets from the chicken; also remove the piece of fat which is found just inside the vent and put this fat into a roasting pan – it can be rendered down and used when cooking the roast potatoes. Wipe out the inside of the bird thoroughly. Separate the liver from the rest of the giblets, chop it and set it aside to use in the gravy.

2 Put the giblets and the neck into a pan with the sliced onion and sliced carrot, the bunch of parsley and thyme and a good sprinkling of salt and pepper. Add enough cold water to cover generously, bring to the boil and leave to simmer gently for about 1 hour. Strain the chicken stock and discard the giblets. Preheat the oven to 200°C/400°F/Gas 6.

3 Meanwhile, make the herb stuffing: cook the chopped onion in the butter in a large pan over a low heat without colouring for a few minutes until it is just beginning to soften.

4 Remove from the heat, and add the breadcrumbs, fresh herbs and grated lemon rind. Mix thoroughly. Mix in the lemon juice, beaten egg, if using, and salt and pepper. (The egg will bind the stuffing and make it firmer when cooked, but it can be omitted if you prefer a lighter, more crumbly texture.)

5 Spoon the stuffing into the neck cavity of the chicken, without packing it in too tightly, and secure the opening with a small skewer. Spread the breast with the butter, then put the chicken fat or oil into a roasting pan and lay the bird in it. Season and lay the bacon rashers over the top of the bird to protect it in the oven.

6 Weigh the stuffed chicken and work out the cooking time at 20 minutes per 450g/1lb and 20 minutes over, then put into the preheated oven. After 20 minutes, reduce the temperature to 180°C/350°F/Gas 4 for another 45–60 minutes, or until cooked. Test by inserting a sharp knife between the body and thigh: if the juices run clear with no hint of blood, it is cooked.

7 Transfer the cooked chicken to a serving dish and allow it to rest for 10 minutes while you make the gravy.

8 To make the gravy, pour off the excess fat from the roasting pan, then add the finely chopped liver and stir over low heat for 1 minute, or until it has turned light brown. Sprinkle in just enough flour to absorb the remaining chicken fat and cook gently, stirring to blend, for 1 or 2 minutes. Gradually add some of the giblet stock, scraping the pan to dissolve the residues and stirring well to make a smooth gravy.

9 Bring to the boil, stirring, gradually adding more stock until the consistency is as you like it. Adjust the seasoning, and then pour into a heated sauceboat to hand round separately.

10 Carve the chicken. Serve on heated plates with the herb stuffing and gravy.

Per portion Energy 562kcal/2342kJ; Protein 40.9g; Carbohydrate 23.2g, of which sugars 2.7g; Fat 34.5g, of which saturates 11.9g; Cholesterol 216mg; Calcium 72mg; Fibre 1.5g; Sodium 381mg.

Lemon and garlic pot roast chicken

Pot roasting is at the heart of rustic cooking. Easy to prepare and slow cooked, this is a great family dish. Serve with baked rice, mashed potatoes or thick bread.

Serves 4

30ml/2 tbsp olive oil

25g/1oz/2 tbsp butter

175g/6oz/1 cup smoked lardons, or roughly chopped streaky (fatty) bacon

8 garlic cloves, peeled

4 onions, quartered

10ml/2 tsp plain (all-purpose) flour

600ml/1 pint/2½ cups chicken stock

2 lemons, thickly sliced

45ml/3 tbsp chopped fresh thyme

1 chicken, about 1.3–1.6kg/3–3½lb

2 x 400g/14oz cans flageolet, cannellini or haricot (navy) beans, drained and rinsed

salt and ground black pepper

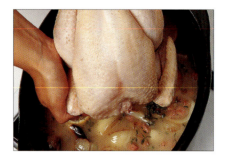

3 Bring to the boil, stirring constantly until thickened, then place the chicken on top. Season well. Transfer the casserole to the oven. Cook for 1 hour, basting the chicken once or twice during cooking to ensure it stays moist.

4 Baste the chicken again. Stir the beans into the casserole and return it to the oven for a further 30 minutes, or until the chicken is cooked through and tender. Carve the chicken into thick slices and serve with the beans.

1 Preheat the oven to 190°C/375°F/ Gas 5. Heat the oil and butter in a flameproof casserole that is large enough to hold the chicken with a little room around the sides. Add the lardons and cook until golden. Remove with a slotted spoon and drain on kitchen paper.

2 Add the garlic and onions and brown over a high heat. Stir in the flour, then the stock. Return the lardons to the pan with the lemon, thyme and seasoning.

Per portion Energy 887kcal/3696kJ; Protein 62.5g; Carbohydrate 45.5g, of which sugars 12.9g; Fat 51.7g, of which saturates 16g; Cholesterol 256mg; Calcium 187mg; Fibre 13.9g; Sodium 1519mg.

Chicken baked with forty cloves of garlic

Don't be put off by the amount of garlic in this traditional dish. The garlic heads become soft, sweet and fragrant when cooked, and impart a mouth-watering aroma.

Serves 4–5

5–6 whole heads of garlic

15g/½oz/1 tbsp butter

45ml/3 tbsp olive oil

1.8–2kg/4–4½lb chicken

150g/5oz/1¼ cups plain (all-purpose) flour, plus 5ml/1 tsp

75ml/5 tbsp white port, Pineau de Charentes or other white, fortified wine

2–3 fresh tarragon or rosemary sprigs

30ml/2 tbsp crème fraîche

few drops of lemon juice

salt and ground black pepper

1 Separate three of the heads of garlic into cloves and peel. Remove the first layer of papery skin from the remaining heads of garlic and leave whole. Preheat the oven to 180°C/350°F/Gas 4.

2 Heat the butter and 15ml/1 tbsp of the olive oil in a flameproof casserole that is just large enough to take the chicken and garlic. Add the chicken and cook over a medium heat, turning frequently, for 10 minutes, until it is browned all over. Sprinkle in 5ml/1 tsp flour and cook for 1 minute. Add the port or wine. Tuck in the whole heads of garlic and the peeled cloves with the herb sprigs.

3 Pour the remaining oil over the chicken and season to taste with salt and pepper. Rub all over to coat.

4 Mix the main batch of flour with enough water to make a firm dough. Roll it out into a long sausage and press around the rim of the casserole, then press on the lid, folding the dough up and over it to create a tight seal. Cook in the oven for 1½ hours.

5 To serve, lift off the lid to break the seal and remove the chicken and whole garlic to a serving platter and keep warm. Remove and discard the herb sprigs, then place the casserole on the hob and whisk to combine the garlic cloves with the juices. Add the crème fraîche and a little lemon juice to taste. Process the sauce in a food processor or blender if a smoother result is required. Serve the garlic purée with the chicken.

Per portion Energy 787kcal/3276kJ; Protein 51.3g; Carbohydrate 33.2g, of which sugars 1g; Fat 50.6g, of which saturates 14.5g; Cholesterol 248mg; Calcium 77mg; Fibre 2.2g; Sodium 212mg.

Coq au vin

A quintessential French country casserole, this dish is a fricassée made with a cock bird, cooked long and slow in red wine to tenderize the meat. Making it fills the house with appetite-arousing aromas. Serve with boiled potatoes or little fried bread croûtons.

Serves 6

45ml/3 tbsp light olive oil

12 shallots

225g/8oz rindless streaky (fatty) bacon rashers (strips), chopped

3 garlic cloves, finely chopped

225g/8oz small mushrooms, halved

3 boneless chicken breast portions

6 boneless chicken thighs

1 bottle red wine

salt and ground black pepper

45ml/3 tbsp chopped fresh parsley, to garnish

For the bouquet garni

3 sprigs each of fresh parsley, thyme and sage

1 bay leaf

4 peppercorns

For the beurre manié

25g/1oz/2 tbsp butter, softened

25g/1oz/¼ cup plain (all-purpose) flour

Cook's tip Coq au Vin can be made with any full-bodied red wine. A truly authentic recipe would include some of the birds' blood to thicken the sauce, which ends up an almost black sauce.

1 Heat the oil in a large, flameproof casserole, add the shallots and cook for 5 minutes, or until golden. Increase the heat, add the bacon, garlic and halved mushrooms and cook for 10 minutes more, stirring frequently.

2 Use a draining spoon to transfer the cooked ingredients to a plate. Halve the chicken breast portions, then brown, along with the thighs, in the oil remaining in the pan. As they cook, turn them to ensure they are golden brown all over. Return the shallots, garlic, mushrooms and bacon to the casserole and pour in the red wine.

3 Tie the ingredients for the bouquet garni in a bundle in a small piece of muslin (cheesecloth) and add to the casserole. Bring to the boil, reduce the heat and cover the casserole, then simmer for about 35 minutes.

4 To make the beurre manié, cream the butter and flour together in a small bowl using your fingers or a spoon to make a smooth paste.

5 Add small lumps of this paste to the bubbling casserole, stirring well until each piece has melted into the liquid before adding the next. When all the paste has been added, bring back to the boil and simmer for 5 minutes.

6 Season the casserole to taste with salt and pepper and serve garnished with chopped fresh parsley and accompanied by boiled potatoes.

Per portion Energy 496kcal/2067kJ; Protein 39.2g; Carbohydrate 5g, of which sugars 1.8g; Fat 26.9g, of which saturates 8.5g; Cholesterol 153mg; Calcium 47mg; Fibre 1.1g; Sodium 600mg.

Chicken and root vegetable casserole

Tender chunks of starchy root vegetables are the ideal winter comfort food. When cooked slowly in a casserole with chicken, green lentils and creamy mustard sauce, the natural sugars in the vegetables become mellow and intense, giving an irresistible flavour.

Serves 4

350g/12oz onions

350g/12oz leeks

225g/8oz carrots

450g/1lb swede (rutabaga)

30ml/2 tbsp oil

4 chicken portions, about 900g/2lb total weight

115g/4oz/½ cup green lentils

475ml/16fl oz/2 cups chicken stock

300ml/½ pint/1¼ cups apple juice

10ml/2 tsp cornflour (cornstarch)

45ml/3 tbsp crème fraîche

10ml/2 tsp wholegrain mustard

30ml/2 tbsp chopped fresh tarragon

salt and ground black pepper

fresh tarragon sprigs, to garnish

3 Add the onions to the casserole and cook for 5 minutes, stirring, until they begin to soften and colour. Add the leeks, carrots, swede and lentils to the casserole and stir over a medium heat for 2 minutes.

4 Return the chicken to the pan, then add the stock, apple juice and seasoning. Bring to the boil and cover. Reduce the heat and cook for 50–60 minutes, or until the chicken and lentils are tender.

5 In a small bowl, blend the cornflour with about 30ml/2 tbsp water to make a smooth paste and then add to the casserole with the crème fraîche, wholegrain mustard and chopped tarragon.

6 Adjust the seasoning to taste, then simmer the casserole gently for about 2 minutes, stirring constantly, until thickened slightly. Garnish with the tarragon sprigs, and then serve in individual bowls.

1 Prepare the onions, leeks, carrots and swede and roughly chop them into even pieces.

2 Heat the oil in a large flameproof casserole. Season the chicken portions with plenty of salt and pepper and brown them in the hot oil until golden. Drain on kitchen paper.

Per portion Energy 477kcal/2010kJ; Protein 46.8g; Carbohydrate 45.7g, of which sugars 24.9g; Fat 13.2g, of which saturates 4.5g; Cholesterol 118mg; Calcium 151mg; Fibre 8.1g; Sodium 141mg.

Puff pastry chicken pies

These versatile little pies can be filled with different kinds of meat. Although chicken is the most popular, they are also good with a mixture of game and chicken, or with fish or shellfish. They make a tempting afternoon snack, or you could have two or three of them, either hot or cold, with a refreshing salad for a delicious light lunch.

Makes about 12

1 chicken, weighing 1.6–2kg/3½–4½lb

45ml/3 tbsp olive oil

1 sausage, weighing about 250g/9oz

150g/5oz bacon

1 garlic clove

10 black peppercorns

1 onion stuck with 2 cloves

1 bunch of parsley, chopped

4 thyme or marjoram sprigs

juice of 1 lemon or 60ml/4 tbsp white wine vinegar

butter, for greasing

500g/1¼lb puff pastry, thawed if frozen

plain (all-purpose) flour, for dusting

2 egg yolks, lightly beaten

salt

1 Cut the chicken into pieces. Heat the oil in a large, heavy pan. Add the chicken pieces and cook over a medium-low heat, turning occasionally, for about 10 minutes, until golden brown on all sides.

2 Add the sausage, bacon, garlic, peppercorns, onion, parsley, thyme and lemon juice or vinegar. Pour in enough water to cover and bring to the boil. Lower the heat, cover and simmer for 1–1½ hours, until tender.

3 Remove all the meat from the stock with a slotted spoon. Then return the stock to the heat and cook, uncovered, until slightly reduced. Strain the stock into a bowl and season with salt to taste.

4 Remove and discard the chicken skin and bones and cut the meat into small pieces. Cut the sausage and bacon into small pieces. Mix all the meat together. Preheat the oven to 200°C/400°F/Gas 6. Grease a 12-cup muffin tin (pan) with butter.

5 Roll out the pastry thinly on a lightly floured surface and stamp out 12 rounds with a 7.5cm/3in cutter.

6 Gather the trimmings together and roll out thinly again, then stamp out 12 rounds with a 6cm/2½in cutter. Place the larger rounds in the cups of the prepared tin, pressing the pastry to the side with your thumb, and divide the meat among them.

7 Spoon in a little of the stock, then brush the edges with beaten egg yolk and cover with the smaller rounds, pinching the edges to seal.

8 Brush the remaining egg yolk over the top to glaze and make a small hole in the centre of each pie with a wooden cocktail stick (toothpick).

9 Bake for 15–25 minutes, until golden brown. Remove from the oven and leave to cool before serving.

Variation You can use the following dough as an alternative to puff pastry. Sift 500g/1¼lb/5 cups plain (all-purpose) flour into a bowl and make a well in the centre. Add 5 eggs and about 150g/5oz/⅔ cup of the leftover chicken fat to the well and mix together, adding some stock if necessary. Blend well, then shape the dough into a ball and leave to rest, wrapped in clear film (plastic wrap), for 30 minutes before rolling out.

Per pie Energy 368kcal/1534kJ; Protein 24.5g; Carbohydrate 18.3g, of which sugars 1.2g; Fat 22.8g, of which saturates 4.3g; Cholesterol 109mg; Calcium 44mg; Fibre 0.2g; Sodium 547mg.

Creamy chicken and mushroom pie

A family favourite, this classic pie includes porcini mushrooms, which give an intense mushroom flavour, topped with a melt-in-the-mouth pastry crust.

Serves 6

15g/½oz/¼ cup dried porcini mushrooms

50g/2oz/¼ cup butter

30ml/2 tbsp plain (all-purpose) flour

250ml/8fl oz/1 cup hot chicken stock

60ml/4 tbsp single (light) cream

1 onion, coarsely chopped

2 carrots, sliced

2 celery sticks, coarsely chopped

50g/2oz/¾ cup fresh mushrooms, quartered

450g/1lb cooked chicken meat, cubed

50g/2oz/½ cup fresh or frozen peas

salt and ground black pepper

beaten egg, to glaze

For the pastry

225g/8oz/2 cups plain (all-purpose) flour

1.5ml/¼ tsp salt

115g/4oz/½ cup cold butter, diced

65g/2½oz/⅓ cup white vegetable fat, diced

60–120ml/4–8 tbsp chilled water

1 To make the pastry, sift the flour and salt into a bowl. Cut or rub in the butter and white vegetable fat until the mixture resembles fine breadcrumbs. Sprinkle with 90ml/ 6 tbsp chilled water and mix until the dough holds together. If the dough is too crumbly, add a little more water, 15ml/1 tbsp at a time.

2 Gather the dough into a ball and flatten it into a round. Wrap and chill for at least 30 minutes.

3 To make the filling, put the mushrooms in a bowl. Cover with hot water and soak for 30 minutes. Drain in a muslin- (cheesecloth-) lined sieve (strainer), then dry on kitchen paper. Preheat the oven to 190°C/375°F/Gas 5.

4 Melt half of the butter in a heavy pan. Whisk in the flour and cook until bubbling, whisking constantly. Add the hot stock and whisk over a medium heat until the mixture boils. Cook for 2–3 minutes, then whisk in the cream. Season to taste, and set aside.

5 Heat the remaining butter in a non-stick frying pan and cook the onion and carrots over a low heat for 5 minutes. Add the celery and fresh mushrooms and cook for 5 minutes more. Stir in the cooked chicken, peas and drained porcini mushrooms.

6 Add the chicken mixture to the hot cream sauce and stir to mix. Adjust the seasoning if necessary. Spoon the mixture into a 2.5 litre/4 pint/2½ quart oval baking dish.

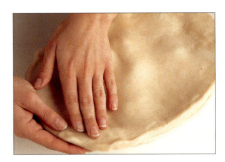

7 Roll out the pastry to a thickness of about 3mm/⅛in. Cut out an oval 2.5cm/1in larger all around than the dish. Lay the pastry over the filling. Gently press around the edge of the dish to seal, then trim off the excess pastry. Crimp the edge of the pastry by pushing the forefinger of one hand into the edge and, using the thumb and forefinger of the other hand, pinch the pastry. Continue all round the pastry edge.

8 Press together the pastry trimmings and roll out again. Cut out mushroom shapes with a knife and stick them on to the pastry lid with beaten egg. Glaze the lid with egg and cut several slits in the pastry to allow the steam to escape. Bake the pie for about 30 minutes, until the pastry has browned. Serve hot.

Per portion Energy 576kcal/2403kJ; Protein 23.8g; Carbohydrate 39.6g, of which sugars 4.7g; Fat 36.9g, of which saturates 20.3g; Cholesterol 127mg; Calcium 104mg; Fibre 3.1g; Sodium 334mg.

Devilled chicken

A 19th-century way to use up cooked meats, 'devilling' adds spicy seasoning to pep up leftovers. This recipe uses the technique to give freshly prepared chicken a sticky, hot flavour.

Serves 4–6

6 chicken drumsticks

6 chicken thighs

15ml/1 tbsp oil

45ml/3 tbsp chutney, finely chopped

15ml/1 tbsp Worcestershire sauce

10ml/2 tsp English (hot) mustard

1.5ml/$\frac{1}{4}$ tsp cayenne pepper

1.5ml/$\frac{1}{4}$ tsp ground ginger

salt and ground black pepper

1 With a sharp knife, make several deep slashes in the chicken pieces, cutting down to the bone.

2 In a large bowl, mix the oil, chutney, Worcestershire sauce, mustard, cayenne, ginger and seasoning. Add the chicken pieces and toss them in the mixture, until well coated. Cover and leave to stand for 1 hour.

3 Preheat the oven to 200°C/400°F/ Gas 6. Arrange the chicken pieces in a single layer on a non-stick baking sheet, brushing them with any extra sauce.

Variation Instead of chutney, try using the same quantity of tomato ketchup or mushroom ketchup, or a teaspoon of finely chopped fresh chilli.

4 Put the chicken pieces into the hot oven and cook for about 35 minutes until they are a crisp, deep golden brown and cooked through (test them by inserting a small sharp knife or skewer – the juices should run clear). Turn them over once or twice during cooking to encourage even browning.

Per portion Energy 299kcal/1254kJ; Protein 47.4g; Carbohydrate 0.3g, of which sugars 0.3g; Fat 12g, of which saturates 2.6g; Cholesterol 236mg; Calcium 41mg; Fibre 0.6g; Sodium 207mg.

Guinea fowl and spring vegetable ragoût

Equally delicious when made with chicken or rabbit, this light stew makes the best of spring vegetables, including tender baby leeks. Finish with plenty of chopped parsley.

Serves 4

45ml/3 tbsp olive oil

115g/4oz pancetta, cut into lardons

30ml/2 tbsp plain (all-purpose) flour

2 × 1.2–1.6kg/2½–3½lb guinea fowl, each jointed in 4 portions

1 onion, chopped

1 head of garlic, separated into cloves and peeled

1 bottle dry white wine

fresh thyme sprig

1 fresh bay leaf

a few parsley stalks

250g/9oz baby carrots

250g/9oz baby turnips

6 slender leeks, cut into 7.5cm/3in lengths

250g/9oz shelled peas

15ml/1 tbsp French herb mustard

15g/½oz flat leaf parsley, chopped

15ml/1 tbsp chopped fresh mint

salt and ground black pepper

1 Heat 30ml/2 tbsp of the oil in a large frying pan and cook the pancetta over a medium heat until lightly browned, stirring occasionally. Remove the pancetta from the pan and set aside.

2 Season the flour with salt and pepper and toss the guinea fowl portions in it. Fry the portions in the oil remaining in the pan until they are browned on all sides. Transfer to a flameproof casserole. Preheat the oven to 180°C/350°F/Gas 4. Add the remaining oil to the pan and cook the onion gently until soft.

3 Add the garlic to the pan and fry for 4 minutes. Stir in the pancetta and wine.

4 Tie the thyme, bay leaf and parsley into a bundle and add to the pan. Bring to the boil, then simmer gently for 3–4 minutes. Pour over the guinea fowl and add seasoning. Cover and cook in the oven for 40 minutes.

5 Add the baby carrots and turnips to the casserole and cook, covered, for another 30 minutes, until the vegetables are just tender. Stir in the leeks and cook for a further 20 minutes, or until the vegetables are cooked.

6 Meanwhile, blanch the peas in boiling water for 2 minutes, then drain. Transfer the guinea fowl and vegetables to a warmed serving dish. Place the casserole on the hob and boil the juices vigorously over a high heat until they are reduced by about half.

7 Stir in the peas and cook gently for 2–3 minutes, then stir in the mustard and adjust the seasoning. Stir in most of the parsley and the mint. Pour this sauce over the guinea fowl or return the joints and vegetables to the casserole. Sprinkle the remaining parsley over the top and serve.

Per portion Energy 862kcal/3579kJ; Protein 52g; Carbohydrate 23.4g, of which sugars 11g; Fat 50.5g, of which saturates 13.6g; Cholesterol 227mg; Calcium 138mg; Fibre 8.3g; Sodium 558mg.

Classic roast turkey with country stuffing

Traditionally served at Christmas or Thanksgiving, roast turkey is a splendid celebration dish. The rich herb stuffing in this recipe is made with calf's liver, but lamb's liver would be fine, too. Serve with cranberry jelly, which will taste even better if you make it yourself.

Serves 6

1 turkey, about 4.5–5.5kg/10–12lb, washed and patted dry with kitchen paper

25g/1oz/2 tbsp butter, melted

salt and ground black pepper, to taste

cranberry jelly, to serve

For the stuffing

200g/7oz/3½ cups fresh white breadcrumbs

175ml/6fl oz/¾ cup milk

25g/1oz/2 tbsp butter

1 egg, separated

1 calf's liver, about 600g/1lb 6oz, finely chopped

2 onions, finely chopped

90ml/6 tbsp chopped fresh dill

10ml/2 tsp clear honey

salt and ground black pepper, to taste

1 To make the stuffing, put the breadcrumbs and milk in a large bowl and soak until swollen and soft.

2 Melt the butter in a frying pan and mix 5ml/1 tsp with the egg yolk.

3 Heat the remaining butter in a frying pan and add the finely chopped calf's liver and onions. Fry gently for 5 minutes, until the onions are golden brown. Remove from the heat and leave to cool.

4 Preheat the oven to 180°C/350°F/Gas 4. Add the cooled liver mixture to the soaked breadcrumbs and milk, then add the butter and egg yolk mixture, with the chopped dill, clear honey and seasoning.

5 In a clean bowl, whisk the egg white to soft peaks, then fold into the stuffing mixture, stirring gently to combine thoroughly.

6 Season the turkey inside and out with salt and pepper. Stuff the cavity with the stuffing mixture, then weigh to calculate the cooking time. Allow 20 minutes per 500g/1¼lb, plus an additional 20 minutes. Tuck the legs of the turkey inside the cavity and tie the end shut with string. Brush the outside with melted butter and transfer to a roasting pan. Place in the oven and roast for the calculated time.

7 Baste the turkey regularly during cooking, and cover with foil for the final 30 minutes if the skin becomes too brown. To test whether the turkey is cooked, pierce the thickest part of the thigh with a knife; the juices should run clear.

8 Remove the turkey from the oven, cover with foil and leave to rest for about 15 minutes. Carve into thin slices, then spoon over the juices and serve with the stuffing and cranberry jelly.

Per portion Energy 740kcal/3126kJ; Protein 112.3g; Carbohydrate 35.9g, of which sugars 7.3g; Fat 13.5g, of which saturates 6.6g; Cholesterol 507mg; Calcium 122mg; Fibre 1.7g; Sodium 517mg.

Roast farmyard duck with apples and cider

The combination of the apples and cider in this recipe makes a fine sauce which complements the rich meat of roast duck or goose perfectly. Serve with a selection of vegetables, including roast potatoes and, perhaps, some red cabbage.

Serves 4

2kg/4½lb oven-ready duck or duckling

300ml/½ pint/1¼ cups dry (hard) cider

60ml/4 tbsp double (heavy) cream

sea salt and ground black pepper

For the stuffing

75g/3oz/6 tbsp butter

115g/4oz/2 cups fresh white breadcrumbs

450g/1lb cooking apples, peeled, cored and diced

15ml/1 tbsp sugar, or to taste

freshly grated nutmeg

1 Preheat the oven to 200°C/400°F/ Gas 6. To make the stuffing, melt the butter in a pan and fry the breadcrumbs until golden brown. Add the apples to the breadcrumbs with salt, pepper, the sugar and a pinch of nutmeg. Mix well.

2 Wipe the duck out with a clean, damp cloth, and remove any obvious excess fat (including the flaps just inside the vent). Rub the skin with salt. Stuff the duck with the prepared mixture, then secure the vent with a small skewer.

3 Weigh the stuffed duck and calculate the cooking time, allowing 20 minutes per 450g/1lb. Prick the skin all over with a fork to allow the fat to run out during the cooking time, then lay it on top of a wire rack in a roasting pan, sprinkle with freshly ground black pepper and put it into the preheated oven to roast.

4 About 20 minutes before the end of the estimated cooking time, remove the duck from the oven and pour off all the fat that has accumulated under the rack (reserve it for frying). Slide the duck off the rack into the roasting pan and pour the cider over it. Return to the oven and finish cooking, basting occasionally.

5 When the duck is cooked, remove it from the pan and keep warm while you make the sauce. Set the roasting pan over a medium heat and boil the cider to reduce it by half. Stir in the cream, heat through and season. Meanwhile, remove the stuffing from the duck. Carve the duck into slices or quarter it using poultry shears. Serve with a portion of stuffing and the cider sauce.

Per portion Energy 572kcal/2397kJ; Protein 31.5g; Carbohydrate 34.6g, of which sugars 13.1g; Fat 33.1g, of which saturates 17.8g; Cholesterol 211mg; Calcium 74mg; Fibre 2.4g; Sodium 498mg.

Duck with damson ginger sauce

Wild damsons or plums have a sharp taste that make a lovely fruity sauce to serve with these simple and quick-to-cook pan-fried duck breasts. This delicious sauce would also be good with other rich meats such as venison, pheasant or goose.

Serves 4

250g/9oz fresh damsons

5ml/1 tsp ground ginger

45ml/3 tbsp sugar

10ml/2 tsp wine vinegar or sherry vinegar

4 duck breast portions

15ml/1 tbsp oil

salt and ground black pepper

1 Put the damsons in a pan with the ginger and 45ml/3 tbsp water. Bring to the boil, cover and simmer gently for about 5 minutes, or until the fruit is soft. Stir frequently and add a little extra water if the fruit looks as if it is drying out or sticking to the bottom of the pan.

2 Stir in the sugar and vinegar. Press the mixture through a sieve (strainer) to remove stones (pits) and skin. Taste the sauce and add more sugar (if necessary) and seasoning to taste.

3 Meanwhile, with a sharp knife, score the fat on the duck breast portions in several places without cutting into the meat. Brush the oil over both sides of the duck. Sprinkle a little salt and pepper on the fat side only.

4 Preheat a griddle pan or heavy frying pan. When hot, add the duck breast portions, skin side down, and cook over medium heat for about 5 minutes or until the fat is evenly browned and crisp.

5 Turn over and cook the meat side for 4–5 minutes. Lift out and leave to rest for 5–10 minutes.

6 Slice the duck on the diagonal and serve with the sauce.

Cook's tip Both the duck and the sauce are good served cold too. Serve with simple steamed vegetables, crisp salads or in sandwiches.

Per portion Energy 275kcal/1157kJ; Protein 29.9g; Carbohydrate 17.5g, of which sugars 17.5g; Fat 12.5g, of which saturates 2.4g; Cholesterol 165mg; Calcium 39mg; Fibre 1.1g; Sodium 167mg.

Roast pheasant with sherry mustard sauce

It is best to use only young pheasants for roasting – older birds are too tough and are only suitable for casseroles. Serve this succulent dish with potatoes braised in wine with garlic and onions, bread sauce and winter vegetables such as Brussels sprouts or red cabbage.

Serves 4

2 young oven-ready pheasants

50g/2oz/¼ cup softened butter

200ml/7fl oz/scant 1 cup sherry

15ml/1 tbsp Dijon mustard

salt and ground black pepper

Cook's tip To keep the meat moist, add bacon rashers (strips) to the pheasants before putting them in the oven. Remove 20 minutes before the end of cooking.

1 Preheat the oven to 200°C/400°F/ Gas 6. Put the pheasants in a roasting pan and spread the butter all over both birds. Season with salt and pepper.

2 Roast the pheasants for 50 minutes, basting often to stop the birds from drying out. When the pheasants are cooked, take them out of the pan and leave to rest on a board, covered with foil.

3 Meanwhile, place the roasting pan over a medium heat. Add the sherry and season with salt and pepper. Simmer for 5 minutes, until the sherry has slightly reduced, then stir in the mustard. Carve the pheasants and serve with the sherry and mustard sauce.

Per portion Energy 692kcal/2897kJ; Protein 81.7g; Carbohydrate 1.2g, of which sugars 1.1g; Fat 34.2g, of which saturates 14.5g; Cholesterol 27mg; Calcium 133mg; Fibre 0g; Sodium 456mg.

Roast young grouse with rowanberries

As with venison, rowan jelly goes well with this meat. Young grouse can be identified by their pliable breastbone, legs and feet, and their claws will be sharp. They have very little fat, so bacon is used here to protect the breasts during the initial roasting.

Serves 2

2 young grouse

6 rashers (strips) bacon

2 sprigs of rowanberries
or 1 lemon, quartered, plus
30ml/2 tbsp extra rowanberries
(optional)

50g/2oz/¼ cup butter

150ml/¼ pint/⅔ cup red wine

150ml/¼ pint/⅔ cup water

5ml/1 tsp rowan jelly

salt and ground black pepper

1 Preheat the oven to 200°C/400°F/ Gas 6. Wipe the grouse with kitchen paper and place in a roasting pan. Lay the bacon over the breasts.

2 If you have rowanberries, place one sprig in the cavity of each grouse as well as a little butter. Otherwise put a lemon quarter in each cavity.

3 Roast the grouse in the preheated oven for 10 minutes, then remove the bacon and pour in the wine. Return to the oven for 10 minutes.

4 Baste the birds with the juices and cook for a further 5 minutes. Remove the birds from the pan and keep warm. Add the water and rowan jelly to the pan and simmer gently until the jelly melts. Strain into another pan, add the rowanberries, if using, and simmer until the sauce just begins to thicken. Season with salt and ground black pepper.

Variation If rowanberries are hard to find, you can replace them with dried cranberries or sour cherries, which will give a similar result.

Per portion Energy 423kcal/1763kJ; Protein 43.8g; Carbohydrate 1.5g, of which sugars 1.5g; Fat 24g, of which saturates 10.8g; Cholesterol 51mg; Calcium 43mg; Fibre 0g; Sodium 902mg.

Pheasant and wild mushroom ragoût

This rich and delicious way to prepare pheasant uses shallots, garlic cloves, port and a mixture of wild mushrooms for a good variety of flavour and texture.

Serves 4

4 pheasant breasts, skinned

15ml/1 tbsp oil

12 shallots, halved

2 garlic cloves, crushed

75g/3oz wild mushrooms, sliced

75ml/2½fl oz/⅓ cup port

150ml/¼ pint/⅔ cup chicken stock

sprigs of fresh parsley and thyme

1 bay leaf

grated rind of 1 lemon

200ml/7fl oz/scant 1 cup double (heavy) cream

salt and ground black pepper

1 Dice and season the pheasant breasts. Heat the oil in a heavy pan and colour the pheasant meat quickly. Remove from the pan and set aside.

2 Add the halved shallots to the pan, fry quickly to colour a little, then add the crushed garlic and sliced wild mushrooms. Reduce the heat and cook gently for 5 minutes.

3 Pour the port and stock into the pan and add the herbs and lemon rind. Reduce the liquid a little. When the shallots are nearly cooked, add the cream, reduce to thicken, then return the meat. Allow to cook for a few minutes before serving.

Cook's tip Serve with pilaff rice: fry a chopped onion, stir in 2.5cm/1in cinnamon stick, 2.5ml/½ tsp crushed cumin seeds, 2 crushed cardamom pods, a bay leaf and 5ml/1 tsp turmeric. Add 225g/8oz/generous 1 cup long grain rice. Stir until well coated. Pour in 600ml/1 pint/2½ cups boiling water, cover, then simmer gently for 15 minutes. Transfer to a serving dish, cover with a dish towel and leave for 5 minutes.

Per portion Energy 530kcal/2200kJ; Protein 34.1g; Carbohydrate 7.4g, of which sugars 5.9g; Fat 33g, of which saturates 20.2g; Cholesterol 69mg; Calcium 91mg; Fibre 1.1g; Sodium 114mg.

Grouse with orchard fruit stuffing

In the late summer and autumn, when grouse are in season, orchard fruits such as apples, plums and pears make a perfect stuffing. Try serving with creamy mashed potatoes.

Serves 2

juice of ½ lemon

2 young grouse

50g/2oz/¼ cup butter

4 Swiss chard leaves

50ml/2fl oz/¼ cup Marsala

salt and ground black pepper

For the stuffing

2 shallots, finely chopped

1 tart cooking apple, peeled, cored and chopped

1 pear, peeled, cored and chopped

2 plums, halved, stoned (pitted) and chopped

large pinch of mixed (apple pie) spice

Cook's tip In this recipe, the birds are steamed rather than boiled, so it is important that the casserole has a heavy base and a tight-fitting lid, otherwise the liquid may evaporate and the chard will burn on the base of the pan.

1 Sprinkle the lemon juice over the grouse and season well. Melt half the butter in a flameproof casserole, add the grouse and cook for 10 minutes, or until browned. Use tongs to remove the grouse from the casserole and set aside.

2 Add the shallots to the fat remaining in the casserole and cook until softened but not coloured. Add the apple, pear, plums and mixed spice, and cook for about 5 minutes, or until the fruits are just beginning to soften. Remove the casserole from the heat and spoon the hot fruit mixture into the body cavities of the birds, filling them well.

3 Truss the birds neatly with string. Smear the remaining butter over the birds and wrap them in the chard leaves, then replace them in the casserole.

4 Pour in the Marsala and heat until simmering. Cover tightly and simmer for 20 minutes, or until the birds are tender, taking care not to overcook them. Leave to rest in a warm place for about 10 minutes before serving.

Per portion Energy 508kcal/2121kJ; Protein 46.9g; Carbohydrate 19.5g, of which sugars 18.7g; Fat 24.3g, of which saturates 13.8g; Cholesterol 53mg; Calcium 185mg; Fibre 4.2g; Sodium 406mg.

Game pie

This impressive country pie can be made with whichever game birds are available. Add in some freshly foraged mushrooms and serve the pie with puréed Jerusalem artichokes and winter greens such as purple sprouting broccoli or Brussels sprouts.

Serves 8–10

2 game birds, such as skinless pheasant and/or pigeon

225g/8oz lean stewing steak

115g/4oz streaky (fatty) bacon, trimmed

butter, for frying

2 medium onions, finely chopped

1 large garlic clove, crushed

15ml/1 tbsp plain (all-purpose) flour

about 300ml/½ pint/¼ cup pigeon or pheasant stock

15ml/1 tbsp tomato purée (paste) (optional)

15ml/1 tbsp chopped fresh parsley

a little grated lemon rind

15ml/1 tbsp rowan or redcurrant jelly

50–115g/2–4oz button (white) mushrooms, halved or quartered if large

a small pinch of freshly grated nutmeg or ground cloves (optional)

milk or beaten egg, to glaze

sea salt and ground black pepper

For the rough-puff pastry

225g/8oz/2 cups plain (all-purpose) flour

2.5ml/½ tsp salt

5ml/1 tsp lemon juice

115g/4oz/½ cup butter, in walnut-sized pieces

1 To make the rough-puff pastry, sieve (sift) the flour and salt into a large mixing bowl. Add the lemon juice and the butter pieces and just enough cold water to bind the ingredients together. Turn the mixture on to a floured board and roll the pastry into a long strip. Fold it into three and press the edges together. Half-turn the pastry, rib it with the rolling pin to equalize the air in it and roll it into a strip once again. Repeat this folding and rolling process three more times.

2 Slice the pheasant or pigeon breasts from the bone and cut the meat into fairly thin strips. Trim away any fat from the stewing steak and slice it in the same manner. Cut the streaky bacon into thin strips, and then cook it very gently in a heavy frying pan until the fat runs. Add some butter and brown the sliced pigeon or pheasant and stewing steak in it, a little at a time.

3 Remove the meats from the pan and set aside. Cook the onions and garlic in the fat for 2–3 minutes over a medium heat. Remove and set aside with the meats, then stir the flour into the remaining fat. Cook for 1–2 minutes, and then gradually stir in enough stock to make a fairly thin gravy. Add the tomato purée, if using, parsley, lemon rind and rowan or redcurrant jelly and the mushrooms. Season to taste and add the nutmeg or cloves, if you like.

4 Return the browned meats, chopped onion and garlic to the pan containing the gravy, and mix well before turning into a deep 1.75 litre/3 pint/7½ cup pie dish. Leave to cool. Meanwhile, preheat the oven to 220°C/425°F/Gas 7.

5 Roll the prepared pastry out to make a circle 2.5cm/1in larger all round than the pie dish, and cut out to make a lid for the pie. Wet the rim of the pie dish and line with the remaining pastry strip. Dampen the strip and cover with the lid, pressing down well to seal.

6 Trim away any excess pastry and knock up the edges with a knife. Make a hole in the centre for the steam to escape and use any pastry trimmings to decorate the top. Glaze the top of the pie with milk or beaten egg. Bake in the oven for about 20 minutes, until the pastry is well-risen, then reduce the oven to 150°C/300°F/Gas 2 for another 1½ hours, until cooked. Protect the pastry from over-browning if necessary by covering it with a double layer of wet baking parchment. Serve.

Cook's tip Frozen puff pastry could replace the home-made rough-puff pastry, if you prefer.

Per portion Energy 448kcal/1871kJ; Protein 28.3g; Carbohydrate 29.5g, of which sugars 5.3g; Fat 24.9g, of which saturates 9.5g; Cholesterol 55mg; Calcium 67mg; Fibre 1.5g; Sodium 393mg.

Raised game pie

The perfect picnic food traditionally taken on country shoots, this stylish dish makes a spectacular centrepiece when baked in a fluted raised pie mould. The hot water crust pastry is very easy to make, and the pie can be served with piccalilli and pickled onions.

Serves 10

25g/1oz/2 tbsp butter

1 onion, finely chopped

2 garlic cloves, finely chopped

900g/2lb mixed boneless game meat, such as skinless pheasant and/or pigeon breast, venison and rabbit, diced

30ml/2 tbsp chopped mixed fresh herbs such as parsley, thyme and marjoram

salt and ground black pepper

For the pâté

50g/2oz/¼ cup butter

2 garlic cloves, finely chopped

450g/1lb chicken livers, rinsed, trimmed and chopped

60ml/4 tbsp brandy

5ml/1 tsp ground mace

For the hot water crust pastry

675g/1½lb/6 cups strong plain (all-purpose) flour

5ml/1 tsp salt

115ml/3½fl oz/scant ½ cup milk

115ml/3½fl oz/scant ½ cup water

115g/4oz/½ cup lard, diced

115g/4oz/½ cup butter, diced

beaten egg, to glaze

For the jelly

300ml/½ pint/1¼ cups game or beef consommé

2.5ml/½ tsp powdered gelatine

1 Melt the butter in a small pan until foaming, then add the onion and garlic, and cook until softened but not coloured. Remove from the heat and mix with the diced game meat and the chopped mixed herbs. Season well, cover and chill.

2 To make the pâté, melt the butter in a pan until foaming. Add the garlic and chicken livers and cook until the livers are just browned. Remove the pan from the heat and stir in the brandy and mace. Purée the mixture in a blender or food processor until smooth, then set aside and leave to cool.

3 To make the pastry, sift the flour and salt into a bowl and make a well in the centre. Place the milk and water in a pan. Add the lard and butter and heat gently until melted, then bring to the boil and remove from the heat as soon as the mixture begins to bubble. Pour the hot liquid into the well in the flour and beat until smooth. Cover and leave until cool enough to handle.

4 Preheat the oven to 200°C/400°F/Gas 6. Roll out two-thirds of the pastry and use to line a 23cm/9in raised pie mould. Spoon in half the game mixture and press it down evenly. Add the pâté, then top with the remaining game.

5 Roll out the remaining pastry to form a lid. Brush the edge of the pastry lining the mould with water and cover the pie with the lid. Trim off any excess. Pinch the edges together to seal. Make two holes in the centre of the lid and glaze with egg. Use pastry trimmings to roll out leaves to garnish the pie. Brush with egg.

6 Bake the pie for 20 minutes, cover with foil and cook for a further 10 minutes. Reduce the oven temperature to 150°C/300°F/Gas 2. Glaze the pie again with beaten egg and cook for a further 1½ hours, keeping the top covered loosely with foil.

7 Remove the pie from the oven and leave to stand for 15 minutes. Increase the oven temperature to 200°C/400°F/Gas 6. Stand the mould on a baking sheet and remove the sides. Glaze the sides of the pie with beaten egg and cover the top with foil, then cook for a final 15 minutes to brown the sides. Cool completely, then chill the pie overnight.

8 For the jelly, heat the game or beef consommé in a small pan until just starting to bubble, whisk in the gelatine until dissolved and leave to cool until just setting. Using a small funnel, carefully pour the jellied consommé into the holes in the pie. Chill. This pie will keep in the refrigerator for up to 3 days.

Per portion Energy 731kcal/3058kJ; Protein 44g; Carbohydrate 54.3g, of which sugars 2.5g; Fat 32g, of which saturates 17.9g; Cholesterol 223mg; Calcium 163mg; Fibre 2.3g; Sodium 444mg.

Slow-braised rabbit

Long, slow cooking is the secret to the tender rabbit in this dish. It is delicious served with potatoes boiled in their skins and lightly cooked green vegetables such as leeks.

Serves 4–6

1 rabbit, prepared and jointed by the butcher

30ml/2 tbsp seasoned flour

30ml/2 tbsp olive oil or vegetable oil

25g/1oz/2 tbsp butter

115g/4oz streaky (fatty) bacon

1 onion, roughly chopped

2 or 3 carrots, sliced

1 or 2 celery sticks, trimmed and sliced

300ml/½ pint/1¼ cups chicken stock

300ml/½ pint/1¼ cups dry (hard) cider or stout

a small bunch of parsley leaves, chopped

salt and ground black pepper

1 Soak the joints in cold salted water for at least 2 hours, then pat them dry with kitchen paper and toss them in seasoned flour. Preheat the oven to 200°C/400°F/Gas 6.

2 Heat the oil and butter together in a heavy flameproof casserole. Shake off (and reserve) any excess flour from the rabbit joints and brown them on all sides. Lift out and set aside.

3 Add the bacon to the casserole and cook for a few minutes, then remove and set aside with the rabbit.

4 Add the vegetables to the casserole and cook gently until just colouring, then sprinkle over any remaining seasoned flour to absorb the fats in the casserole. Stir over a low heat for 1 minute, to cook the flour. Add the stock and cider or stout, stirring, to make a smooth sauce.

5 Return the rabbit and bacon to the casserole, and add half of the chopped parsley and a light seasoning of salt and pepper. Mix gently together, then cover with a lid and put into the preheated oven. Cook for 15–20 minutes, then reduce the temperature to 150°C/300°F/Gas 2 for about 1½ hours, or until the rabbit is tender. Add the remaining parsley and serve.

Per portion Energy 368kcal/1535kJ; Protein 32.9g; Carbohydrate 10.5g, of which sugars 5.8g; Fat 19.7g, of which saturates 8g; Cholesterol 133mg; Calcium 88mg; Fibre 1.4g; Sodium 567mg.

Rabbit salmorejo

Slow-cooked rabbit was a crucial part of the Spanish peasant diet, and this dish includes pounded garlic, bread and vinegar, giving it a classic Mediterranean character.

Serves 4

675g/1½lb rabbit, jointed

300ml/½ pint/1¼ cups dry white wine

15ml/1 tbsp sherry vinegar

several oregano sprigs

2 bay leaves

30ml/2 tbsp plain (all-purpose) flour

90ml/6 tbsp olive oil

175g/6oz baby (pearl) onions, peeled and left whole

4 garlic cloves, sliced

150ml/¼ pint/⅔ cup chicken stock

1 dried chilli, seeded and finely chopped

10ml/2 tsp paprika

salt and ground black pepper

fresh flat leaf parsley sprigs, to garnish (optional)

1 Put the rabbit in a bowl. Add the wine, vinegar, oregano and bay leaves and toss together. Marinate for several hours or overnight in the refrigerator.

2 Drain the rabbit, reserving the marinade, and pat it dry with kitchen paper. Season the flour and use to dust the marinated rabbit.

3 Heat the oil in a large, wide flameproof casserole or frying pan. Fry the rabbit pieces until golden on all sides, then remove them and set aside.

4 Fry the onions until they are beginning to colour, then reserve on a separate plate.

5 Add the garlic to the pan and fry, then add the strained marinade, with the chicken stock, chilli and paprika.

6 Return the rabbit and the reserved onions to the pan. Bring to a simmer, then cover and simmer gently for about 45 minutes until the rabbit is tender. Check the seasoning, adding more vinegar and paprika if necessary. Serve the dish garnished with a few sprigs of flat leaf parsley, if you like.

Cook's tip Rather than cooking on the stove, transfer the stew to an ovenproof dish and bake in the oven at 180°C/350°F/Gas 4 for about 50 minutes.

Per portion Energy 311kcal/1294kJ; Protein 23.2g; Carbohydrate 9.5g, of which sugars 2.6g; Fat 20.4g, of which saturates 4.1g; Cholesterol 83mg; Calcium 65mg; Fibre 0.9g; Sodium 52mg.

Wild venison stew

This simple, yet deeply flavoured stew makes a wonderful supper dish, incorporating rich red wine and sweet redcurrant jelly with the depth of the bacon. This recipe also works beautifully with diced beef or wild boar, and can be made the day before and reheated.

Serves 4

1.3kg/3lb stewing venison (shoulder or topside), trimmed and diced

50g/2oz/¼ cup butter

225g/8oz piece of streaky (fatty) bacon, cut into 2cm/¾in lardons

2 large onions, chopped

1 large carrot, peeled and diced

1 large garlic clove, crushed

30ml/2 tbsp plain (all-purpose) flour

½ bottle red wine

dark stock

1 bay leaf

sprig of fresh thyme

200g/7oz button (white) mushrooms, sliced

30ml/2 tbsp redcurrant jelly

salt and ground black pepper

1 Dry the venison thoroughly using kitchen paper. Set to one side.

2 Melt the butter in a large, heavy pan then brown the bacon lardons over a medium-high heat, stirring occasionally. Reduce the heat slightly to medium and add the onions and carrot, stir in and brown lightly.

3 Add the venison to the pan along with the garlic and stir into the mixture. Sprinkle on the flour and mix well.

4 Pour in the wine and dark stock to cover, along with the herbs, mushrooms and redcurrant jelly.

5 Cover the pan and simmer over a low heat until the meat is cooked, approximately 1½–2 hours. Serve immediately with creamy mashed potato and green vegetables of your choice.

Cook's tip This dish can be cooked and then left until required – even for a couple of days if need be. The flavours will be enhanced if it has been left for a while. Simply reheat and serve when needed.

Per portion Energy 727kcal/3045kJ; Protein 83.8g; Carbohydrate 17.5g, of which sugars 14.4g; Fat 31.3g, of which saturates 13.8g; Cholesterol 226mg; Calcium 70mg; Fibre 2.9g; Sodium 985mg.

Venison pie with root vegetable mash

A variation on cottage pie, this tasty game pie has tender pieces of venison cooked in a rich gravy, and is topped with creamy root vegetabes such as sweet potatoes, parsnips and swede. It makes an excellent winter supper dish, served with steamed green vegetables.

Serves 6

30ml/2 tbsp olive oil

2 leeks, trimmed and chopped

1kg/2¼lb minced (ground) venison

30ml/2 tbsp chopped
fresh parsley

300ml/½ pint/1¼ cups game
consommé

salt and ground black pepper

For the topping

1.5kg/3¼lb mixed root vegetables,
such as sweet potatoes, parsnips and
swede (rutabaga), coarsely chopped

15ml/1 tbsp horseradish sauce

25g/1oz/2 tbsp butter

1 Heat the oil in a pan. Add the leeks and cook for about 8 minutes, or until softened and beginning to brown.

2 Add the minced venison to the pan and cook for about 10 minutes, stirring frequently, or until the meat is well browned. Stir in the chopped parsley, consommé and seasoning, then bring to the boil, cover and simmer for about 20 minutes, stirring occasionally.

3 Meanwhile, preheat the oven to 200°C/400°F/Gas 6 and prepare the topping. Cook the vegetables in boiling, salted water to cover for 15–20 minutes. Drain and mash with the horseradish sauce, butter and pepper.

4 Spoon the venison mixture into an ovenproof dish and top with the mashed vegetables. Bake for 20 minutes, or until piping hot and beginning to brown.

Per portion Energy 307kcal/1291kJ; Protein 39.8g; Carbohydrate 13.2g, of which sugars 12.5g; Fat 12g, of which saturates 4.1g; Cholesterol 93mg; Calcium 154mg; Fibre 5.8g; Sodium 176mg.

Meat dishes

Freshly baked pies, slow-cooked pot roasts and flavoursome casseroles sum up all that is best in country cooking. From simple Sunday roasts to comfort food such as Shepherd's Pie and Lancashire Hotpot, there is a meat dish for every occasion in this chapter. Many of the recipes use economic cuts of meat and seasonal vegetables, so you can really make the most of the revival in home cooking.

Roast loin of pork with apple and spinach

Pork and apple are a well-loved combination, and loin of pork is a prime roasting joint. In this recipe the pork is stuffed with apples, but these could be replaced with apricots or prunes.

Serves 6–8

1.6–1.8kg/3½–4lb loin of pork, boned and skinned

1 onion, sliced

juice of 1 orange

15ml/1 tbsp wholegrain mustard

30ml/2 tbsp demerara (raw) sugar

salt and ground black pepper

For the stuffing

50g/2oz spinach

50g/2oz/¼ cup dried apricots, chopped

50g/2oz Cheddar cheese, grated

1 cooking apple, peeled and grated

grated rind of ½ orange

1 Blanch the spinach in boiling water, chop, and put in a bowl with the other stuffing ingredients. Mix well together. Preheat the oven to 180°C/350°F/Gas 4.

2 Place the loin of pork, fat side down, on a board and place the stuffing down the centre. Roll the meat up and tie with cotton string. Season and put it into a roasting pan with the onion and 60ml/4 tbsp water. Cook uncovered for about 35 minutes per 450g/1lb.

3 About 40 minutes before the end of the estimated cooking time, pour off the cooking liquid into a small pan and discard the onion. Add the orange juice to the cooking liquid.

4 Spread the joint with mustard and sprinkle with the sugar. Return it to the oven and increase to 200°C/400°F/Gas 6 for 15 minutes or until crisp.

5 Meanwhile, boil up the juices and reduce to make a thin sauce. Serve with the sliced meat.

Per portion Energy 330kcal/1385kJ; Protein 49.4g; Carbohydrate 6.9g, of which sugars 6.3g; Fat 11.6g, of which saturates 4.9g; Cholesterol 145mg; Calcium 105mg; Fibre 1.2g; Sodium 227mg.

Roast pork belly with caramelized vegetables

Topped with crackling, this melting pork is served with root vegetables. The layer of fat keeps the meat moist. To ensure crisp crackling, make sure the skin is dry before roasting.

Serves 4–6

1 small swede (rutabaga), weighing about 500g/1lb 2oz

1 onion

1 parsnip

2 carrots

15ml/1 tbsp olive oil

1.5kg/3lb 6oz belly of pork, well scored

15ml/1 tbsp fresh thyme leaves or 5ml/1 tsp dried thyme

sea salt flakes and ground black pepper

Cook's tip Ask your butcher to score (slash) the pork rind really well, or use a strong sharp blade and (with care) do it yourself.

1 Preheat the oven to 220°C/425°F/ Gas 7. Cut the vegetables into small cubes (about 2cm/$\frac{3}{4}$in) and stir them with the oil in a roasting pan, tossing them until evenly coated. Pour in 300ml/$\frac{1}{2}$ pint/1$\frac{1}{4}$ cups water.

2 Sprinkle the pork rind with thyme, salt and pepper, rubbing them well into the scored slashes in the pork belly. Place the pork on top of the vegetables, pressing it down so that it sits level, with the skin side uppermost.

3 Put the pork and vegetables into the hot oven and cook for about 30 minutes, by which time the liquid will have almost evaporated to leave a nice golden crust in the bottom of the pan. Remove the pan from the oven.

4 Add 600ml/1 pint/2½ cups cold water to the vegetables in the pan. Reduce the oven temperature to 180°C/350°F/Gas 4.

5 Cook for 1½ hours, or until the pork is tender and the juices run clear when the centre of the meat is pierced with a sharp knife. Check the oven during the final 30 minutes to make sure the liquid does not dry up, adding a little water if necessary.

6 If the crackling is not yet crisp enough, increase the oven temperature to 220°C/425°F/Gas 7 and continue cooking for another 10–20 minutes, adding extra water if necessary – just enough to prevent the vegetables from burning on the bottom of the pan.

7 With a sharp knife, slice off the crackling. Serve it with thick slices of the pork, some vegetables and the golden juices spooned over.

Per portion Energy 1014kcal/4194kJ; Protein 39.5g; Carbohydrate 9.4g, of which sugars 7.3g; Fat 91.2g, of which saturates 33.1g; Cholesterol 180mg; Calcium 81mg; Fibre 3.3g; Sodium 202mg.

Cider-glazed ham

Succulent, moist and with plenty of flavour, this old-fashioned English country recipe keeps the meat tender with a lovely sticky glaze, which is complemented by the fruit and port sauce. It is perfect to share with friends and family at Christmas or any time of the year.

Serves 8–10

2kg/4½lb middle gammon (cured ham) joint

1 large or 2 small onions

about 30 whole cloves

3 bay leaves

10 black peppercorns

1.3 litres/2½ pints/5⅔ cups medium-dry (hard) cider

45ml/3 tbsp soft light brown sugar

bunch of flat leaf parsley, to garnish

For the cranberry sauce

350g/12oz/3 cups cranberries

175g/6oz/¾ cup soft light brown sugar

grated rind and juice of 2 clementines

30ml/2 tbsp port

1 Weigh the gammon and calculate the cooking time at 20 minutes per 450g/1lb, then place it in a large flameproof casserole or pan. Stud the onion or onions with 5–10 of the cloves and add to the casserole or pan with the bay leaves and peppercorns. Add 1.2 litres/2 pints/5 cups of the cider and enough water just to cover the gammon.

2 Heat until simmering and then carefully skim off the scum that rises to the surface using a large spoon or ladle. Start timing the cooking from the moment the stock begins to simmer.

3 Cover the gammon with a lid or foil and simmer gently for the calculated time. Towards the end of the cooking time, preheat the oven to 220°C/425°F/Gas 7.

4 Heat the sugar and remaining cider in a pan; stir until the sugar has dissolved. Simmer for 5 minutes to make a dark, sticky glaze. Remove the pan from the heat and leave to cool for 5 minutes.

Cook's tips

• Leave the gammon until it is just cool enough to handle before removing the rind. Snip off the string using a sharp knife or scissors, then carefully slice off the rind, leaving a thin, even layer of fat. Use a narrow-bladed, sharp knife for the best results.

• A large stockpot is ideal for cooking a big piece of meat like this gammon, but a deep roasting pan will do in an emergency, with foil as a cover and turning the meat often for even cooking.

5 Lift the gammon out of the pan. Carefully and evenly, cut the rind from the meat, then score the fat into a diamond pattern. Place the gammon in a large roasting pan or ovenproof dish.

6 Press a clove into the centre of each diamond, then carefully spoon over the glaze. Bake for 20–25 minutes, or until the fat is brown, glistening and crisp.

7 To make the sauce, simmer all the ingredients in a pan for 20 minutes, stirring. Transfer to a jug (pitcher). Serve the gammon hot or cold, garnished with parsley and the cranberry sauce.

Per portion Energy 447kcal/1873kJ; Protein 44.1g; Carbohydrate 25.6g, of which sugars 25.6g; Fat 18.8g, of which saturates 6.3g; Cholesterol 58mg; Calcium 35mg; Fibre 1.3g; Sodium 2203mg.

Pan-fried liver with bacon, sage and onions

Calf's liver would also be ideal for this recipe, but make sure not to overcook the liver or it will become tough. Serve with green leaves and a potato and root vegetable mash. You could also try adding mashed swede, parsnip or roast pumpkin to basic mashed potatoes.

Serves 4

450g/1lb lamb's liver

30ml/2 tbsp plain (all-purpose) flour

15ml/1 tbsp oil, plus extra if necessary

8 rindless streaky (fatty) bacon rashers (slices)

2 onions, thinly sliced

4 fresh sage leaves, finely chopped

150ml/½ pint/⅔ cup chicken or vegetable stock

salt and ground black pepper

Variations
• Other liver such as venison or ox could also be used in this recipe.
• A delicious addition would be a splash of Madeira or Marsala wine to add a sweet and sticky sauce – replace the stock with the wine and bubble down.

1 Pat the liver with kitchen paper, then trim it and cut on the diagonal to make thick strips. Season the flour and toss the liver in it until it is well coated, shaking off any excess flour.

2 Heat the oil in a large frying pan and add the bacon. Cook over medium heat until the fat runs out of the bacon and it is browned and crisp. Lift out and keep warm.

3 Add the onions and sage to the frying pan. Cook over medium heat for about 10–15 minutes, stirring occasionally, until the onions are soft and golden brown.

4 Carefully lift the onions out of the pan with a draining spoon and keep them warm.

5 Increase the heat and, adding extra oil if necessary, add the liver in a single layer. Cook for 4 minutes, turning once, until browned both sides.

6 Return the onions to the pan and pour in the stock. Bring to the boil and bubble gently for a minute or two, seasoning to taste. Serve topped with the bacon.

Per portion Energy 310kcal/1293kJ; Protein 28.7g; Carbohydrate 13.7g, of which sugars 5.7g; Fat 15.9g, of which saturates 4.4g; Cholesterol 500mg; Calcium 44mg; Fibre 1.6g; Sodium 400mg.

Pot-roast ham with mustard and cabbage

An updated version of traditional boiled bacon and cabbage, this recipe also takes its inspiration from the Italian country dish of pork cooked in milk. This technique helps to counteract the saltiness of the ham, and also keeps the meat deliciously moist.

Serves 4–6

1.3kg/3lb piece of gammon (smoked or cured ham) or boiling bacon

30ml/2 tbsp oil

2 large onions, sliced

1 bay leaf

750ml/1¼ pints/3 cups milk, plus extra if necessary

15ml/1 tbsp cornflour (cornstarch), dissolved in 15ml/1 tbsp milk

45ml/3 tbsp wholegrain mustard

15–30ml/2–3 tbsp single (light) cream (optional)

1 head of cabbage, such as Savoy, trimmed, ribs removed and leaves finely sliced

ground black pepper

1 Soak the bacon joint in cold water overnight. Heat 15ml/1 tbsp oil in a pan, add the onions and cook gently.

2 Place the joint on the bed of cooked onions. Add the bay leaf and milk, and season with pepper. Bring to the boil, cover and cook for about 1½ hours. Remove the meat from the pan and keep warm. Strain the cooking liquid. Reserve 300ml/½ pint/1¼ cups for the sauce and put the rest aside for soup.

3 Add the cornflour mixture to the reserved liquid and bring to the boil, stirring constantly. As it begins to thicken, stir in the wholegrain mustard and cream, if using.

4 Rinse the cabbage in cold running water and drain well.

5 Heat the remaining oil in a wok or large frying pan and stir-fry the cabbage for 2–3 minutes until cooked but still crunchy.

6 Slice the ham and serve on warmed serving plates with the mustard sauce and crisply cooked cabbage.

Per portion Energy 541kcal/2253kJ; Protein 58.4g; Carbohydrate 7.4g, of which sugars 5g; Fat 30.8g, of which saturates 9.4g; Cholesterol 77mg; Calcium 76mg; Fibre 2.1g; Sodium 2.87g.

Ham with Italian vegetables and eggs

An easy and tasty family supper dish, this is very straightforward to prepare, and you can vary the vegetables as you like. Serve with plenty of crusty Italian bread, such as ciabatta.

Serves 4

30ml/2 tbsp olive oil

1 onion, roughly chopped

2 garlic cloves, crushed

175g/6oz cooked ham

225g/8oz courgettes (zucchini)

1 red (bell) pepper, seeded and thinly sliced

1 yellow (bell) pepper, seeded and thinly sliced

10ml/2 tsp paprika

400g/14oz can chopped tomatoes

15ml/1 tbsp sun-dried tomato purée (paste)

4 eggs

115g/4oz/1 cup coarsely grated Cheddar cheese

salt and ground black pepper

crusty bread, to serve

1 Heat the olive oil in a deep frying pan. Add the onion and garlic and cook for 4 minutes, stirring frequently, or until just beginning to soften.

2 While the onions and garlic are cooking, cut the ham and courgettes into 5cm/2in long batons. Set the ham aside.

3 Add the courgettes and peppers to the onion and garlic and continue to cook over a medium heat for 3–4 minutes.

4 Stir in the paprika, tomatoes, tomato purée, ham and seasoning. Bring to the boil and simmer gently for about 15 minutes.

5 Reduce the heat to low. Make four wells in the tomato mixture, break an egg into each and season. Cook over a gentle heat until the white begins to set.

6 Preheat the grill (broiler). Sprinkle the cheese over the vegetables and grill (broil) for about 5 minutes until the eggs are set. Serve immediately with bread.

Per portion Energy 350kcal/1457kJ; Protein 24.4g; Carbohydrate 11.4g, of which sugars 10.7g; Fat 22.8g, of which saturates 9.3g; Cholesterol 244mg; Calcium 276mg; Fibre 3.1g; Sodium 817mg.

Bacon, egg and leek pie

The mild onion flavour of leeks is lovely with the bacon and eggs. The creamy filling is topped with flaky puff pastry, but shortcrust pastry would also work well.

Serves 4–6

15ml/1 tbsp olive oil

200g/7oz lean back bacon rashers (strips), trimmed of rinds and cut into thin strips

250g/9oz/2 cups leeks, thinly sliced

40g/1½oz/⅓ cup plain (all-purpose) flour

1.5ml/¼ tsp freshly grated nutmeg

450ml/¾ pint/scant 2 cups milk, plus extra for brushing

4 eggs

1 sheet ready-rolled puff pastry

salt and ground black pepper

1 Preheat the oven to 200°C/400°F/ Gas 6. Put the oil and bacon in a pan and cook for 5 minutes, stirring occasionally, until the bacon is golden brown. Add the leeks. Stir, cover and cook over medium heat for 5 minutes until softened, stirring once or twice. Stir in the flour and nutmeg. Remove from the heat and gradually stir in the milk.

2 Return to the heat and cook, stirring, until the sauce thickens and boils. Season, then pour into a shallow ovenproof pie dish, measuring 25cm/ 10in in diameter. Make four wells in the sauce and break an egg into each one.

3 Brush the edges of the dish with milk. Lay the pastry over the dish. Trim off the excess pastry and use it to make the trimmings. Brush the backs with milk and stick them on the top of the pie.

4 Brush the pastry with milk and make a small central slit to allow steam to escape. Put into the oven and cook for about 40 minutes until the pastry is puffed up and golden brown, and the eggs have set.

Per portion Energy 202kcal/842kJ; Protein 13.4g; Carbohydrate 9.7g, of which sugars 4.4g; Fat 12.5g, of which saturates 4.2g; Cholesterol 149mg; Calcium 125mg; Fibre 1.1g; Sodium 592mg.

Sausage and potato casserole

Be sure to use good meaty sausages for this traditional Irish recipe, slow cooking all the ingredients together to give the best results. Serve with some steamed buttered spinach.

Serves 4

15ml/1 tbsp vegetable oil

4 bacon rashers (strips), cut into 2.5cm/1in pieces

2 large onions, chopped

2 garlic cloves, crushed

8 large pork sausages

4 large baking potatoes, thinly sliced

1.5ml/¼ tsp fresh sage

300ml/½ pint/1¼ cups vegetable stock

salt and ground black pepper

soda bread, to serve

1 Preheat the oven to 180°C/350°F/ Gas 4. Grease a large ovenproof dish and set aside. Heat the oil in a frying pan. Add the bacon and fry for 2 minutes. Add the onions and fry for 5 minutes until golden. Add the garlic and fry for 1 minute, then remove the mixture from the pan and set aside. Then fry the sausages in the pan for 5 minutes until golden brown.

2 Arrange the potatoes in the base of the prepared dish. Spoon the bacon and onion mixture on top. Season with the salt and pepper and sprinkle with the fresh sage.

3 Pour on the stock and top with the sausages. Cover and bake for 1 hour. Serve hot with fresh soda bread.

Per portion Energy 553kcal/2305kJ; Protein 17.4g; Carbohydrate 48.7g, of which sugars 10g; Fat 33.4g, of which saturates 11.8g; Cholesterol 51mg; Calcium 74mg; Fibre 4g; Sodium 1019mg.

Toad-in-the-hole

Resembling toads peeping out of holes, this country favourite can be made with any variety of sausage. Try venison or wild boar, and replace the chives with shredded fresh sage leaves.

Serves 4–6

175g/6oz/1½ cups plain (all-purpose) flour

30ml/2 tbsp chopped fresh chives (optional)

2 eggs

300ml/½ pint/1¼ cups milk

50g/2oz/¼ cup white vegetable fat or lard

450g/1lb good-quality pork sausages

salt and ground black pepper

Cook's tip To ensure really light and crisp batter, ensure that the pan is very hot before adding the batter.

1 Preheat the oven to 220°C/425°F/ Gas 7. Sift the flour into a bowl with a pinch of salt and pepper. Make a well in the centre of the flour. Whisk the chives, if using, with the eggs and milk, then pour this into the well in the flour. Gradually whisk the flour into the liquid to make a smooth batter. Cover and leave to stand for at least 30 minutes.

2 Put the fat into a small roasting pan and place in the oven for 3–5 minutes. Add the pork sausages and cook for 15 minutes. Turn the sausages twice during cooking.

3 Pour the batter over the sausages and return to the oven. Cook for about 20 minutes, or until the batter is risen and golden. Serve immediately.

Per portion Energy 497kcal/2070kJ; Protein 14.5g; Carbohydrate 32.1g, of which sugars 3.8g; Fat 35.4g, of which saturates 13.6g; Cholesterol 109mg; Calcium 141mg; Fibre 1.3g; Sodium 616mg.

Lamb with honey, rosemary and cider

Country lamb with honey and rosemary are traditional partners. Here, they are teamed with cider and cooked until the meat is meltingly soft and the sweet juices are deliciously caramelized and golden. Slow-cooking this economic cut of lamb ensures that the finished dish is beautifully tender, and the addition of cider gives a lovely tangy flavour. Serve with some golden roast potatoes and green vegetables, such as spinach leaves or beans.

Serves 4–6

1.5kg/3lb 6oz shoulder of lamb

2 garlic cloves, halved

fresh rosemary sprigs

75ml/5 tbsp clear honey

300ml/½ pint/1¼ cups dry (hard) cider, plus extra if necessary

lemon juice (optional)

salt and ground black pepper

1 Preheat the oven to 220°C/425°F/Gas 7. Rub the lamb with the cut garlic. Put the meat and the garlic in a deep roasting pan. Season with salt and pepper.

2 Make small slashes in the meat with a knife and push in a few small sprigs of rosemary.

3 Stir the honey into the cider until it has fully dissolved and then pour it over the lamb.

4 Put the roasting pan into the hot oven and cook the lamb for 20–30 minutes until it has browned and the juices have reduced, begun to caramelize and turn golden brown. Keep checking to make sure the liquid does not dry up and brown too much. If so, add a little water.

5 Stir 300ml/½ pint water into the pan juices and spoon them over the lamb. Cover with a large tent of foil, scrunching the edges around the rim of the pan to seal them.

6 Put the pan back into the oven, reduce the temperature to 180°C/350°F/Gas 4 and cook for about another hour.

7 Remove the foil and spoon the juices over the lamb again. Turn the oven temperature back up to 220°C/425°F/Gas 7 and continue cooking, uncovered, for a further 10–15 minutes, until the lamb is crisp and brown.

8 Lift the lamb on to a serving plate and leave in a warm place to rest for 15 minutes before carving.

9 While the lamb is resting, spoon any excess fat off the top of the juices in the pan. Then taste the juices and adjust the seasoning, if necessary, adding lemon juice to taste. Put the roasting pan on the hob and bring just to the boil.

10 Serve the carved lamb with the juices spooned over.

Cook's tip Though it looks attractive when the rosemary stands proud of the lamb, it is likely to burn. So make sure the slashes are deep and that you push the rosemary sprigs into the lamb.

Variation Medium dry white wine, apple juice, light vegetable stock or water could be used in place of cider.

Per portion Energy 524kcal/2180kJ; Protein 35.3g; Carbohydrate 10.9g, of which sugars 10.9g; Fat 36.5g, of which saturates 17g; Cholesterol 153mg; Calcium 17mg; Fibre 0g; Sodium 130mg.

Roast shoulder of lamb with garlic potatoes

The potatoes are basted in the lamb juices while cooking, and become wonderfully garlicky, fragrant and sticky. Return the potatoes to the oven to keep warm while you leave the lamb to rest before carving, then serve along with a selection of seasonal vegetables.

Serves 4–6

675g/1½lb waxy potatoes, peeled and cut into large dice

12 garlic cloves, unpeeled

1 whole shoulder of lamb

45ml/3 tbsp olive oil

salt and ground black pepper

Cook's tip Shoulder of lamb is naturally sweet as it has fat distributed within the meat. When buying the lamb, make sure it still has the bone as this will add to the flavour when it is cooking.

1 Preheat the oven to 180°C/350°F/ Gas 4. Put the potatoes and garlic cloves into a large roasting pan and season with salt and pepper. Pour over 30ml/2 tbsp of the oil and toss the potatoes and garlic to coat.

2 Place a rack over the roasting pan, so that it is not touching the potatoes. Place the lamb on the rack and drizzle over the remaining oil. Season with salt and pepper.

3 Roast the lamb and potatoes for about 2–2½ hours, or until the lamb is cooked through.

4 Halfway through the cooking time, carefully take the lamb and the rack off the roasting pan and turn the potatoes to ensure even cooking. Transfer the lamb, potatoes and garlic to a warmed serving platter.

Per portion Energy 668kcal/2775kJ; Protein 29.2g; Carbohydrate 20.8g, of which sugars 1.7g; Fat 52.6g, of which saturates 24.1g; Cholesterol 113mg; Calcium 22mg; Fibre 1.8g; Sodium 123mg.

Lamb and pearl barley casserole

The combination of pearl barley and carrots add texture, bulk and flavour to this comforting stew, giving a thick, flavourful sauce for the meat. Comfort food is at its best when served with boiled or baked potatoes and a green vegetable, such as spring cabbage.

Serves 6

675g/1½lb stewing lamb

15ml/1 tbsp oil

2 onions, sliced

675g/1½lb carrots, thickly sliced

4–6 celery sticks, sliced

45ml/3 tbsp pearl barley, rinsed

stock or water

salt and ground black pepper

chopped fresh parsley,
to garnish

1 Trim the lamb and cut it into bitesize pieces. Heat the oil in a flameproof casserole and brown the lamb.

2 Add the vegetables to the casserole and fry them briefly with the meat. Add the barley and enough stock or water to cover, and season to taste.

3 Cover the casserole and simmer gently or cook in a slow oven, 150°C/300°F/Gas 2 for 1–1½ hours until the meat is tender. Add extra stock or water during cooking if necessary. Serve garnished with the chopped fresh parsley.

Cook's tip The best lamb for stewing is neck or shoulder, with some fat on the meat to keep it moist during cooking.

Per portion Energy 304kcal/1263kJ; Protein 23.2g; Carbohydrate 13g, of which sugars 11.3g; Fat 18g, of which saturates 7.5g; Cholesterol 84mg; Calcium 53mg; Fibre 3.6g; Sodium 110mg.

Lamb stew with shallots and new potatoes

Italian gremolata made with lemon rind, garlic and parsley is a piquant garnish
for the lamb. Traditionally served with osso buco, it is also good served with fish.

Serves 6

1kg/2¼lb boneless shoulder of lamb, trimmed of fat and cut into 5cm/ 2in cubes

1 garlic clove, finely chopped

finely grated rind of ½ lemon and juice of 1 lemon

90ml/6 tbsp olive oil

45ml/3 tbsp plain (all-purpose) flour

1 large onion, sliced

5 anchovy fillets in olive oil, drained

2.5ml/½ tsp caster (superfine) sugar

300ml/½ pint/1¼ cups white wine

475ml/16fl oz/2 cups lamb stock or half stock and half water

1 fresh bay leaf

fresh thyme sprig

fresh parsley sprig

500g/1¼lb small new potatoes

250g/9oz shallots, peeled but left whole

45ml/3 tbsp double (heavy) cream (optional)

salt and ground black pepper

For the gremolata

1 garlic clove, finely chopped

finely shredded rind of ½ lemon

45ml/3 tbsp chopped fresh flat leaf parsley

1 Mix the lamb with the garlic and the rind and juice of ½ lemon. Season with pepper and mix in 15ml/1 tbsp olive oil, then leave to marinate for 12–24 hours.

2 Drain the lamb, reserving the marinade, and pat the lamb dry with kitchen paper. Preheat the oven to 180°C/350°F/Gas 4.

3 Heat 30ml/2 tbsp olive oil in a large, heavy frying pan. Season the flour with salt and pepper and toss the lamb in it to coat, shaking off any excess. Seal the lamb on all sides in the hot oil. Do this in batches, transferring each batch of lamb to an ovenproof pan or flameproof casserole as you brown it. You may need to add an extra 15ml/1 tbsp olive oil to the pan.

4 Reduce the heat, add another 15ml/1 tbsp oil to the pan and cook the onion gently over a very low heat, stirring frequently, for 10 minutes, until softened and golden but not browned.

5 Add the anchovies and caster sugar, and cook, mashing the anchovies into the soft onion with a wooden spoon until well combined.

6 Add the reserved marinade, increase the heat a little and cook for about 1–2 minutes, then pour in the wine and stock or stock and water and bring to the boil. Simmer gently for about 5 minutes, then pour over the lamb.

7 Tie the bay leaf, thyme and parsley together and add to the lamb. Season with salt and pepper, then cover tightly and cook in the oven for 1 hour. Stir the potatoes into the stew and cook for a further 20 minutes.

8 Meanwhile, to make the gremolata, chop all the ingredients together finely. Place in a dish, cover and set aside.

9 Heat the remaining oil in a frying pan and brown the shallots on all sides, then stir them into the lamb.

10 Cover and cook for a further 30–40 minutes, until the lamb is tender. Transfer the lamb and vegetables to a dish and keep warm. Discard the herbs.

11 Boil the cooking juices to reduce and concentrate them, then add the cream, if using, and simmer for 2–3 minutes.

12 Adjust the seasoning, adding a little lemon juice to taste. Pour this sauce over the lamb, sprinkle the gremolata on top and serve immediately.

Per portion Energy 553kcal/2311kJ; Protein 37g; Carbohydrate 26.2g, of which sugars 5.3g; Fat 30.6g, of which saturates 10.4g; Cholesterol 128mg; Calcium 79mg; Fibre 2.7g; Sodium 261mg.

Lancashire hotpot

Authentically made with mutton and lamb's kidney, this dish is now more often made with neck of lamb and vegetables, including turnips, carrots and leeks and potato.

Serves 4

40g/1½oz/3 tbsp dripping, or 45ml/3 tbsp oil

8 middle neck lamb chops, about 1kg/2¼lb total weight

175g/6oz lamb's kidneys, cut into large pieces

1kg/2¼lb potatoes, thinly sliced

3 carrots, thickly sliced

450g/1lb leeks, sliced

3 celery sticks, sliced

15ml/1 tbsp chopped fresh thyme

30ml/2 tbsp chopped fresh parsley

small sprig of rosemary

600ml/1 pint/2½ cups veal stock

salt and ground black pepper

Variations
• Pork chops can be used instead of lamb. Use thick loin chops or boneless sparerib chops, as preferred.
• Try adding the shredded leaves from a couple of sprigs of sage instead of the rosemary.

1 Preheat the oven to 170°C/325°F/Gas 3. Heat the dripping or oil in a frying pan and brown the lamb chops and lamb's kidneys in batches, then reserve the fat.

2 In a large casserole, make alternate layers of lamb chops, kidneys, three-quarters of the potatoes and the carrots, leeks and celery, sprinkling the herbs and seasoning over each layer as you go. Tuck the rosemary sprig down the side.

3 Arrange the remaining potatoes on top. Pour over the stock, brush with the reserved fat, then cover and bake for 2½ hours. Increase the oven temperature to 220°C/425°F/Gas 7. Uncover and cook for 30 minutes until well browned on top.

Per portion Energy 724kcal/3035kJ; Protein 51.6g; Carbohydrate 50g, of which sugars 8.7g; Fat 36.7g, of which saturates 13.6g; Cholesterol 278mg; Calcium 75mg; Fibre 7.3g; Sodium 233mg.

Mustard thatch lamb pie

This is a shepherd's pie with a twist. Adding mustard to the potato topping gives extra bite and a crunchy, golden topping. Serve with minted new peas or steamed broccoli.

Serves 4

800g/1¾lb floury potatoes, diced

60ml/4 tbsp milk

15ml/1 tbsp wholegrain
or French mustard

a little butter

450g/1lb lean lamb, minced (ground)

1 onion, chopped

2 celery sticks, thinly sliced

2 carrots, diced

30ml/2 tbsp cornflour blended into
150ml/¼ pint/⅔ cup lamb stock

15ml/1 tbsp Worcestershire sauce

30ml/2 tbsp chopped fresh rosemary,
or 10ml/2 tsp dried

salt and ground black pepper

fresh vegetables, to serve

1 Cook the potatoes in a large pan of boiling lightly salted water until tender. Drain well and mash until smooth, then stir in the milk, mustard, butter and seasoning to taste. Meanwhile, preheat the oven to 200°C/400°F/Gas 6.

2 Fry the lamb in a non-stick pan, breaking it up with a fork, until browned. Add the onion, celery and carrots and cook for 2–3 minutes, stirring, to stop the mixture sticking to the base.

3 Stir in the stock and cornflour mixture. Bring to the boil, stirring constantly, then remove from the heat. Stir in the Worcestershire sauce and rosemary and season with salt and pepper to taste.

4 Turn the lamb mixture into a 1.75 litre/3 pint/7 cup ovenproof dish and spread over the potato topping evenly, swirling with the edge of a palette knife. Bake for 30–35 minutes until golden on the top. Serve hot with a selection of fresh vegetables.

Variations
• The original shepherd's pie is made with lamb. It can be made with minced beef, in which case it is a cottage pie.
• To vary the potato topping, try adding horseradish – either creamed or, for an even stronger flavour, freshly grated.

Per portion Energy 371kcal/1561kJ; Protein 26.5g; Carbohydrate 37.9g, of which sugars 7.7g; Fat 13.7g, of which saturates 6.2g; Cholesterol 86mg; Calcium 68mg; Fibre 3.3g; Sodium 194mg.

Rib of beef with Yorkshire puddings

A quintessential Sunday-lunch classic, this is the well-loved 'roast beef of old England', traditionally served with crisp Yorkshire puddings, golden roast potatoes and a selection of seasonal green and root vegetables, all covered in mouth-watering gravy and accompanied by a tangy horseradish cream. In Yorkshire the puddings are often served before the meat, with the gravy, as a first course. Either way, this dish will have your guests asking for more.

Serves 6–8

rib of beef joint, weighing about 3kg/6½lb

oil, for brushing

salt and ground black pepper

For the Yorkshire puddings

115g/4oz/1 cup plain (all-purpose) flour

1.5ml/¼ tsp salt

1 egg

200ml/7fl oz/scant 1 cup milk

oil or beef dripping, for greasing

For the horseradish cream

60–75ml/4–5 tbsp finely grated fresh horseradish

300ml/½ pint/1¼ cups sour cream

30ml/2 tbsp cider vinegar or white wine vinegar

10ml/2 tsp caster (superfine) sugar

For the gravy

600ml/1 pint/2½ cups good beef stock

Cook's tip To avoid the pungent smell (and tears) produced by grating horseradish, use a jar of preserved grated horseradish.

1 Preheat the oven to 220°C/425°F/ Gas 7. Weigh the joint and calculate the cooking time required as follows: 10–15 minutes per 500g/1¼lb for rare beef, 15–20 minutes for medium and 20–25 minutes for well done.

2 Put the joint into a large roasting pan. Brush it all over with oil and season with salt and pepper. Put into the hot oven and cook for 30 minutes, until the beef is browned. Lower the oven temperature to 160°C/325°F/Gas 3 and cook for the calculated time, spooning the juices over the meat occasionally during cooking.

3 For the Yorkshire pudding, sift the flour and salt into a bowl and break the egg into it. Make the milk up to 300ml/½ pint/1¼ cups with water and gradually whisk into the flour to make a smooth batter. Leave to stand while the beef cooks. Generously grease eight Yorkshire pudding tins (muffin pans) measuring about 10cm/4in.

4 For the horseradish cream, put all the ingredients into a bowl and mix well. Cover and chill until required.

5 At the end of its cooking time, remove the beef from the oven, cover with foil and leave to stand for 30–40 minutes while you cook the Yorkshire puddings and make the gravy.

6 Increase the oven temperature to 220°C/425°F/Gas 7 and put the prepared tins on the top shelf for 5 minutes until very hot. Pour in the batter and cook for about 15 minutes until well risen, crisp and golden brown.

7 To make the gravy, transfer the beef to a warmed serving plate. Pour off the fat from the roasting pan, leaving the meat juices. Add the stock to the pan, bring to the boil and bubble until reduced by about half. Season to taste.

8 Carve the beef and serve with the gravy, Yorkshire puddings, roast potatoes and horseradish cream.

Per portion Energy 1037kcal/4338kJ; Protein 129g; Carbohydrate 15.1g, of which sugars 4.1g; Fat 51.5g, of which saturates 24.3g; Cholesterol 352mg; Calcium 123mg; Fibre 0.5g; Sodium 249mg.

Pot roast beef with stout

Use a boned and rolled joint such as brisket, silverside or topside for this slow-cooked dish, where the vegetables are cooked with the beef and the meat becomes meltingly tender.

Serves 6

30ml/2 tbsp vegetable oil

900g/2lb rolled brisket of beef

2 medium onions, roughly chopped

2 celery sticks, thickly sliced

450g/1lb carrots, cut into large chunks

675g/1½lb potatoes, peeled and cut into large chunks

30ml/2 tbsp plain (all-purpose) flour

450ml/¾ pint/ 2 cups beef stock

300ml/½ pint/1¼ cups stout

1 bay leaf

45ml/3 tbsp chopped fresh thyme

5ml/1 tsp soft light brown sugar

30ml/2 tbsp wholegrain mustard

15ml/1 tbsp tomato purée (paste)

salt and ground black pepper

1 Preheat the oven to 180°C/350°F/ Gas 4. Heat the oil in a large flameproof casserole and brown the beef until golden brown all over.

2 Lift the beef from the pan and drain on kitchen paper. Add the onions to the pan and cook for about 4 minutes, until just beginning to soften and brown.

3 Add the celery, carrots and potatoes to the casserole and cook over a medium heat for 2–3 minutes, or until they are just beginning to colour.

4 Add the flour and cook for a further 1 minute, stirring constantly. Gradually pour in the beef stock and the stout. Heat until the mixture comes to the boil, stirring frequently.

5 Stir in the bay leaf, thyme, sugar, mustard, tomato purée and seasoning. Place the meat on top, cover tightly and transfer the casserole to the hot oven.

6 Cook for about 2½ hours, or until tender. Adjust the seasoning, to taste. To serve, carve the beef into thick slices and serve with the vegetables and plenty of gravy.

Per portion Energy 415kcal/1743kJ; Protein 36g; Carbohydrate 35.6g, of which sugars 13.1g; Fat 14g, of which saturates 4.4g; Cholesterol 81mg; Calcium 66mg; Fibre 4.2g; Sodium 284mg.

Braised beef and country vegetables

A dish which, in the past, would have been gently left to cook all day, this casserole is just as impressive slow cooked for a few hours. It is delicious with suet dumplings or crusty bread.

Serves 4–6

1kg/2¼lb lean stewing steak, cut into 5cm/2in cubes

45ml/3 tbsp plain (all-purpose) flour

45ml/3 tbsp oil

1 large onion, thinly sliced

1 large carrot, thickly sliced

2 celery sticks, finely chopped

300ml/½ pint/¼ cup beef stock

30ml/2 tbsp tomato purée (paste)

5ml/1 tsp dried mixed herbs

15ml/1 tbsp dark muscovado (molasses) sugar

225g/8oz baby potatoes, halved

2 leeks, thinly sliced

salt and ground black pepper

Variation Replace the potatoes with dumplings. Sift 175g/6oz/1½ cups self-raising (self-rising) flour and stir in 75g/3oz/½ cup shredded suet (US chilled, grated shortening), 30ml/2 tbsp chopped parsley and seasoning. Stir in water to make a soft dough and divide the mixture into 12 balls. In step 6, stir in the leeks and put the dumplings on top. Cover and cook for 15–20 minutes more.

1 Preheat the oven to 150°C/300°F/ Gas 2. Season the flour and use to coat the beef cubes.

2 Heat the oil in a large, flameproof casserole. Add a small batch of meat, cook quickly until browned on all sides and, with a slotted spoon, lift out. Repeat with the remaining beef.

3 Add the onion, carrot and celery to the casserole. Cook over medium heat for about 10 minutes, stirring frequently, until they begin to soften and brown slightly on the edges.

4 Return the meat to the casserole and add the stock, tomato purée, herbs and sugar, at the same time scraping up any sediment that has stuck to the casserole. Heat until the liquid nearly comes to the boil.

5 Cover with a tight fitting lid and put into the hot oven. Cook for 2–2½ hours, or until the beef is tender.

6 Gently stir in the potatoes and leeks, cover and continue cooking for a further 30 minutes or until the potatoes are soft.

Per portion Energy 450kcal/1880kJ; Protein 41.3g; Carbohydrate 23.6g, of which sugars 10.3g; Fat 21.7g, of which saturates 7.3g; Cholesterol 97mg; Calcium 63mg; Fibre 3.5g; Sodium 137mg.

Boeuf Bourguignon

Beef cooked 'Burgundy style' in red wine with chopped bacon, baby onions and mushrooms and simmered for hours at a low temperature produces a rich, dark gravy and melt-in-the-mouth meat. Serve with creamy mashed potato and croûtons of bread fried in duck fat.

Serves 6

175g/6oz rindless streaky (fatty) bacon rashers (strips), chopped

900g/2lb lean braising steak, such as top rump of beef or braising steak

30ml/2 tbsp plain (all-purpose) flour

45ml/3 tbsp sunflower oil

25g/1oz/2 tbsp butter

12 shallots

2 garlic cloves, crushed

175g/6oz/2½ cups mushrooms, sliced

450ml/¾ pint/scant 2 cups robust red wine

150ml/¼ pint/⅔ cup beef stock or consommé

1 bay leaf

2 sprigs each of fresh thyme, parsley and marjoram

salt and ground black pepper

Variation Instead of the rindless streaky (fatty) bacon rashers (strips), use lardons, which are available from supermarkets.

1 Preheat the oven to 160°C/325°F/Gas 3. Heat a large flameproof casserole, then add the bacon and cook, stirring occasionally, until the pieces are crisp and golden brown.

2 Meanwhile, cut the meat into 2.5cm/1in cubes. Season the flour and use to coat the meat. Use a draining spoon to remove the bacon from the casserole and set aside. Add and heat the oil, then brown the beef in batches and set aside with the bacon.

3 Add the butter to the fat remaining in the casserole. Cook the shallots and crushed garlic until just starting to colour, then add the sliced mushrooms and cook for a further 5 minutes. Replace the bacon and meat, and stir in the wine and stock or consommé. Tie the bay leaf, thyme, parsley and marjoram together into a bouquet garni and add to the casserole.

4 Cover and cook in the oven for 1½ hours, or until the meat is tender, stirring once or twice. Season to taste and serve the casserole with creamy mashed root vegetables, such as celeriac and potatoes.

Cook's tip Boeuf Bourguignon freezes very well. Transfer the mixture to a dish so that it cools quickly, then pour it into a rigid plastic container. Push all the cubes of meat down into the sauce or they will dry out. Freeze for up to 2 months. Thaw overnight in the refrigerator, then transfer to a flameproof casserole and add 150ml/¼ pint/⅔ cup water. Stir well, bring to the boil, stirring occasionally, and simmer steadily for at least 10 minutes, or until the meat is piping hot.

Per portion Energy 749kcal/3117kJ; Protein 63.3g; Carbohydrate 15.2g, of which sugars 8.8g; Fat 40.3g, of which saturates 14g; Cholesterol 167mg; Calcium 69mg; Fibre 2.8g; Sodium 868mg.

Braised oxtail

While oxtail requires long, slow cooking to tenderize the meat, the resulting complex, dark flavours are well worth the effort. This dish is traditionally served with plain boiled potatoes to soak up the rich gravy, though mashed potatoes would be good too.

Serves 6

2 oxtails, trimmed, cut into pieces, total weight about 1.5kg/3lb 6oz

30ml/2 tbsp flour seasoned with salt and pepper

45ml/3 tbsp oil

2 large onions, sliced

2 celery sticks, sliced

4 medium carrots, sliced

1 litre/1¾ pints/4 cups beef stock

15ml/1 tbsp tomato purée (paste)

finely grated rind of 1 small orange

2 bay leaves

few sprigs of fresh thyme

salt and ground black pepper

chopped fresh parsley, to garnish

1 Preheat the oven to 150°C/300°F/ Gas 2. Coat the pieces of oxtail in the seasoned flour, shaking off and reserving any excess.

2 Heat 30ml/2 tbsp oil in a large flameproof casserole and add the oxtail in batches, cooking quickly until browned all over. Lift out and set aside. Add the remaining oil to the pan, and stir in the onions, celery and carrots.

3 Cook the vegetables quickly, stirring occasionally, until beginning to brown. Tip in any reserved flour, then add the stock, tomato purée and orange rind.

Cook's tip This dish benefits from being made in advance. When cooled completely, any fat can be removed before reheating.

4 Heat until bubbles begin to rise to the surface, then add the herbs, cover and put into the hot oven. Cook for 3½–4 hours until the oxtail is very tender.

5 Remove from the oven and leave to stand, covered, for 10 minutes before skimming off the surface fat. Adjust the seasoning and garnish with parsley.

Per portion Energy 341kcal/1426kJ; Protein 30.9g; Carbohydrate 13.6g, of which sugars 7.7g; Fat 18.6g, of which saturates 0.7g; Cholesterol 0mg; Calcium 54mg; Fibre 2.3g; Sodium 203mg.

Rustic meat loaf

Made with beef, pork and veal mince, this tasty meat loaf has plenty of fresh herbs
and seasoning, and is lovely served with a home-made tomato sauce.

Serves 6

25g/1oz/2 tbsp butter
or margarine

1 onion, finely chopped

2 garlic cloves, finely chopped

50g/2oz/½ cup finely
chopped celery

450g/1lb lean ground beef

225g/8oz veal mince

225g/8oz lean pork mince

2 eggs

50g/2oz/1 cup fine fresh
breadcrumbs

25g/1oz/½ cup chopped
fresh parsley

30ml/2 tbsp chopped fresh basil

2.5ml/½ tsp fresh or dried
thyme leaves

2.5ml/½ tsp salt

2.5ml/½ tsp pepper

30ml/2 tbsp Worcestershire sauce

50ml/2fl oz/¼ cup chilli sauce
or tomato ketchup

6 bacon rashers (strips)

1 Preheat oven to 180°C/350°F/Gas 4.
Melt the butter or margarine in a small
frying pan over a low heat. Add the
onion, garlic and celery and cook until
softened, 8–10 minutes. Remove from
the heat and leave to cool slightly.

2 In a large mixing bowl, combine
the onion, garlic and celery with
all the other ingredients except the
bacon. Mix together lightly, using a
fork or your fingers. Do not overwork
or the meat loaf will be too compact.

3 Form the meat mixture into an
oval loaf. Carefully transfer it to
a shallow baking tin (pan).

4 Lay the bacon across the meat loaf.
Bake for 1¼ hours, basting occasionally
with the juices and bacon fat in the pan.

5 Remove from the oven and drain
off the fat. Leave the meat loaf to
stand for 10 minutes before serving.
Carefully lift the meat loaf on to a
serving dish and slice thickly.

Per portion Energy 286kcal/1189kJ; Protein 18.6g; Carbohydrate 11.9g, of which sugars 5.1g; Fat 18.5g, of which saturates 8.3g; Cholesterol 119mg; Calcium 62mg; Fibre 1g; Sodium 572mg.

Shepherd's pie

A thrifty way to use up leftover roast lamb, this is one of the best-known country dishes.
It can also be made with beef instead of lamb, in which case it is known as cottage pie.

Serves 4

1kg/2½lb potatoes, peeled

60ml/4 tbsp milk

about 25g/1oz/2 tbsp butter

15ml/1 tbsp oil

1 large onion, finely chopped

1 medium carrot, finely chopped

450g/1lb cold cooked lamb,
minced (ground)

150ml/½ pint/⅔ cup lamb stock

30ml/2 tbsp finely chopped
fresh parsley

salt and ground black pepper

Variations
• To make a cottage pie, replace
the lamb and lamb stock with beef.
• Add extra ingredients to the meat
base, such as chopped garlic, a few
mushrooms, a spoonful of tomato
purée (paste) or ketchup, or a splash
of Worcestershire sauce.
• Mix the potatoes with mashed
parsnip, squash or swede (rutabaga),
and a dollop of wholegrain mustard.

1 Preheat the oven to 190°C/375°F/
Gas 5. Boil the potatoes in salted water
for about 20 minutes or until soft.
Drain, and mash with the milk, adding
butter and seasoning to taste.

2 Heat the oil in a frying pan and
add the onion and carrot. Cook over
medium heat for 5–10 minutes, stirring
occasionally, until soft. Stir in the
minced lamb, stock and parsley.

3 Spread the meat mixture in an
ovenproof dish and spoon the mashed
potato evenly over the top. Cook in the
hot oven for about 30 minutes until
the potatoes are crisped and browned.

Per portion Energy 487kcal/2045kJ; Protein 29.4g; Carbohydrate 50.1g, of which sugars 15.2g; Fat 20.2g, of which saturates 8.4g; Cholesterol 69mg; Calcium 54mg; Fibre 5.3g; Sodium 379mg.

Beef in red wine with a potato crust

This recipe makes the best of braising beef by marinating it in red wine and topping it with a cheesy grated potato crust that bakes to a golden, crunchy consistency. For a change, instead of grating the potatoes, slice them thinly and layer over the top of the beef with onion rings and crushed garlic. The dish makes a satistfying meal on its own.

Serves 4

675g/1½lb stewing beef, diced

300ml/½ pint/1¼ cups red wine

3 juniper berries, crushed

slice of orange peel

30ml/2 tbsp olive oil

2 onions, cut into chunks

2 carrots, cut into chunks

1 garlic clove, crushed

225g/8oz/3 cups button (white) mushrooms

150ml/¼ pint/⅔ cup beef stock

30ml/2 tbsp cornflour (cornstarch)

salt and ground black pepper

For the crust

450g/1lb potatoes, grated

15ml/1 tbsp olive oil

30ml/2 tbsp creamed horseradish

50g/2oz/½ cup mature (sharp) Cheddar cheese, grated

salt and ground black pepper

1 Place the diced beef in a non-metallic bowl. Add the wine, berries, and orange peel and season with pepper. Mix the ingredients, then cover and leave to marinate for at least 4 hours or overnight.

2 Preheat the oven to 160°C/325°F/Gas 3. Drain the beef, reserving the marinade.

3 Heat the oil in a large flameproof casserole and fry the meat in batches for 5 minutes to seal. Add the onions, carrots and garlic and cook for 5 minutes. Stir in the mushrooms, red wine marinade and beef stock. Simmer.

4 Mix the cornflour with water to make a smooth paste. Stir into the pan. Season, cover and cook for 1½ hours.

5 Make the crust 30 minutes before the end of the cooking time for the beef. Start by blanching the grated potatoes in boiling water for 5 minutes. Drain well and then squeeze out all the extra liquid.

6 Stir in the remaining ingredients and then sprinkle evenly over the surface of the beef. Increase the oven temperature to 200°C/400°F/Gas 6 and cook the dish for a further 30 minutes so that the top is crispy and slightly browned.

Cook's tip Use a large grater on the food processor for the potatoes, or alternatively, grate them by hand with a traditional grater. They will hold their shape better while being blanched than if you use a finer blade.

Per portion Energy 474kcal/1973kJ; Protein 43g; Carbohydrate 6.1g, of which sugars 5.6g; Fat 28.8g, of which saturates 8.7g; Cholesterol 106mg; Calcium 53mg; Fibre 2.6g; Sodium 564mg.

Steak, mushroom and ale pie

This dish is a firm favourite on menus at restaurants specializing in traditional country fare. Preparing the filling the day before and allowing the meat and vegetables to rest overnight ensures a particularly tasty filling. The pie can be ready relatively quickly simply by topping with the pastry and baking. Serve with seasonal vegetables or a side salad.

Serves 4

25g/1oz/2 tbsp butter

1 large onion, finely chopped

115g/4oz/1½ cups chestnut or button (white) mushrooms, halved

900g/2lb lean beef in one piece, such as rump or braising steak

30ml/2 tbsp plain (all-purpose) flour

45ml/3 tbsp sunflower oil

300ml/½ pint/1¼ cups stout or brown ale

300ml/½ pint/1¼ cups beef stock or consommé

500g/1¼lb puff pastry, thawed if frozen

beaten egg, to glaze

salt and ground black pepper

1 Melt the butter in a large, flameproof casserole, add the onion and cook gently, stirring occasionally, for about 5 minutes, or until it is softened. Add the halved mushrooms and continue cooking for a further 5 minutes, stirring.

2 Meanwhile, trim the meat and cut it into 2.5cm/1in cubes. Season the flour and toss the meat in it.

3 Remove the onion mixture from the casserole and set aside. Add the oil, then brown the steak in batches.

4 Replace the vegetables, then stir in the stout or ale and stock or consommé. Bring to the boil, reduce the heat and simmer for 1 hour, stirring occasionally. Season to taste and transfer to a 1.5 litre/2½ pint/6½ cup pie dish. Cover and leave to cool. If possible, chill the meat filling overnight, as this allows the flavour to develop. Preheat the oven to 230°C/450°F/Gas 8.

5 Roll out the pastry in the shape of the dish and about 4cm/1½in larger all around. Cut a 2.5cm/1in strip from the edge of the pastry. Brush the rim of the dish with water and press the pastry strip on it. Brush the pastry rim with beaten egg and cover the pie with the pastry lid. Press the lid firmly in place, then trim of the excess.

6 Use the blunt edge of a knife to tap the outside edge of the pastry, pressing it down with your finger as you seal in the filling. (This technique is known as knocking up.)

7 Pinch the pastry between your fingers to flute the edge. Roll out any remaining pastry trimmings and cut out shapes to garnish the pie, brushing the shapes with a little beaten egg before pressing them lightly in place.

8 Make a hole in the middle of the pie to allow steam to escape, brush the top carefully with beaten egg and chill for 10 minutes to rest the pastry.

9 Bake the pie for 15 minutes, then reduce the oven temperature to 200°C/400°F/Gas 6 and bake for a further 15–20 minutes, or until the pastry is risen and golden. Let the pie rest for a minute or two before serving.

Per portion Energy 1061kcal/4423kJ; Protein 58.8g; Carbohydrate 59.3g, of which sugars 7.6g; Fat 65.3g, of which saturates 24g; Cholesterol 164mg; Calcium 129mg; Fibre 3.2g; Sodium 622mg.

Steak and kidney pudding

One of the best-known English country dishes, this tasty pudding is a 19th-century recipe that originally contained oysters, but mushrooms are more often used today. Although it has a relatively long cooking time, the finished result is well worth the wait.

Serves 6

500g/1¼lb lean stewing steak, cut into cubes

225g/8oz beef kidney or lamb's kidneys, skin and core removed and cut into small cubes

1 medium onion, finely chopped

30ml/2 tbsp finely chopped fresh herbs, such as parsley and thyme

30ml/2 tbsp plain (all-purpose) flour

275g/10oz/2½ cups self-raising (self-rising) flour

150g/5oz/1 cup shredded suet (US chilled, grated shortening)

finely grated rind of 1 small lemon

about 120ml/4fl oz/½ cup beef stock or water

salt and ground black pepper

1 Put the stewing steak into a large bowl and add the kidneys, onion and chopped herbs. Sprinkle the plain flour and seasoning over the top and mix well.

2 To make the pastry, sift the self-raising flour into another large bowl. Stir in the suet and lemon rind. Add sufficient cold water to bind the ingredients and gather into a soft dough.

3 On a lightly floured surface, knead the dough gently, and then roll out to make a circle measuring about 35cm/14in across. Cut out one-quarter of the circle, roll up and put aside.

4 Lightly butter a 1.75 litre/3 pint heatproof bowl. Line the bowl with the rolled out dough, pressing the cut edges together and allowing the pastry to overlap the top of the bowl slightly.

5 Spoon the steak mixture into the lined bowl, packing it in carefully, so as not to split the pastry.

6 Pour in sufficient stock to reach no more than three-quarters of the way up the filling. (Any stock remaining can be heated and poured into the cooked pudding to thin the gravy if desired.)

7 Roll out the reserved pastry into a circle to form a lid and lay it over the filling, pinching the edges together to seal them well.

8 Cover with baking parchment, pleated in the centre to allow the pudding to rise, then cover again with a large sheet of foil (again pleated at the centre). Tuck the edges under and press them tightly to the sides of the basin until securely sealed (alternatively, tie with string). Steam for about 5 hours.

9 Carefully remove the foil and paper, slide a knife around the sides of the pudding and turn out on to a warmed serving plate.

Per portion Energy 436kcal/1835kJ; Protein 31.1g; Carbohydrate 49.5g, of which sugars 4.8g; Fat 13.9g, of which saturates 3.6g; Cholesterol 166mg; Calcium 201mg; Fibre 1.9g; Sodium 380mg.

Veal casserole with broad beans

This delicate stew, flavoured with sherry and plenty of garlic, is a spring casserole made with new vegetables – menestra de ternera. For a delicious flavour, be sure to add plenty of parsley just before serving. Lamb would be equally good cooked in this way.

Serves 6

45ml/3 tbsp olive oil

1.3–1.6kg/3–3½lb veal, cut into 5cm/2in cubes

1 large onion, chopped

6 large garlic cloves, unpeeled

1 bay leaf

5ml/1 tsp paprika

250ml/8fl oz/1 cup fino sherry

100g/4oz/scant 1 cup shelled, skinned broad (fava) beans

60ml/4 tbsp fresh flat leaf parsley

salt and ground black pepper

1 Heat 30ml/2 tbsp oil in a large flameproof casserole. Add half the meat and brown well on all sides. Transfer to a plate. Brown the rest of the meat and remove from the pan.

2 Add the remaining oil to the pan and cook the onion until soft. Return the meat to the casserole and stir well to mix with the onion.

3 Add the garlic cloves, bay leaf, paprika and sherry. Season. Bring to simmering point, then cover and cook very gently for 30–40 minutes.

4 Add the broad beans to the casserole about 10 minutes before the end of the cooking time. Chop the flat leaf parsley. Check the seasoning and stir in the parsley just before serving.

Per portion Energy 352kcal/1473kJ; Protein 47.4g; Carbohydrate 3.6g, of which sugars 1.3g; Fat 11.6g, of which saturates 2.8g; Cholesterol 182mg; Calcium 34mg; Fibre 1.2g; Sodium 244mg.

Veal and ham pie

Historically, the English love pies made with mutton and pork. This splendid version contains diced veal, gammon and hard-boiled eggs. The flavours of the two meats marry perfectly in the delicate filling. Serve with green cabbage leaves and buttery mashed potato.

Serves 4

450g/1lb boneless shoulder of veal, diced

225g/8oz lean gammon (smoked or cured ham), diced

15ml/1 tbsp plain (all-purpose) flour

large pinch each of dry mustard and ground black pepper

25g/1oz/2 tbsp butter

15ml/1 tbsp sunflower oil

1 onion, chopped

600ml/1 pint/2½ cups chicken or veal stock

2 eggs, hard-boiled and sliced

30ml/2 tbsp chopped fresh parsley

For the pastry

175g/6oz/1½ cups plain (all-purpose) flour

75g/3oz/6 tbsp butter

iced water, to mix

beaten egg, to glaze

1 Preheat the oven to 180°C/350°F/ Gas 4. Mix the veal and gammon in a bowl. Season the flour with the mustard and pepper, then add it to the meat and toss well. Heat the butter and oil in a casserole until sizzling, then cook the meat mixture in batches until golden on all sides. Remove the meat from the pan.

2 Cook the onion in the fat remaining in the casserole until softened, but not coloured. Gradually stir in the stock, then replace the meat mixture and stir. Cover and cook in the oven for 1½ hours, or until the veal is tender.

3 To make the pastry, sift the flour into a bowl and rub in the butter with your fingers. Mix in enough iced water to bind the mixture into clumps, then press these together with your fingertips to make a dough.

4 Spoon the cooked veal and gammon mixture into a 1.5 litre/2½ pint/6¼ cup pie dish. Arrange the slices of hard-boiled egg over the top and sprinkle with the chopped parsley.

5 Roll out the pastry on a lightly floured work surface to about 4cm/1½in larger than the top of the pie dish.

6 Cover the pie dish with the pastry lid. Press the pastry around the rim to seal in the filling and cut off any excess. Use the blunt edge of a knife to tap the outside edge of the pastry, pressing it down with your finger as you seal in the filling. Pinch the pastry between your fingers to flute the edge.

7 Roll out any remaining pastry and cut out decorative shapes to garnish the top of the pie. Brush with beaten egg and bake for 30–40 minutes, or until the pastry is well-risen and golden brown. Serve hot with steamed green cabbage and creamy mashed potato.

Per portion Energy 621kcal/2595kJ; Protein 42.4g; Carbohydrate 39.2g, of which sugars 2.6g; Fat 33.8g, of which saturates 17.2g; Cholesterol 281mg; Calcium 128mg; Fibre 2.3g; Sodium 1007mg.

Vegetable side dishes

Tasty and nutritious, vegetables are vital to good health and well-being. Served simply with a little unsalted butter or a drizzle of olive oil and a scatter of chopped herbs, they are hard to beat. Seasonal treats such as asparagus and new potatoes are best eaten as fresh as possible, so always seek out local suppliers or enrol in a vegetable box scheme that will give access to what's in season.

Spring vegetables with tarragon

This is almost a salad since the vegetables are only lightly cooked. The bright, fresh flavours are enhanced with the aniseed flavour of tarragon. Serve alongside fish, seafood or chicken.

Serves 4

5 spring onions (scallions)

50g/2oz/¼ cup butter

1 garlic clove, crushed

115g/4oz asparagus tips

115g/4oz mangetouts (snowpeas), trimmed

115g/4oz broad (fava) beans

2 Little Gem (Bibb) lettuces

5ml/1 tsp finely chopped fresh tarragon

salt and ground black pepper

1 Cut the spring onions into quarters lengthways and fry gently over a medium-low heat in half the butter with the garlic.

2 Add the asparagus tips, mangetouts and broad beans. Mix the vegetables gently, making sure they are all well coated in oil.

3 Just cover the base of the pan with water, season, and allow to simmer gently for a few minutes, until the vegetables are tender.

4 Cut the lettuce into quarters and add to the pan. Cook for 3 minutes then, off the heat, swirl in the remaining butter and the tarragon, and serve.

Per portion Energy 149kcal/619kJ; Protein 4.7g; Carbohydrate 6.1g, of which sugars 3g; Fat 12g, of which saturates 7.3g; Cholesterol 29mg; Calcium 55mg; Fibre 3.5g; Sodium 89mg.

Fresh green beans and tomato sauce

A standard country summer dish in Greece made with whichever beans are available, this pretty side dish is most often served with feta cheese, olives and flat bread.

Serves 4

800g/1¾lb green beans, trimmed

150ml/¼ pint/⅔ cup extra virgin olive oil

1 large onion, thinly sliced

2 garlic cloves, chopped

2 small potatoes, peeled and chopped into cubes

675g/1½lb tomatoes or a 400g/14oz can plum tomatoes, chopped

150ml/¼ pint/⅔ cup hot water

45–60ml/3–4 tbsp chopped fresh parsley

salt and ground black pepper

1 If the green beans are very long, cut them in half. Drop them into a bowl of cold water so that they are completely submerged. Leave them to absorb the water for a few minutes. To test if the beans are fresh, snap one in half. If it breaks crisply it is fresh; if it bends rather than breaking, the beans are not fresh.

2 Heat the olive oil in a large pan, add the onion and sauté until translucent. Add the garlic, then, when it becomes aromatic, stir in the potatoes and sauté the mixture for a few minutes.

3 Add the tomatoes and the hot water and cook for 5 minutes. Drain the beans, rinse them and drain again, then add them to the pan with a little salt and pepper to season. Cover and simmer for 30 minutes.

4 Stir in the chopped parsley, with a little more hot water if the mixture is dry. Cook for 10 minutes more, until the beans are very tender. Serve hot with slices of feta cheese, if you like.

Per portion Energy 350kcal/1,448kJ; Protein 6.6g; Carbohydrate 21.9g, of which sugars 13.4g; Fat 26.9g, of which saturates 4g; Cholesterol 0mg; Calcium 121mg; Fibre 7.7g; Sodium 25mg.

Sautéed broad beans with bacon

Particularly associated with Andalucía, where broad beans are served to bulls destined for the bullring, this classic country dish is eaten all over Spain. Use young tender broad beans or, if using larger beans, remove the skins to reveal the bright green inner bean.

Serves 4

30ml/2 tbsp olive oil

1 small onion, finely chopped

1 garlic clove, finely chopped

50g/2oz rindless smoked streaky (fatty) bacon, roughly chopped

225g/8oz broad (fava) beans, thawed if frozen

5ml/1 tsp paprika

15ml/1 tbsp sweet sherry

salt and ground black pepper

1 Heat the olive oil in a large frying pan or sauté pan. Add the chopped onion, garlic and bacon and fry over a high heat for about 5 minutes, stirring frequently, until the onion is softened and the bacon browned.

2 Add the beans and paprika to the pan and stir-fry for 1 minute. Add the sherry, lower the heat, cover and cook for 5–10 minutes until the beans are tender. Season with salt and pepper to taste and serve hot or warm.

Per portion Energy 139kcal/577kJ; Protein 6.8g; Carbohydrate 8.2g, of which sugars 1.6g; Fat 9g, of which saturates 1.9g; Cholesterol 8mg; Calcium 38mg; Fibre 3.9g; Sodium 163mg.

Creamed leeks

Versatile leeks are a great winter vegetable, adding a subtle onion flavour to many dishes, including soups, casseroles, stews and stir-fries. Serve these creamed leeks on their own, or as a tasty accompaniment to grilled meats, such as chops, chicken or gammon.

Serves 4–6

4 large or 8 medium leeks

300ml/½ pint/1¼ cups milk

8 streaky (fatty) rashers (strips) of bacon, trimmed and sliced (optional)

1 egg, lightly beaten

150ml/¼ pint/⅔ cup single (light) cream

15ml/1 tbsp mild Irish mustard

75g/3oz/¾ cup grated cheese (optional)

salt and ground black pepper

1 Slice the leeks into fairly large chunks. Put them into a pan with the milk. Season and bring to the boil. Reduce the heat and simmer for 15–20 minutes, or until tender. Drain well and turn the leeks into a buttered shallow baking dish, reserving the cooking liquor.

2 Meanwhile, if using the bacon, put it into a frying pan and cook gently to allow the fat to run, then turn up the heat a little and cook for a few minutes until it crisps up. Remove from the pan with a slotted spoon and sprinkle the bacon over the leeks.

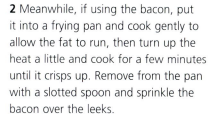

3 Rinse the pan used for the leeks. Blend the beaten egg, single cream and Irish mustard together and mix it with the reserved cooking liquor. Return to the pan and heat gently without boiling, allowing the sauce to thicken a little. Taste and adjust the seasoning with salt and ground black pepper. Pour the sauce over the leeks and bacon.

4 Sprinkle the baking dish with grated cheese, if using, and brown for a few minutes under a hot grill (broiler). (Alternatively, the leeks may be served immediately without browning them.) Serve with plain grilled (broiled) meat or poultry, if you like.

Variations
• The bacon may be grilled (broiled) and served separately, if you prefer.
• Omit the cheese topping and use the leeks and bacon to dress hot tagliatelle or spaghetti, or use in a risotto.
• The leeks could also be spread on to toast topped with cheese and grilled for a light lunch.

Per portion Energy 238kcal/993kJ; Protein 18.6g; Carbohydrate 9g, of which sugars 7.9g; Fat 14.4g, of which saturates 7.3g; Cholesterol 90mg; Calcium 172mg; Fibre 3.5g; Sodium 830mg.

Butter-braised lettuce, peas and spring onions

A well-loved French country recipe, this dish is traditionally served with grilled fish or meat. Try adding shredded fresh mint or substituting mangetouts or sugar snaps for the peas.

Serves 4

50g/2oz/¼ cup butter

4 Little Gem (Bibb) lettuces, halved lengthways

2 bunches spring onions (scallions), trimmed

400g/14oz shelled peas (about 1kg/2¼lb in pods)

salt and ground black pepper

Variations
• Braise about 250g/9oz baby carrots with the lettuce.
• Cook 115g/4oz chopped smoked bacon in the butter. Use 1 bunch spring onions (scallions) and some chopped parsley.

1 Melt half the butter in a wide, heavy pan over a low heat. Add the lettuces and spring onions.

2 Turn the vegetables in the butter, then sprinkle in salt and plenty of ground black pepper. Cover, and cook the vegetables very gently for 5 minutes, stirring once.

3 Add the peas and turn them in the buttery juices. Pour in 120ml/4fl oz/ ½ cup water, then cover and cook over a gentle heat for a further 5 minutes. Uncover and increase the heat to reduce the liquid to a few tablespoons.

4 Stir in the remaining butter. Transfer to a warmed serving dish and serve.

Per portion Energy 161kcal/670kJ; Protein 9.1g; Carbohydrate 15.9g, of which sugars 6.8g; Fat 7.4g, of which saturates 3.7g; Cholesterol 13mg; Calcium 73mg; Fibre 6.5g; Sodium 47mg.

Cauliflower cheese

A mature, strong farmhouse cheddar cheese gives an authentic taste to this simple country classic, or try making this recipe with half cauliflower and half broccoli florets.

Serves 4

1 medium cauliflower

25g/1oz/2 tbsp butter

25g/1oz/4 tbsp plain (all-purpose) flour

300ml/½ pint/1¼ cups milk

115g/4oz mature (sharp) Cheddar or Cheshire cheese, grated

salt and ground black pepper

1 Trim the cauliflower and cut it into florets. Bring a pan of lightly salted water to the boil, drop in the cauliflower and cook for 5–8 minutes or until just tender. Drain and transfer the florets into an ovenproof dish.

2 To make the sauce, melt the butter in a pan, stir in the flour and cook gently, stirring constantly, for about 1 minute (do not allow it to brown). Remove from the heat and gradually stir in the milk. Return the pan to the heat and cook, stirring, until the mixture thickens and comes to the boil. Simmer gently for 1–2 minutes.

3 Stir in three-quarters of the cheese and season to taste. Spoon the sauce over the cauliflower and sprinkle the remaining cheese on top. Put under a hot grill (broiler) until golden brown.

Cook's tip Boost the cheese flavour by adding a little English (hot) mustard to the cheese sauce.

Per portion Energy 318kcal/1318kJ; Protein 17.4g; Carbohydrate 4.4g, of which sugars 3.9g; Fat 25.8g, of which saturates 16.3g; Cholesterol 71mg; Calcium 371mg; Fibre 1.8g; Sodium 453mg.

Carrot and parsnip purée

The most widely used and versatile of root vegetables, carrots blend beautifully with all the others. In this easy-to-make recipe they are mashed together with tasty parsnips, creating a smooth and flavourful combination. Celeriac, swede or sweet potatoes all purée well too.

Serves 6–8

350g/12oz carrots

450g/1lb parsnips

pinch of freshly grated nutmeg or ground mace

15g/½oz/1 tbsp butter

about 15ml/1 tbsp single (light) cream, or top of the milk (optional)

1 small bunch parsley leaves, chopped (optional), plus extra to garnish

salt and ground black pepper

1 Peel the carrots and slice fairly thinly. Peel the parsnips and cut into bitesize chunks (they are softer and will cook more quickly than the carrots). Boil the two vegetables, separately, in salted water, until tender.

2 Drain them well and put them through a mouli-légumes (food mill) with the grated nutmeg or mace, a good seasoning of salt and ground black pepper and the butter. Purée together and taste for seasoning.

▶ **3** If you like, blend in some cream or top of the milk to taste, and add chopped parsley for extra flavour.

4 Transfer the carrot and parsnip purée to a warmed serving bowl, sprinkle with freshly chopped parsley to garnish and serve hot.

Cook's tip Any leftover purée can be thinned to taste with good-quality chicken stock and heated to make a quick home-made soup.

Per portion Energy 92kcal/385kJ; Protein 1.8g; Carbohydrate 14.1g, of which sugars 8.7g; Fat 3.5g, of which saturates 1.8g; Cholesterol 7mg; Calcium 48mg; Fibre 4.9g; Sodium 38mg

Spiced red cabbage with apple

A hardy vegetable, red cabbage can be grown in tough conditions – it was ubiquitous in the European rural diet, and especially popular throughout Germany. This colourful, sharp and sweet-flavoured side dish is ideal served alongside roast pork, goose and game.

Serves 4–6

1kg/2¼lb red cabbage

2 cooking apples

2 onions, chopped

5ml/1 tsp freshly grated nutmeg

1.5ml/¼ tsp ground cloves

1.5ml/¼ tsp ground cinnamon

15ml/1 tbsp soft dark brown sugar

45ml/3 tbsp red wine vinegar

25g/1oz/2 tbsp butter, diced

salt and ground black pepper

chopped flat leaf parsley, to garnish

2 Layer the shredded cabbage in a large ovenproof dish with the onions, apples, spices, sugar, and salt and ground black pepper. Pour over the vinegar and add the diced butter.

3 Cover the dish with a lid and cook in the preheated oven for about 1½ hours, stirring a couple of times, until the cabbage is very tender. Serve immediately, garnished with the parsley.

1 Preheat the oven to 160°C/325°F/Gas 3. Cut away and discard the large white ribs from the outer cabbage leaves using a large, sharp knife, then finely shred the cabbage. Peel, core and coarsely grate the apples.

Cook's tip This dish can be cooked in advance. Bake the cabbage for 1½ hours, then leave to cool. Store in a cool place covered with clear film (plastic wrap). To complete the cooking, bake it in the oven at 160°C/325°F/Gas 3 for about 30 minutes, stirring occasionally.

Per portion Energy 160kcal/668kJ; Protein 4.3g; Carbohydrate 23.8g, of which sugars 22.4g; Fat 5.8g, of which saturates 3.3g; Cholesterol 13mg; Calcium 140mg; Fibre 6.6g; Sodium 58mg.

Asparagus with hollandaise sauce

The asparagus season is short, and this country dish makes the most of its delicate and distinctive flavour. Asparagus can be served simply with melted butter drizzled over the top, but this delicious whisked white wine hollandaise sauce makes it really special.

Serves 4

2 bunches of asparagus

30ml/2 tbsp white wine vinegar

2 egg yolks

115g/4oz butter, melted

juice of ½ lemon

salt and ground black pepper

Cook's tips
• Asparagus should be cooked and eaten as soon as possible, preferably on the day it is picked.
• Make stock with the woody ends of the asparagus rather than throwing them away and add it to vegetable soups or sauces, or use for risotto.

1 Snap off the tough ends of the asparagus. Drop the spears into fast boiling water, cooking for 1–2 minutes until just tender. Test the thickest part of the stalk with a small sharp knife; take care not to overcook.

2 In a pan, bring the vinegar to the boil and bubble until it has reduced to just 15ml/1 tbsp. Remove from the heat and add 15ml/1 tbsp cold water.

3 Whisk the egg yolks into the vinegar and water mixture, then put the pan over a very low heat and continue whisking until the mixture is frothy and thickened.

4 Remove from the heat again and slowly whisk in the melted butter. Add the lemon juice and seasoning to taste. Serve the sauce immediately with the drained asparagus.

Per portion Energy 276kcal/1135kJ; Protein 5.3g; Carbohydrate 2.7g, of which sugars 2.6g; Fat 27.1g, of which saturates 15.9g; Cholesterol 162mg; Calcium 51mg; Fibre 2.1g; Sodium 180mg.

Jerusalem artichokes au gratin

An under-appreciated vegetable, the Jerusalem artichoke – sometimes known as the 'sun choke' – has a distinctive nutty flavour and an appealing crunch. This creamy gratin side dish is the perfect accompaniment to roast meat or fried fish.

Serves 4

250ml/8fl oz/1 cup sour cream

50ml/2fl oz/¼ cup single (light) cream

675g/1½lb Jerusalem artichokes, coarsely chopped

40g/1½oz/½ cup grated Danbo cheese

60ml/4 tbsp fresh breadcrumbs

salt

Variation If you can't find Danbo, a mellow yet flavoursome semi-hard cheese, look for Elbo, Havarti, or use a good English Cheddar.

1 Preheat the oven to 190°C/375°F/ Gas 5. Lightly grease an ovenproof dish. Stir together the sour cream and single cream in a mixing bowl, season with salt and stir to mix.

2 Add the Jerusalem artichokes to the cream and toss to coat evenly with the mixture. Spread the artichokes over the bottom of the prepared dish.

3 Sprinkle evenly with the cheese, then the breadcrumbs. Bake for about 30 minutes, until the cheese melts and the top is brown and bubbling.

Per portion Energy 296kcal/1230kJ; Protein 6.9g; Carbohydrate 27.6g, of which sugars 15.5g; Fat 18.1g, of which saturates 11.1g; Cholesterol 52mg; Calcium 186mg; Fibre 4.4g; Sodium 240mg.

Baked tomatoes with mint

This is a high summer recipe that makes the most of falling-off-the-vine ripe tomatoes and fresh mint. Serve this attractive dish with grilled lamb or fish. It is ideal for a barbecue.

Serves 4

6 large ripe tomatoes

300ml/½ pint/1¼ cups double (heavy) cream

2 sprigs of fresh mint

olive oil, for brushing

a few pinches of caster (superfine) sugar

30ml/2 tbsp grated Bonnet cheese

salt and ground black pepper

Cook's tip Bonnet is a hard variety of goat's cheese but any other hard, well-flavoured cheese will do.

1 Preheat the oven to 220°C/425°F/Gas 7. Bring a pan of water to the boil and have a bowl of iced water ready. Cut the cores out of the tomatoes and make a cross at the base. Plunge the tomatoes into the boiling water for 10 seconds and then straight into the iced water. Leave to cool completely.

2 Put the cream and mint in a pan and bring to the boil. Reduce the heat and allow to simmer until it has reduced by about half.

3 Peel the cooled tomatoes and slice them thinly. Pat dry on kitchen paper.

4 Brush a shallow gratin dish lightly with a little olive oil. Layer the sliced tomatoes in the dish, overlapping slightly, and season with salt and ground black pepper. Sprinkle a little sugar over the top.

5 Strain the reduced cream evenly over the top of the tomatoes. Sprinkle on the cheese and bake in the preheated oven for 15 minutes, or until the top is browned and bubbling. Serve immediately in the gratin dish.

Per portion Energy 443kcal/1831kJ; Protein 5g; Carbohydrate 6.7g, of which sugars 6.7g; Fat 44.1g, of which saturates 27.4g; Cholesterol 113mg; Calcium 123mg; Fibre 1.8g; Sodium 105mg.

Oven-roast red onions

Serve these sticky, sweet and fragrant onions with roast chicken or warm as part of a mezze. Alternatively, crumble over some fresh herb cheese and serve with crusty bread.

Serves 4

4 large or 8 small red onions

45ml/3 tbsp olive oil

6 juniper berries, crushed

8 small rosemary sprigs

30ml/2 tbsp balsamic vinegar

salt and ground black pepper

Cook's tips

• To help hold back the tears, chill the onions first for about 30 minutes, then remove the root end last. The root contains the largest concentration of the sulphuric compounds that make the eyes water.

• If you don't have an onion baker, use a ceramic baking dish and cover with foil.

1 Soak a clay onion baker in cold water for 15 minutes, then drain. If the base of the baker is glazed, only the lid will need to be soaked.

2 Cut the onions from the tip to the root, cutting the large onions into quarters and the small onions in half. Trim the roots from the onions and remove the skins, if you like.

3 Rub the onions with olive oil, salt and pepper and the juniper berries. Place the onions in the baker, inserting the rosemary in among the onions. Pour the remaining olive oil and vinegar over.

4 Cover and place in an unheated oven. Set the oven to 200°C/400°F/Gas 6 and cook for 40 minutes. Remove the lid and cook for a further 10 minutes.

Per portion Energy 128kcal/530kJ; Protein 1.8g; Carbohydrate 11.9g, of which sugars 8.4g; Fat 8.6g, of which saturates 1.2g; Cholesterol 0mg; Calcium 38mg; Fibre 2.1g; Sodium 5mg.

Farmhouse cheese-baked courgettes

This is an easy dish that makes a great accompaniment to a wide range of meat and fish dishes or a good vegetarian lunch. Use piquant farmhouse cheddar or mature goat's cheese.

Serves 4

4 courgettes (zucchini)

30ml/2 tbsp grated hard farmhouse cheese, such as Gabriel or Desmond

about 25g/1oz/2 tbsp butter

salt and ground black pepper

1 Preheat the oven to 180°C/350°F/ Gas 4. Slice the courgettes in half, lengthways. Trim the ends and discard.

2 Butter a shallow baking dish and arrange the courgettes, cut side up, inside the dish.

3 Sprinkle the cheese over the courgettes, and sprinkle over a few knobs (pats) of butter. Bake in the preheated oven for about 20 minutes, or until the courgettes are tender and the cheese is bubbling and golden brown. Serve immediately.

Per portion Energy 96kcal/395kJ; Protein 3.8g; Carbohydrate 1.9g, of which sugars 1.8g; Fat 8g, of which saturates 5g; Cholesterol 21mg; Calcium 82mg; Fibre 0.9g; Sodium 93mg.

Greek courgette and potato bake

This is an early autumn dish known in Greece as Briami. Serve the oven-baked courgettes with bread, olives and grilled lamb, feta or halloumi cheese for a satisfying vegetarian meal.

Serves 6

675g/1½lb courgettes (zucchini)

450g/1lb potatoes, peeled and cut into chunks

1 onion, finely sliced

3 garlic cloves, chopped

1 large red (bell) pepper, seeded and cubed

400g/14oz can chopped tomatoes

150ml/¼ pint/⅔ cup extra virgin olive oil

150ml/¼ pint/⅔ cup hot water

5ml/1 tsp dried oregano

45ml/3 tbsp chopped fresh flat leaf parsley, plus a few extra sprigs, to garnish

salt and ground black pepper

1 Preheat the oven to 190°C/375°F/ Gas 5. Scrape the courgettes lightly under running water to dislodge any grit and then slice them into thin rounds. Put them in a large baking dish and add the chopped potatoes, onion, garlic, red pepper and tomatoes.

2 Mix well, then stir in the olive oil, hot water and dried oregano.

3 Spread the mixture evenly, then season with salt and pepper. Bake for 30 minutes, then stir in the parsley and a little more water.

4 Return to the oven and cook for 1 hour, increasing the temperature to 200°C/400°F/Gas 6 for the final 10–15 minutes, so that the potatoes brown.

Per portion Energy 374kcal/1,554kJ; Protein 6.6g; Carbohydrate 28.6g, of which sugars 11.2g; Fat 26.7g, of which saturates 4g; Cholesterol 0mg; Calcium 86mg; Fibre 5.1g; Sodium 29mg.

Irish colcannon

This traditional Irish dish is often served at Hallowe'en with a ring hidden inside it to predict the wedding of the person who finds it. You can use curly kale, cabbage or cavolo nero for a variation. Serve topped with a fried or poached egg, or with a stew or roast.

Serves 6–8

450g/1lb potatoes, peeled and boiled

450g/1lb curly kale or cabbage, cooked

milk, if necessary

50g/2oz/2 tbsp butter, plus extra for serving

1 large onion, finely chopped

salt and ground black pepper

Variation If making this dish for Hallowe'en, slip in a wrapped ring just before serving to your guests.

1 Mash the potatoes. Chop the kale or cabbage, add it to the potatoes and mix. Stir in a little milk if the mash is too stiff.

2 Melt a little butter in a frying pan over a medium heat and add the onion. Cook until softened. Remove and mix well with the potato and kale or cabbage.

3 Add the remainder of the butter to the hot pan. When very hot, turn the potato mixture on to the pan and spread it out. Fry until brown, then cut it roughly into pieces and continue frying until they are crisp and brown. Serve in bowls or as a side dish, with plenty of butter.

Per portion Energy 306kcal/1281kJ; Protein 5.4g; Carbohydrate 40.6g, of which sugars 13.6g; Fat 14.6g, of which saturates 8.8g; Cholesterol 36mg; Calcium 104mg; Fibre 5.9g; Sodium 127mg.

Potatoes roasted with goose fat and garlic

Goose or duck fat gives the best flavour for roasting potatoes. In addition to the garlic, try adding a couple of bay leaves and a sprig of rosemary or thyme to the roasting pan. For a vegetarian version, use a large knob of butter and a splash of olive oil.

Serves 4

675g/1½lb floury potatoes, such as Maris Piper, peeled

30ml/2 tbsp goose fat

12 garlic cloves, unpeeled

salt and ground black pepper

1 Preheat the oven to 190°C/375°F/ Gas 5. Cut the potatoes into large chunks and cook in a pan of salted, boiling water for 5 minutes. Drain well and give the colander a good shake to fluff up the edges of the potatoes. Return the potatoes to the pan and place it over a low heat for 1 minute to steam off any excess water.

2 Meanwhile, spoon the goose fat into a roasting pan and place in the oven until hot, about 5 minutes. Add the potatoes to the pan with the garlic and turn to coat in the fat. Season well with salt and ground black pepper and roast for 40–50 minutes, turning occasionally, until the potatoes are golden and tender.

Per portion Energy 185kcal/778kJ; Protein 2.9g; Carbohydrate 27.2g, of which sugars 2.2g; Fat 7.9g, of which saturates 3.2g; Cholesterol 7mg; Calcium 10mg; Fibre 1.7g; Sodium 19mg.

New potato salad with chives

The potatoes in this dish absorb the oil and vinegar dressing as they cool, and are then tossed in mayonnaise. Small waxy potatoes, which can be kept whole, are particularly suitable for this recipe. Serve them with cold poached salmon or roast chicken.

2 Meanwhile, finely chop the white parts of the spring onions together with a little of the green part.

3 Whisk the oil with the vinegar and mustard. Drain the potatoes. Immediately, while the potatoes are still hot and steaming, toss them lightly with the oil mixture and the spring onions. Leave to cool.

4 Stir the mayonnaise and chives into the cooled potatoes and turn into a serving bowl. Chill the salad until you are ready to serve.

Serves 4–6

675g/1½lb small new potatoes, unpeeled

4 spring onions (scallions)

45ml/3 tbsp olive oil

15ml/1 tbsp cider vinegar or wine vinegar

2.5ml/½ tsp ready-made English (hot) mustard

175ml/6fl oz/¾ cup mayonnaise

45ml/3 tbsp chopped fresh chives

salt and ground black pepper

Variation Add a handful of chopped parsley or mint to the salad with the mayonnaise instead of chives.

1 Cook the new potatoes in boiling salted water for about 15 minutes, or until tender.

Per portion Energy 182kcal/761kJ; Protein 2.5g; Carbohydrate 22.5g, of which sugars 1.9g; Fat 9.7g, of which saturates 1.5g; Cholesterol 0mg; Calcium 20mg; Fibre 1.7g; Sodium 17mg.

Blue cheese coleslaw

In this recipe, shredded crisp cabbage is tossed in a dressing flavoured with English blue cheese. White or red cabbage, or a mixture of the two, works well in this crunchy salad. Use a favourite blue cheese, and serve piled into hot baked potatoes or with roast chicken.

Serves 4–8

45ml/3 tbsp mayonnaise

45ml/3 tbsp thick natural (plain) yogurt

50g/2oz blue cheese, such as Stilton or Oxford Blue

15ml/1 tbsp lemon juice or cider vinegar

about 500g/1¼lb white cabbage

1 medium carrot

1 small red onion

2 small celery sticks

1 crisp eating apple

salt and ground black pepper

watercress sprigs, to garnish

2 Trim and shred the cabbage finely, grate the carrot, chop the onion finely and cut the celery into very thin slices. Core and dice the apple.

Variation Try making the coleslaw with a half-and-half mixture of red cabbage and white cabbage.

3 Add the cabbage, carrot, onion, celery and apple to the bowl and toss until all the ingredients are well mixed and coated with the dressing.

4 Cover the bowl and refrigerate for 2–3 hours or until ready to serve. Stir before serving; garnish with watercress.

1 To make the dressing, put the mayonnaise and yogurt into a large bowl and crumble in the cheese. Stir well, adding a squeeze of lemon juice and a little seasoning to taste.

Cook's tips
• Make the dressing by blending the ingredients in a food processor.
• If you have a slicing attachment, the cabbage can be finely shredded using a food processor.

Per portion Energy 86kcal/359kJ; Protein 2.7g; Carbohydrate 5.1g, of which sugars 4.8g; Fat 6.3g, of which saturates 1.9g; Cholesterol 9mg; Calcium 78mg; Fibre 1.6g; Sodium 116mg.

Marinated bean and courgette salad

This bright green, fresh and healthy salad makes the most of a summer glut of courgettes. Add some chopped soft herbs, such as chervil, dill or tarragon, and crumble over fresh ricotta or cubed mozzarella cheese. Serve as an accompaniment to meat and chicken dishes.

Serves 4

2 courgettes (zucchini), halved lengthways and sliced

400g/14oz can flageolet or cannellini beans, drained and rinsed

grated rind and juice of 1 unwaxed lemon

45ml/3 tbsp garlic-infused olive oil

salt and ground black pepper

1 Cook the courgettes in boiling salted water for 2–3 minutes, or until just tender. Drain well and refresh under cold running water.

2 Transfer the courgettes into a bowl with the beans and stir in the oil, lemon rind and juice and some salt and pepper. Chill for 30 minutes before serving.

Per portion Energy 106kcal/444kJ; Protein 5.5g; Carbohydrate 11.9g, of which sugars 3.5g; Fat 4.4g, of which saturates 0.7g; Cholesterol 0mg; Calcium 62mg; Fibre 4.4g; Sodium 228mg.

Vine tomato salad with peppers and oregano

Home-grown tomatoes fresh from the vine would be ideal here, but any ripe, juicy fruits combined with the marinated peppers would make a lovely appetizer or side dish for a summer buffet. Sprinkle over a few fresh basil leaves instead of the oregano, if you prefer.

Serves 4–6

2 marinated (bell) peppers, drained

6 ripe tomatoes, sliced

15ml/1 tbsp chopped fresh oregano

75ml/5 tbsp olive oil

30ml/2 tbsp white wine vinegar

sea salt

Cook's tip To marinate (bell) peppers, wrap one green and one red pepper in foil and place on a baking sheet. Cook in a preheated oven at 180°C/350°F/Gas 4, or under a preheated grill (broiler), turning occasionally, for 20–30 minutes, until tender. Unwrap and when cool, peel the peppers, then halve and seed. Cut the flesh into strips and pack into a screw-top jar. Add olive oil to cover, close and store in the refrigerator for up to 6 days.

1 If the marinated peppers are in large pieces, cut them into strips. Arrange the tomato slices and pepper strips on a serving dish, sprinkle with the oregano and season to taste with sea salt.

2 Whisk together the olive oil and vinegar in a jug (pitcher), decant into a bottle and pour the dressing over the salad. Serve immediately or cover and chill in the refrigerator until required.

Per portion Energy 119kcal/494kJ; Protein 1.4g; Carbohydrate 6.9g, of which sugars 6.7g; Fat 9.7g, of which saturates 1.5g; Cholesterol 0mg; Calcium 17mg; Fibre 2.1g; Sodium 12mg.

Puddings and desserts

The aroma of a gently steaming pudding is a delectable part of winter country cooking, while the abundant fruits of summer make luscious desserts. Rice puddings and fruit crumbles are nursery classics and, along with American pies, offer something for every sweet tooth. There are few simpler recipes than those for berry or rhubarb fools – they are easy to make and look very impressive.

Hot bramble and apple soufflés

Hedgerow brambles, blackberries, loganberries or blackcurrants would all work equally well in this deliciously light pudding. Serve with lashings of thick cream or crème anglais.

Makes 6

butter, for greasing

150g/5oz/¾ cup caster (superfine) sugar, plus extra for dusting

350g/12oz/3 cups blackberries

1 large cooking apple, peeled and finely diced

grated rind and juice of 1 orange

3 egg whites

icing (confectioners') sugar, for dusting

1 Preheat the oven to 200°C/400°F/ Gas 6. Generously grease six 150ml/ ¼ pint/⅔ cup individual soufflé dishes with butter and dust with caster sugar, shaking out the excess sugar.

2 Put a baking sheet in the oven to heat. Cook the blackberries, diced apple and orange rind and juice in a pan for 10 minutes or until the apple has pulped down well.

3 Press through a sieve (strainer) into a bowl. Stir in 50g/2oz/¼ cup of the caster sugar. Set aside to cool for about 20–30 minutes.

4 Put a spoonful of the fruit purée into each prepared dish and smooth the surface. Set the dishes aside.

5 Whisk the egg whites in a large grease-free bowl until they form stiff peaks. Very gradually whisk in the remaining caster sugar to make a stiff, glossy meringue mixture.

6 Fold in the remaining fruit purée and spoon the flavoured meringue into the prepared dishes. Level the tops with a palette knife, and run a table knife around the edge of each dish.

7 Place the dishes on the hot baking sheet and bake for 10–15 minutes until the soufflés have risen well and are lightly browned. Dust the tops with icing sugar and serve immediately.

Cook's tip Running a table knife around the inside edge of the dishes before baking helps the soufflés to rise evenly without sticking to the rim.

Per portion Energy 123kcal/522kJ; Protein 2.1g; Carbohydrate 30.1g, of which sugars 30.1g; Fat 0.1g, of which saturates 0g; Cholesterol 0mg; Calcium 38mg; Fibre 2g; Sodium 33mg.

Autumn orchard pudding

This autumn version of a summer pudding makes the most of seasonal orchard fruits.
Serve with cream, lightly whipped with apple brandy or plain crème fraîche.

Serves 6–8

1 loaf white bread, 2 or 3 days old

675g/1½lb/6 cups mixed soft
fruit, such as blackberries,
autumn raspberries, late
strawberries, and peeled and
chopped eating apples

115g/4oz/generous ½ cup
caster (superfine) sugar
or 75ml/5 tbsp honey

1 Remove the crusts from the loaf
and slice the bread thinly. Use several
slices to line the base and sides of a
900ml–1.2 litre/1½–2 pint/3¾–5 cup
pudding bowl or soufflé dish, cutting
them carefully so that the pieces fit
closely together.

2 Put all the fruit into a wide, heavy
pan, sprinkle the sugar or honey over
and bring very gently to the boil. Cook
for 2–3 minutes, or until the sugar has
dissolved and the juices run.

3 Remove the pan from the heat
and set aside 30–45ml/2–3 tbsp of
the juices. Spoon the fruit and the
remaining juices into the prepared
bread-lined dish and cover the top
closely with the remaining slices of
bread. Put a plate that fits neatly inside
the top of the dish on top of the
pudding and weigh it down with a
heavy tin or jar. Leave in the refrigerator
for at least 8 hours, or overnight.

4 Before serving the dish, remove the
weight and plate, cover the bowl with
a serving plate and turn upside down
to unmould the pudding.

5 Use the reserved fruit juice to pour
over any patches of the bread that
have not been completely soaked and
coloured by the fruit juices. Serve cold
cut into wedges with lightly whipped
chilled cream or crème fraîche.

Per portion Energy 261kcal/1112kJ; Protein 7.7g; Carbohydrate 57.5g, of which sugars 27.1g; Fat 1.7g, of which saturates 0.4g; Cholesterol 0mg; Calcium 153mg; Fibre 4.2g; Sodium 398mg.

Sticky honey and ginger baked apples

Baked apples are a country-cooking staple, and there are myriad different versions – they can be made with any type of eating apple and stuffed with vine fruits, spices and citrus fruits. This version uses honey and fresh ginger, and is accompanied by either vanilla sauce, sour cream or double cream. A final touch of luxury would be to fold a little whipped cream into the vanilla sauce before serving, then spooning stem ginger ice cream on top.

Serves 4

4 eating apples, such as Cox's Orange Pippin or Golden Delicious

30ml/2 tbsp finely chopped fresh root ginger

60ml/4 tbsp honey

25g/1oz/2 tbsp unsalted (sweet) butter

60ml/4 tbsp medium white wine

vanilla sauce, sour cream or double (heavy) cream, to serve

For the vanilla sauce

300ml/½ pint/1¼ cups single (light) cream

1 vanilla pod (bean), split lengthways

2 egg yolks

30ml/2 tbsp caster (superfine) sugar

1 To make the vanilla sauce, put the cream and vanilla pod in a pan and heat to just below boiling point. Remove from the heat and leave to infuse for 10 minutes. Remove the vanilla pod.

2 Put the egg yolks and sugar in a bowl and whisk them together until pale and thick, then slowly pour in the cream, whisking all the time.

3 Return the pan to the heat and heat very gently until the cream is thick enough to coat the back of a wooden spoon. (If you draw a finger horizontally across the back of the spoon, the sauce should be thick enough not to run down through the channel.)

4 Remove from the heat and leave to cool. Either stir from time to time, or cover to prevent a skin forming.

5 Preheat the oven to 160°C/325°F/ Gas 3. Remove the cores from the apples leaving the stalk end intact, but remove the actual stalk. Fill each cavity with 2.5ml/½ tbsp chopped ginger and 15ml/1 tbsp honey.

6 Place the apples in an ovenproof dish, with the open end uppermost, and top each one with a knob of butter.

7 Pour in the wine and bake in the oven, basting frequently with the cooking juices, for about 45 minutes, until the apples are tender. Serve the apples with the vanilla sauce, sour cream or double cream.

Cook's tip If the sauce looks as though it may overheat, plunge the base of the pan into a bowl of cold water. This will cool the contents and prevent it curdling.

Per portion Energy 331kcal/1381kJ; Protein 4.3g; Carbohydrate 27.8g, of which sugars 27.8g; Fat 22.3g, of which saturates 13.2g; Cholesterol 155mg; Calcium 89mg; Fibre 1.2g; Sodium 68mg.

Maple and pecan steamed pudding

Imagine a hot sponge cake, straight out of the oven but with less golden crust, a deeper sponge and more crumbliness – that's a steamed pudding. It can be flavoured with anything; maple syrup and pecan nuts are wonderful. Serve with home-made custard.

Serves 6

60ml/4 tbsp pure maple syrup

30ml/2 tbsp fresh brown breadcrumbs

115g/4oz/1 cup shelled pecan nuts, roughly chopped

115g/4oz/½ cup butter, softened

finely grated rind of 1 orange

115g/4oz/heaped ½ cup golden caster (superfine) sugar

2 eggs, beaten

175g/6oz/1½ cups self-raising (self-rising) flour, sifted

pinch of salt

about 75ml/5 tbsp milk

extra maple syrup and home-made custard, to serve

1 Butter a 900ml/1½ pint/3¾ cup heatproof pudding bowl generously. Stir the maple syrup, breadcrumbs and pecans together and spoon into the bowl.

2 Cream the butter with the orange rind and sugar until light and fluffy. Gradually beat in the eggs, then fold in the flour and salt. Stir in enough milk to make a loose mixture that will drop off the spoon if lightly shaken.

3 Carefully spoon the mixture into the bowl on top of the syrup and nuts. Cover with pleated, buttered baking parchment, then with pleated foil (the pleats allow for expansion). Tie string under the lip of the basin to hold the paper in place, then take it over the top to form a handle.

4 Place the bowl in a pan of simmering water, cover and steam for 2 hours, topping up with boiling water as necessary.

5 Remove the string, foil and paper, then turn out the pudding and serve with extra maple syrup and a spoonful of home-made custard.

Per portion Energy 523kcal/2187kJ; Protein 7.7g; Carbohydrate 55.6g, of which sugars 29.9g; Fat 31.6g, of which saturates 12.2g; Cholesterol 108mg; Calcium 160mg; Fibre 1.9g; Sodium 345mg.

Winter fruit crumble

This recipe uses pears and dried fruits under the crumble topping, making it a deliciously warming winter pudding. At other times of the year, try gooseberries or rhubarb flavoured with orange rind. The almond topping adds a wonderfully rich texture.

Serves 6

175g/6oz/1½ cups plain (all-purpose) flour

50g/2oz/½ cup ground almonds

175g/6oz/¾ cup butter, diced

115g/4oz/½ cup soft light brown sugar

40g/1½oz flaked (sliced) almonds

1 orange

about 16 ready-to-eat dried apricots

4 firm ripe pears

1 Preheat the oven to 190°C/375°F/ Gas 5. To make the topping, sift the flour into a bowl and stir in the ground almonds. Add the butter and rub it into the flour until the mixture resembles rough breadcrumbs. Stir in 75g/3oz/ ⅓ cup sugar and the flaked almonds.

2 Finely grate 5ml/1 tsp rind from the orange and squeeze out its juice. Halve the apricots and put them into a shallow ovenproof dish. Peel the pears, remove their cores and cut the fruit into small pieces. Sprinkle the pears over the apricots. Stir the orange rind into the orange juice and sprinkle over the fruit. Sprinkle the remaining brown sugar over the top.

3 Cover the fruit completely with the crumble mixture and smooth over. Put into the hot oven and cook for about 40 minutes until the topping is golden brown and the fruit is soft (test with the point of a sharp knife).

Per portion Energy 615kcal/2569kJ; Protein 9.4g; Carbohydrate 65.7g, of which sugars 42.9g; Fat 36.7g, of which saturates 16.2g; Cholesterol 62mg; Calcium 150mg; Fibre 6.6g; Sodium 190mg.

Rice pudding with nutmeg

Originally a medieval treat at a time when rice and sugar were expensive imports, rice pudding went on to become a Victorian country favourite. This simple pudding can be enlivened by adding a spoonful of preserves or some brandy-soaked dried vine fruits or figs.

Serves 4

50g/2oz/4 tbsp butter, diced, plus extra for greasing

50g/2oz/¼ cup pudding rice

30ml/2 tbsp soft light brown sugar

900ml/1½ pints/3¾ cups milk

small strip of lemon rind

freshly grated nutmeg

Variation Add some sultanas (golden raisins), raisins or ready-to-eat dried apricots and cinnamon to the pudding.

Cook's tip Serve with fresh fruit such as peaches, raspberries or strawberries.

1 Preheat the oven to 150°C/300°F/ Gas 2. Butter a 1.2 litre/2 pint/5 cup shallow ovenproof dish.

2 Put the rice, sugar and butter into the dish and stir in the milk. Add the strip of lemon rind and sprinkle a little nutmeg over the surface. Put the pudding into the hot oven.

3 Cook the pudding for about 2 hours, stirring after 30 minutes and another couple of times during the next 1½ hours, until the rice is tender and the pudding is thick and creamy.

4 If you prefer skin on top, leave the pudding undisturbed for the final 30 minutes, or stir again. Serve with jam.

Per portion Energy 298kcal/1252kJ; Protein 8.8g; Carbohydrate 54.3g, of which sugars 21.5g; Fat 5.2g, of which saturates 1.4g; Cholesterol 143mg; Calcium 71mg; Fibre 0g; Sodium 185mg.

Bread and butter pudding with whiskey sauce

The ultimate comfort food and made to use up stale bread, this dish becomes rather sophisticated with the addition of a boozy whiskey sauce. It is best served with vanilla ice cream or chilled cream – the contrast between the hot and cold is exquisite.

Serves 6

8 slices of white bread, buttered

115–150g/4–5oz/²⁄₃–¾ cup sultanas (golden raisins), or mixed dried fruit

2.5ml/½ tsp grated nutmeg

150g/5oz/¾ cup caster (superfine) sugar

2 large (US extra large) eggs

300ml/½ pint/1¼ cups single (light) cream

450ml/¾ pint/scant 2 cups milk

5ml/1 tsp of vanilla extract

light muscovado (brown) sugar, for sprinkling (optional)

For the whiskey sauce

150g/5oz/10 tbsp butter

115g/4oz/generous ½ cup caster (superfine) sugar

1 egg

45ml/3 tbsp Irish whiskey

1 Preheat the oven to 180°C/350°F/ Gas 4. Remove the crusts from the bread and put four slices, buttered side down, in the base of an ovenproof dish. Sprinkle with the fruit, some of the nutmeg and 15ml/1 tbsp sugar.

2 Place the remaining four slices of bread on top, buttered side down, and sprinkle again with nutmeg and 15ml/1 tbsp sugar.

3 Beat the eggs lightly, add the cream, milk, vanilla extract and the remaining sugar, and mix well to make a custard. Pour this mixture over the bread, and sprinkle light muscovado sugar over the top, if you like to have a crispy crust.

4 Bake in the preheated oven for 1 hour, or until all the liquid has been absorbed and the pudding is risen and brown.

5 Meanwhile, make the whiskey sauce: melt the butter in a heavy pan, add the caster sugar and dissolve over gentle heat. Remove from the heat and add the egg, whisking vigorously, and then add the whiskey. Serve the pudding on hot serving plates, with the whiskey sauce poured over the top.

Per portion Energy 757kcal/3168kJ; Protein 11.7g; Carbohydrate 82g, of which sugars 65.2g; Fat 40.8g, of which saturates 24.3g; Cholesterol 207mg; Calcium 232mg; Fibre 0.9g; Sodium 472mg.

Classic treacle tart

A way of using up stale breadcrumbs, this tart is actually based on golden syrup rather than treacle or molasses. There many variations on the basic recipe, but the hint of lemon in this one makes it particularly good. Serve it warm or cold, with custard or cream.

3 Mix the breadcrumbs with the ginger, if using, and spread the mixture over the bottom of the pastry. Gently warm the syrup with the lemon rind and juice (on the stove or in the microwave) until quite runny and pour evenly over the breadcrumbs.

4 Gather the reserved pastry trimmings into a ball, roll out on a lightly floured surface and cut into long, narrow strips. Twist these into spirals and arrange them in a lattice pattern on top of the tart, pressing them on to the edge to secure. Trim the ends.

5 Put into the hot oven and cook for about 25 minutes until the pastry is golden brown and cooked through and the filling has set.

Serves 6

175g/6oz/1½ cups plain (all-purpose) flour

pinch of salt

40g/1½oz/3 tbsp lard

40g/1½oz/3 tbsp butter, diced

75g/3oz/1½ cups fresh breadcrumbs

2.5ml/½ tsp ground ginger (optional)

225g/8oz/1 cup golden (light corn) syrup

grated rind and juice of 1 lemon

1 Sift the flour and salt into a bowl and add the lard and butter. With the fingertips, rub the fats into the flour until the mixture resembles fine breadcrumbs. Stir in about 45ml/3 tbsp cold water until the mixture can be gathered together into a smooth ball of dough. Wrap the pastry and refrigerate for 30 minutes. Meanwhile, preheat the oven to 190°C/375°F/Gas 5.

2 Roll out the pastry on a lightly floured surface and use to line a 20cm/8in flan tin (pan) or pie plate, reserving the trimmings.

Variations
• You could omit the lemon rind and juice.
• Sometimes finely crushed cornflakes are used in place of the breadcrumbs.

Per portion Energy 420kcal/1764kJ; Protein 4.1g; Carbohydrate 63.5g, of which sugars 35.1g; Fat 18.4g, of which saturates 11.3g; Cholesterol 46mg; Calcium 62mg; Fibre 1.1g; Sodium 344mg.

Bakewell tart

This is a modern version of the Bakewell pudding, which is made with puff pastry and has a custard-like almond filling. It is said to be the result of a 19th-century kitchen accident and is still baked in the original shop in Bakewell, England. Serve with a hot cup of tea.

Serves 4

For the pastry

115g/4oz/1 cup plain (all-purpose) flour

pinch of salt

50g/2oz/4 tbsp butter, diced

For the filling

30ml/2 tbsp raspberry or apricot jam

2 whole eggs and 2 extra yolks

115g/4oz/generous ½ cup caster (superfine) sugar

115g/4oz/½ cup butter, melted

55g/2oz/⅔ cup ground almonds

few drops of almond extract

icing (confectioners') sugar, to dust

1 Sift the flour and salt and rub in the butter until the mixture resembles fine crumbs. Stir in about 30ml/2 tbsp cold water and gather into a smooth ball of dough. Wrap and chill for 30 minutes. Preheat the oven to 200°C/400°F/Gas 6.

2 Roll out the pastry and use to line an 18cm/7in loose-based flan tin (pan). Spread the jam over the pastry.

3 Whisk the eggs, egg yolks and sugar together in a large bowl until the mixture is thick and pale. Gently stir in the melted butter, ground almonds and almond extract. Mix well together to combine.

4 Pour the mixture over the jam in the pastry case (pie shell). Put the tart into the hot oven and cook for 30 minutes until just set and browned. Sift a little icing sugar over the top before serving warm or at room temperature.

Per portion Energy 700kcal/2919kJ; Protein 10.8g; Carbohydrate 57.1g, of which sugars 36.7g; Fat 49.9g, of which saturates 17.1g; Cholesterol 257mg; Calcium 110mg; Fibre 0.9g; Sodium 394mg.

Black cherry clafoutis

Clafoutis is a batter pudding that originated in the Limousin area of central France.
It is often made with cream and traditionally uses slightly tart black cherries, although
other soft fruits such as halved apricots, peaches or plums will also give delicious results.

Serves 6

butter, for greasing

450g/1lb/2 cups black cherries, pitted

25g/1oz/¼ cup plain (all-purpose) flour

50g/2oz/½ cup icing (confectioners')
sugar, plus extra for dusting

4 eggs, beaten

250ml/8fl oz/1 cup full-cream
(whole) milk

30ml/2 tbsp cherry liqueur,
such as kirsch or maraschino

1 Preheat the oven to 180°C/350°F/
Gas 4. Generously grease a 1.2 litre/
2 pint/5 cup dish and add the pitted
black cherries.

2 Sift the flour and icing sugar into a
large mixing bowl, then gradually whisk
in the beaten eggs until the mixture is
smooth. Whisk in the milk until well
blended, then stir in the liqueur.

3 Pour the batter into the baking dish.
Transfer to the oven and bake for about
40 minutes, or until just set and golden
brown. Insert a knife into the centre of
the pudding to test if it is cooked in the
middle; the blade should come out clean.

4 Allow the pudding to cool for at least
15 minutes. Dust liberally with icing
sugar just before serving, either warm
or at room temperature.

Variations
• Try using other liqueurs – almond-
flavoured liqueur is delicious teamed
with cherries, while hazelnut, raspberry
or orange liqueurs also work well.
• Also try other fruits, such as plums,
apricots, blackberries or blueberries.

Per portion Energy 201kcal/843kJ; Protein 6.7g; Carbohydrate 23.8g, of which sugars 20.7g; Fat 8.9g, of which saturates 4.3g; Cholesterol 142mg; Calcium 89mg; Fibre 0.8g; Sodium 91mg.

Old-fashioned deep-dish apple pie

It is impossible to resist a really good home-baked apple pie. If you make your own shortcrust pastry and use eating apples bursting with flavour and loads of butter and sugar, you can't go wrong. Serve this old-fashioned dish with thick cream or nutmeg ice cream.

Serves 6

900g/2lb eating apples

75g/3oz/6 tbsp unsalted (sweet) butter

45–60ml/3–4 tbsp demerara (raw) sugar

3 cloves

2.5ml/½ tsp mixed (apple pie) spice

For the pastry

250g/9oz/2¼ cups plain (all-purpose) flour

pinch of salt

50g/2oz/¼ cup lard or white cooking fat, chilled and diced

75g/3oz/6 tbsp unsalted butter, chilled and diced

30–45ml/2–3 tbsp chilled water

a little milk, for brushing

caster (superfine) sugar, for dredging

clotted cream or ice cream, to serve

1 Preheat the oven to 200°C/400°F/Gas 6. Make the pastry first. Sift the flour and salt into a bowl. Rub in the lard or fat and butter. Stir in enough chilled water to bring the pastry together. Knead lightly, then wrap in clear film (plastic wrap) and chill for 30 minutes.

2 To make the filling, peel, core and thickly slice the apples. Melt the butter in a frying pan, add the sugar and cook for 3–4 minutes, allowing it to melt and caramelize. Add the apples and stir. Cook over a brisk heat until the apples take on a little colour, add the spices and tip out into a bowl to cool slightly.

3 Divide the pastry in two and, on a lightly floured surface, roll out into two rounds that will easily fit a deep 23cm/9in pie plate. Line the plate with one round of pastry. Spoon in the cooled filling and mound up in the centre.

4 Cover the apples with the remaining pastry, sealing and crimping the edges.

5 Make a 5cm/2in long slit through the top of the pastry to allow the steam to escape. Brush the pie with milk and dredge with caster sugar.

6 Place the pie on a baking sheet and bake in the oven for 25–35 minutes until golden and firm. Serve with dollops of thick cream or ice cream.

Per portion Energy 610kcal/2566kJ; Protein 8.1g; Carbohydrate 86.1g, of which sugars 40.2g; Fat 28.5g, of which saturates 8.8g; Cholesterol 14mg; Calcium 168mg; Fibre 8.1g; Sodium 413mg.

Peach and blueberry pie

With its attractive lattice pastry top, this colourful pie is bursting with plump blueberries and juicy peaches. It is good hot, or can be wrapped in its tin and transported to a picnic.

Serves 8

225g/8oz/2 cups plain (all-purpose) flour

2.5ml/½ tsp salt

5ml/1 tsp granulated (white) sugar

150g/5oz/10 tbsp cold butter or margarine, diced

1 egg yolk

30–45ml/2–3 tbsp iced water

30ml/2 tbsp milk, for glazing

For the filling

6 peaches, peeled, pitted and sliced

225g/8oz/2 cups fresh blueberries

150g/5oz/¾ cup granulated sugar

30ml/2 tbsp fresh lemon juice

40g/1½oz/⅓ cup plain (all-purpose) flour

pinch of grated nutmeg

25g/1oz/2 tbsp butter or margarine, cut into pea-size pieces

1 For the pastry, sift the flour, salt and sugar into a bowl. Rub the butter or margarine into the dry ingredients as quickly as possible until the mixture is crumbly and resembles breadcrumbs.

2 Mix the egg yolk with 30ml/2 tbsp of the iced water and sprinkle over the flour mixture. Combine with a fork until the pastry holds together. If the pastry is too crumbly, add a little more water, 5ml/1 tsp at a time. Gather the pastry into a ball and flatten into a disk. Wrap in clear film (plastic wrap) and chill for at least 20 minutes.

3 Roll out two-thirds of the pastry between two sheets of baking parchment to a thickness of about 3mm/⅛in. Use to line a 23cm/9in fluted tin (pan). Trim all around, leaving a 1cm/½in overhang, then trim the edges with a sharp knife.

4 Gather the trimmings and remaining pastry into a ball, and roll out to a thickness of about 6mm/¼in. Using a pastry wheel or sharp knife, cut strips 1cm/½in wide. Chill the pastry case and the strips for 20 minutes. Preheat the oven to 200°C/400°F/ Gas 6.

5 Line the pastry case with baking parchment and fill with dried beans. Bake until the pastry case is just set, 12–15 minutes. Remove from the oven and carefully lift out the paper with the beans. Prick the bottom of the pastry case all over with a fork, then return to the oven and bake for 5 minutes more. Let the pastry case cool slightly before filling. Leave the oven on.

6 In a mixing bowl, combine the peach slices with the blueberries, sugar, lemon juice, flour and nutmeg. Spoon the fruit mixture evenly into the pastry case. Dot with the pieces of butter or margarine.

7 Weave a lattice top with the chilled pastry strips, pressing the ends to the baked pastry-case edge. Brush the strips with the milk.

8 Bake the pie for 15 minutes. Reduce the heat to 180°C/350°F/Gas 4, and continue baking until the filling is tender and bubbling and the pastry lattice is golden, about 30 minutes more. If the pastry gets too brown, cover loosely with a piece of foil. Serve the pie warm or at room temperature.

Cook's tip To peel stone (pit) fruits, place them in a large heat-proof bowl and cover with boiling water. Leave for 2–3 minutes until the skins wrinkle, then drain. The skin should slide off easily.

Per portion Energy 391kcal/1640kJ; Protein 4.7g; Carbohydrate 53g, of which sugars 27.7g; Fat 19.3g, of which saturates 11.7g; Cholesterol 72mg; Calcium 86mg; Fibre 2.9g; Sodium 139mg.

Pecan pie

Almost an American institution, this classic country pie has a golden crust with a dense maple syrup filling topped with pecans halves. Serve warm with whipped cream.

Serves 8

3 eggs

pinch of salt

200g/7oz/scant 1 cup soft dark brown sugar

120ml/4fl oz/½ cup golden (light corn) syrup

30ml/2 tbsp fresh lemon juice

75g/3oz/6 tbsp butter, melted

150g/5oz/1¼ cups chopped pecan nuts

50g/2oz/½ cup pecan halves

For the pastry

175g/6oz/1½ cups plain (all-purpose) flour

15ml/1 tbsp caster (superfine) sugar

5ml/1 tsp baking powder

2.5ml/½ tsp salt

75g/3oz/6 tbsp cold unsalted (sweet) butter, cut in pieces

1 egg yolk

45–60ml/3–4 tbsp whipping cream

1 For the pastry, sift the flour, sugar, baking powder and salt into a bowl. Add the butter and cut in with a pastry blender until the mixture resembles coarse breadcrumbs.

2 In a bowl, beat together the egg yolk and cream until blended. Pour the mixture into the flour mixture and stir with a fork.

3 Gather the pastry into a ball. On a lightly floured surface, roll out 3mm/⅛in thick and transfer to a 23cm/9in fluted tin (pan).

4 Trim the overhang and flute the edge with your fingers. Chill for at least 20 minutes.

5 Preheat a baking sheet in the middle of a 200°C/400°F/Gas 6 oven. In a bowl, lightly whisk the eggs and salt. Add the sugar, syrup, lemon juice and butter. Mix well and stir in the chopped nuts.

6 Pour into the pastry case (pie shell) and arrange the pecan halves in concentric circles on top. Bake for 10 minutes. Reduce the heat to 170°C/325°F/Gas 3 and continue baking for 25 minutes.

Per portion Energy 587kcal/2449kJ; Protein 7.5g; Carbohydrate 56.7g, of which sugars 39.6g; Fat 38.3g, of which saturates 13.4g; Cholesterol 142mg; Calcium 82mg; Fibre 1.9g; Sodium 185mg.

Thanksgiving pumpkin pie

A version of this dish was baked by the earliest American settlers, and Thanksgiving would not be complete without it. Using canned pumpkin makes it a very easy pie to make.

Serves 8

450g/1lb cooked or canned pumpkin

250ml/8fl oz/1 cup whipping cream

2 eggs

115g/4oz/½ cup soft dark brown sugar

60ml/4 tbsp golden (light corn) syrup

7.5ml/1½ tsp ground cinnamon

5ml/1 tsp ground ginger

1.5ml/¼ tsp ground cloves

2.5ml/½ tsp salt

For the pastry

175g/6oz/1½ cups plain (all-purpose) flour

2.5ml/½ tsp salt

75g/3oz/6 tbsp cold butter, cut into pieces

40g/1½oz/3 tbsp cold white vegetable fat (shortening), cut into pieces

45–60ml/3–4 tbsp iced water

1 egg, beaten

1 For the pastry, sift the flour and salt into a bowl. Cut in the butter and fat until it resembles coarse crumbs. Bind with iced water. Wrap in clear film (plastic wrap) and chill for 20 minutes.

2 Roll out the dough and line a 23cm/9in fluted pie tin (pan). Trim off the overhang. Roll out the trimmings and cut out leaf shapes.

3 Chill for about 20 minutes. Preheat the oven to 200°C/400°F/Gas 6.

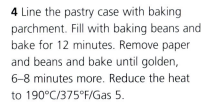

4 Line the pastry case with baking parchment. Fill with baking beans and bake for 12 minutes. Remove paper and beans and bake until golden, 6–8 minutes more. Reduce the heat to 190°C/375°F/Gas 5.

5 Beat together the pumpkin, cream, eggs, sugar, golden syrup, spices and salt. Pour into the pastry case and bake for 25 minutes. Brush the pastry leaves with egg and place around the top of the pie. Bake for 10–15 minutes more.

Per portion Energy 434kcal/1809kJ; Protein 6.2g; Carbohydrate 35.3g, of which sugars 19.4g; Fat 30.8g, of which saturates 13.8g; Cholesterol 94mg; Calcium 108mg; Fibre 1.2g; Sodium 60mg.

Boston cream pie

Actually a sponge cake filled with custard rather than cream and topped with a dark chocolate glaze, this cake is a reworking of the early American pudding cake pie.

Serves 8

225g/8oz/2 cups self-raising (self-rising) flour

15ml/1 tbsp baking powder

2.5ml/½ tsp salt

115g/4oz/½ cup butter, softened

200g/7oz/1 cup granulated (white) sugar

2 eggs

5ml/1 tsp vanilla extract

175ml/6fl oz/¾ cup milk

For the filling

250ml/8fl oz/1 cup milk

3 egg yolks

90g/3½oz/½ cup granulated (white) sugar

25g/1oz/¼ cup plain (all-purpose) flour

15g/1/2oz/1 tbsp butter

15ml/1 tbsp brandy or 5ml/1 tsp vanilla extract

For the chocolate glaze

25g/1oz cooking (unsweetened) chocolate

25g/1oz/2 tbsp butter or margarine

90g/3½oz/½ cup icing (confectioners') sugar, plus extra for dusting

2.5ml/½ tsp vanilla extract

about 15ml/1 tbsp hot water

1 Preheat the oven to 190°F/375°F/ Gas 5. Grease two 20cm/8in shallow round cake tins (pans), and line the bottoms with greased baking parchment.

2 Sift the flour with the baking powder and salt.

3 Beat the butter and granulated sugar together until light and fluffy. Add the eggs one at a time, beating well after each addition. Stir in the vanilla. Add the milk and dry ingredients alternately, mixing only enough to blend thoroughly. Do not over-beat the mixture.

4 Divide the mixture between the prepared tins and spread it out evenly. Bake until a skewer inserted in the centre comes out clean, about 25 minutes.

5 Meanwhile, make the filling. Heat the milk in a small pan to boiling point. Remove from the heat.

6 In a heatproof mixing bowl, beat the egg yolks. Gradually add the granulated sugar and continue beating until pale yellow. Beat in the flour.

7 Pour the hot milk into the egg yolk mixture in a steady stream, beating constantly. When all the milk has been added, place the bowl over a pan of boiling water, or pour the mixture into the top of a double boiler. Heat for 30 minutes, stirring constantly, until thickened. Remove from the heat. Stir in the butter and brandy or vanilla. Chill for 2–3 hours or until set.

8 When the cake layers have cooled, use a large sharp knife to slice off the domed top to make a flat surface. Place one layer on a serving plate and spread the filling on in a thick layer. Set the other layer on top, cut side down. Smooth the edge of the filling layer so it is flush with the sides of the cake layers.

9 For the glaze, melt the chocolate with the butter or margarine in the top of a double boiler, or in a bowl over hot water. When smooth, remove from the heat and beat in the sugar to make a thick paste. Add the vanilla. Beat in a little of the hot water. If the glaze does not have a spreadable consistency, add more water, 5ml/1 tsp at a time.

10 Spread the glaze evenly over the top of the cake, using a metal spatula. Dust the top with icing sugar. Because of the custard filling, any leftover cake must be chilled in the refrigerator, and can be stored for up to 3 days.

Per portion Energy 499kcal/2099kJ; Protein 6g; Carbohydrate 77g, of which sugars 53.1g; Fat 20.3g, of which saturates 12.1g; Cholesterol 146mg; Calcium 112mg; Fibre 1g; Sodium 296mg.

Poached spiced pears

The fragrant aroma of pears is greatly enhanced by gently poaching them in either spiced liquor or wine. Serve this dish warm or cold, with some cream whipped with icing sugar and Poire William, and perhaps some crisp, sweet biscuits to give a contrasting texture.

Serves 4

115g/4oz/½ cup caster (superfine) sugar

grated rind and juice of 1 lemon

2.5ml/½ tsp ground ginger

1 small cinnamon stick

2 whole cloves

4 firm ripe pears

Variations
• Omit the spices and instead flavour the water with ginger or elderflower cordial.
• Use white wine in place of water.

1 Put the sugar in a pan with 300ml/½ pint/1½ cups water, the lemon rind and juice, ginger and spices. Heat, stirring, until the sugar has dissolved.

2 Peel the pears, cut them in half lengthways and remove their cores.

3 Add the pear halves to the pan and bring just to the boil. Cover and simmer gently for about 5 minutes or until the pears are tender, turning them over in the syrup occasionally during cooking. Remove from the heat and leave to cool in the syrup before serving.

Per portion Energy 93kcal/392kJ; Protein 0.5g; Carbohydrate 23.6g, of which sugars 23.6g; Fat 0.2g, of which saturates 0g; Cholesterol 0mg; Calcium 17mg; Fibre 3.3g; Sodium 6mg.

Chilled berry pudding

A cross between a summer pudding and a trifle, this fragrant, light pudding makes the most of summer soft fruits and is a perfect summer dessert. Be sure to use a good loaf of bread rather than processed sliced bread, to get the best texture and flavour.

Serves 4–6

550g/1lb 4oz mixed soft fruit, such as raspberries, blackberries, blackcurrants, redcurrants

50g/2oz/4 tbsp sugar

large thick slice of bread with crusts removed, about 125g/4½oz/2 cups without crusts

300ml/½ pint/1¼ cups double (heavy) cream

45ml/3 tbsp elderflower cordial

150ml/¼ pint/⅔ cup thick natural (plain) yogurt

Cook's tip During the seasons when fresh summer fruits are not as readily available, a bag of mixed frozen fruit works just as well in this recipe.

1 Reserve a few raspberries, blackberries, blackcurrants or redcurrants for decoration, then put the remainder into a pan with the sugar and 30ml/2 tbsp water. Bring just to the boil, cover and simmer gently for 4–5 minutes, until the fruit is soft and plenty of juice has formed.

2 Cut the bread into cubes, measuring about 2.5cm/1in, and put them into one large dish or individual serving bowls or glasses.

3 Spoon the fruit mixture over the bread and leave to cool.

Variation Instead of mixing yogurt into the topping, try using the same quantity of ready-made custard – it gives a richer, sweeter result to the finished dish.

4 Whip the cream with the cordial until stiff peaks begin to form. Gently stir in the yogurt and spoon the mixture over the top of the fruit.

5 Chill until required. Just before serving, decorate the top with the reserved fruit.

Per portion Energy 382kcal/1592kJ; Protein 5.2g; Carbohydrate 29.9g, of which sugars 20.2g; Fat 27.8g, of which saturates 16.9g; Cholesterol 69mg; Calcium 124mg; Fibre 2.6g; Sodium 144mg.

Gooseberry and elderflower fool

The combination of gooseberry and elderflower is heavenly, but rhubarb and ginger or raspberries are also classic ingredients for fruit fools – you can use whatever is ripe in the kitchen garden. Serve in pretty glasses, with crisp little biscuits to add a contrast of texture.

Serves 4

500g/1¼lb gooseberries

300ml/½ pint/1¼ cups double (heavy) cream

about 115g/4oz/1 cup icing (confectioners') sugar, to taste

30ml/2 tbsp elderflower cordial

mint sprigs, to decorate

crisp biscuits (cookies), to serve

3 Layer the cream mixture and the crushed gooseberries in four dessert dishes or tall glasses, then cover and chill until ready to serve. Decorate the fool with mint sprigs and serve with crisp sweet biscuits.

Variations
• When in season, cook 2–3 elderflower heads with the gooseberries and omit the elderflower cordial.
• For rhubarb fool use squeezed orange juice in place of elderflower cordial.

1 Place the gooseberries in a heavy pan, cover and cook over a low heat, shaking the pan occasionally, until tender. Transfer the gooseberries into a bowl, crush them with a fork or potato masher, then leave to cool completely.

2 Whip the cream until soft peaks form, then fold in half the crushed fruit. Add sugar and elderflower cordial to taste. Sweeten the remaining fruit to taste.

Per portion Energy 366kcal/1521kJ; Protein 3.5g; Carbohydrate 24.2g, of which sugars 21.8g; Fat 28.4g, of which saturates 16.7g; Cholesterol 70mg; Calcium 111mg; Fibre 1.9g; Sodium 41mg.

Rhubarb fool

This is a quick and simple dessert that makes the most of rhubarb when it is in season. You can use early or 'forced' rhubarb, which is a ravishing pink and needs very little cooking. Try adding a few drops of rosewater to the fruit as it cooks, and serve with shortbread.

1 Cut the rhubarb into pieces and wash thoroughly. Stew over a low heat with just the water clinging to it and the sugar. This takes about 10 minutes. Set aside to cool.

2 Pass the rhubarb through a fine sieve (strainer) so you have a thick purée.

3 Use equal parts of the purée, the whipped double cream and ready-made thick custard. Combine the purée and custard first, then fold in the cream. Chill in the refrigerator before serving. Serve with heather honey.

Serves 4

450g/1lb rhubarb, trimmed

75g/3oz/scant ½ cup soft light brown sugar

whipped double (heavy) cream and ready-made thick custard (see step 3)

Variations
• You can use another fruit if you like for this dessert – try bramble fruits or apples. Other stewed fruits also work well, such as prunes or peaches. For something a little more exotic, you could try mangoes.
• For a low-fat option, substitute natural (plain) yogurt for the cream.

Per portion Energy 439kcal/1828kJ; Protein 4.6g; Carbohydrate 34.1g, of which sugars 31.8g; Fat 31.7g, of which saturates 18.9g; Cholesterol 80mg; Calcium 233mg; Fibre 1.6g; Sodium 74mg.

Breads and baking

A country meal is not complete without a piece of bread, and there are few more welcoming aromas than a home-baked loaf. Doing your own baking can give great pleasure and satisfaction, and once the technique for basic dough has been mastered, there are endless variations and adaptations. Also in this chapter are recipes for biscuits, crumpets, scones and cakes – all essential country tea-time treats.

Basic yeast bread

Make this dough into any shape you like, such as braids, cottage loaves or rolls. Use strong bread flour as it has a high gluten content, making a more elastic dough that rises better.

Makes 4 loaves

25g/1oz fresh yeast

10ml/2 tsp caster (superfine) sugar

900ml/1½ pints/3¾ cups tepid water, or milk and water mixed

15ml/1 tbsp salt

1.3kg/3lb/12 cups strong white bread flour, preferably unbleached

50g/2oz/scant ¼ cup white vegetable fat (shortening) or 50ml/2fl oz/¼ cup vegetable oil

1 Cream the yeast and caster sugar together in a measuring jug (cup), add about 150ml/¼ pint/⅔ cup of the measured liquid and leave in a warm place for about 10 minutes to froth up.

2 Meanwhile, mix the salt into the flour and rub in the fat (if using oil, add it to the remaining liquid).

3 Using an electric mixer with a dough hook attachment or working by hand in a mixing bowl, add the yeast mixture and remaining liquid to the flour, and work it in to make a firm dough which leaves the bowl clean.

4 Knead well on a floured surface, or in the mixer, until the dough has become firm and elastic. Return to the bowl, cover lightly with a dish towel and leave in a warm place to rise for an hour, or until it has doubled in size. The dough will be springy and full of air. Meanwhile, oil four 450g/1lb loaf tins (pans).

5 Turn the dough out on to a floured work surface and knock back (punch down), flattening it out with your knuckles to knock the air out. Knead lightly into shape again, divide into four pieces and form into loaf shapes.

6 Place the dough in the loaf tins, pushing down well to fit into the corners, then leave to rise again for another 20–30 minutes. Meanwhile, preheat the oven to 230°C/450°F/ Gas 8.

7 When the dough has risen just above the rims of the tins, bake the loaves in the centre of the oven for 30 minutes, or until browned and shrinking a little from the sides of the tins; when turned out and rapped underneath they should sound hollow. Cool on wire racks.

Variation For Granary (whole-wheat) bread, replace the white flour with Granary flour, or half and half Granary and strong white bread flour.

Per loaf Energy 1223kcal/5185kJ; Protein 30.7g; Carbohydrate 256.4g, of which sugars 7.5g; Fat 15.2g, of which saturates 6.3g; Cholesterol 0mg; Calcium 457mg; Fibre 10.1g; Sodium 1.48g.

Cottage loaf

Snipping both sections of the dough at 5cm/2in intervals looks attractive and also helps this classic country loaf to rise and expand in the oven while it cooks.

4 Turn out on to a lightly floured surface and knock back (punch down). Knead for 2–3 minutes, then divide the dough into two-thirds and one-third; shape each to a ball.

5 Place the balls of dough on the baking sheets. Cover with inverted bowls and leave to rise, in a warm place, for about 30 minutes. Gently flatten the top of the larger round of dough and, with a sharp knife, cut a cross in the centre, about 4cm/1½in across. Brush with a little water and place the smaller round on top.

6 Carefully press a hole through the middle of the top ball, down into the lower part, using your thumb and first two fingers. Cover with lightly oiled clear film (plastic wrap) and leave to rest in a warm place for about 10 minutes. Preheat the oven to 220°C/425°F/Gas 7 and place the bread on the lower shelf. It will finish expanding as the oven heats up. Bake for 35–40 minutes, or until golden brown. Cool on a wire rack.

Makes 1 large round loaf

675g/1½ lb/6 cups unbleached white bread flour

10ml/2 tsp salt

20g/¾ oz fresh yeast

400ml/14fl oz/1⅔ cups lukewarm water

Cook's tips
• To ensure a good-shaped cottage loaf, the dough needs to be firm enough to support the weight of the top ball.
• Alternatively, make smaller, individual rolls – bake them for 25 minutes.

1 Lightly grease two baking sheets. Sift the flour and salt together into a large bowl and make a well in the centre.

2 Mix the yeast in 150ml/¼ pint/⅔ cup of the water until dissolved. Pour into the centre of the flour with the remaining water and mix to a firm dough.

3 Knead on a lightly floured surface for 10 minutes until smooth and elastic. Place in a lightly oiled bowl, cover with lightly oiled clear film and leave to rise, in a warm place, for about 1 hour, or until doubled in bulk.

Per loaf Energy 2302kcal/9788kJ; Protein 63.5g; Carbohydrate 524.5g, of which sugars 10.1g; Fat 8.8g, of which saturates 1.4g; Cholesterol 0mg; Calcium 946mg; Fibre 20.9g; Sodium 3950mg.

Poppyseed bloomer

This satisfying white poppyseed bread, which is a version of the chunky baton loaf found throughout Europe, is made using a slower rising method and with less yeast than usual. It produces a longer-keeping loaf with a fuller flavour. The dough takes about 8 hours to rise, so you'll need to start making the bread early in the morning.

Makes 1 large loaf

675g/1½ lb/6 cups unbleached white bread flour

10ml/2 tsp salt

15g/½ oz fresh yeast

430ml/15fl oz/1⅞ cups water

For the topping

2.5ml/½ tsp salt

30ml/2 tbsp water

poppy seeds, for sprinkling

Cook's tip You can get the cracked appearance of this loaf by spraying the oven with water before baking. If the underside is not crusty at the end, turn the loaf over, switch off the heat and leave in the oven for 5–10 minutes.

1 Lightly grease a baking sheet. Sift the flour and salt together into a large bowl and make a well in the centre.

2 Mix the yeast and 150ml/¼ pint/ ⅔ cup of the water in a bowl. Mix in the remaining water. Add to the centre of the flour. Mix, gradually incorporating the surrounding flour, until the mixture forms a firm dough.

3 Turn out on to a lightly floured surface and knead the dough for at least 10 minutes, until smooth and elastic. Place the dough in a lightly oiled bowl, cover with lightly oiled clear film (plastic wrap) and leave to rise, at cool room temperature, about 15–18°C/60–65°F, for 5–6 hours, or until doubled in bulk.

4 Knock back (punch down) the dough, turn out on to a lightly floured surface and knead it thoroughly and quite hard for about 5 minutes. Return the dough to the bowl, and re-cover. Leave to rise, at cool room temperature, for 2 hours.

5 Knock back again and repeat the thorough kneading. Leave the dough to rest for 5 minutes, then roll out on a lightly floured surface into a rectangle 2.5cm/1in thick. Roll the dough up from one long side and shape it into a square-ended thick baton shape about 33 × 13cm/13 × 5in.

6 Place it seam side up on a lightly floured baking sheet, cover and leave to rest for 15 minutes. Turn the loaf over and place on the greased baking sheet. Plump up by tucking the dough under the sides and ends. Using a sharp knife, cut six diagonal slashes on the top.

7 Leave to rest, covered, in a warm place, for 10 minutes. Meanwhile preheat the oven to 230°C/450°F/Gas 8.

8 Mix the salt and water together and brush this glaze over the bread. Sprinkle with poppy seeds. Spray the oven with water, bake the bread immediately for 20 minutes, then reduce the oven temperature to 200°C/400°F/Gas 6. Bake for 25 minutes more, or until golden. Transfer to a wire rack to cool.

Variation You could also use sesame, cumin or nigella seeds instead of poppy seeds, or a mixture of seeds.

Per loaf Energy 2302kcal/9787kJ; Protein 63.5g; Carbohydrate 524.5g, of which sugars 10.1g; Fat 8.8g, of which saturates 1.3g; Cholesterol 0mg; Calcium 946mg; Fibre 20.9g; Sodium 3950mg.

Brown soda bread

Perhaps the easiest to make of all loaves, soda bread is yeast-free and so doesn't need time to rise. It is baked straightaway and is best eaten on the day it is made. It tastes delicious spread with unsalted butter and topped with a fruity jam or a slice of farmhouse cheese.

Makes 1 loaf

450g/1lb/4 cups wholemeal (whole-wheat) flour

175g/6oz/1½ cups plain (all-purpose) flour

7.5ml/1½ tsp bicarbonate of soda (baking soda)

5ml/1 tsp salt

about 450ml/¾ pint/scant 2 cups buttermilk

Variation Cream of tartar can be added to the dry ingredients to provide the acid instead of buttermilk.

1 Preheat the oven to 200°C/400°F/ Gas 6, and grease a baking sheet. Combine the dry ingredients in a mixing bowl and stir in enough buttermilk to make a fairly soft dough. Turn on to a work surface dusted with wholemeal flour and knead lightly until smooth.

2 Form the dough into a circle, about 4cm/1½in thick. Lay on the baking sheet and mark a deep cross in the top with a floured knife.

3 Bake for about 45 minutes, or until the bread is browned and sounds hollow when tapped on the base. Cool on a wire rack. If a soft crust is preferred, wrap the loaf in a clean dish towel while cooling.

Cook's tip Buttermilk can be cultured easily, using a 'buttermilk plant'. Heat 450ml/¾ pint/scant 2 cups skimmed milk to lukewarm by adding 150ml/ ¼ pint/⅔ cup boiling water, then add 25g/1oz yeast and 10ml/2 tsp sugar.

Pour into a sterilized screw-top or preserving jar, allowing enough space for the contents to be shaken. Place on its side in a warm, dark place and shake several times a day for 4–6 days, while the buttermilk plant is forming, then remove the jar and open it carefully.

Strain the soured milk into a jug (pitcher); the lumpy pieces of yeast left in the strainer become the buttermilk plant and can be washed and used again.

Leftover milk can be added to the jar daily if there is room – it will thicken and sour, taking as little as 2 days in summer, 4–5 in winter.

Remember to always wash all the old milk from the yeast and sterilize the jar.

Per loaf Energy 2262kcal/9643kJ; Protein 88.5g; Carbohydrate 465.4g, of which sugars 31.4g; Fat 18.9g, of which saturates 6.5g; Cholesterol 27mg; Calcium 1.37g; Fibre 34.2g; Sodium 2.18g.

Granary cob loaf

Bread-making can be immensely satisfying when the result is as delicious as this brown
loaf. You need fresh yeast for this recipe, which has a similar texture to putty and crumbles
easily when broken. Buy it in small quantities and store in the refrigerator for up to a month.

Makes 1 round loaf

450g/1lb/4 cups Granary
(whole-wheat) or malthouse flour

12.5ml/2$\frac{1}{2}$ tsp salt

15g/$\frac{1}{2}$oz fresh yeast

wheat flakes or cracked wheat,
for sprinkling

1 Lightly flour a baking sheet. Mix
the flour and 10ml/2 tsp of the salt
together in a large bowl and make a
well in the centre. Place in a very low
oven for 5 minutes to warm.

2 Measure 300ml/$\frac{1}{2}$ pint/1$\frac{1}{4}$ cups
lukewarm water. Mix the yeast with
a little of the water, then blend in
the rest. Pour the yeast mixture into the
centre of the flour and mix to a dough.

3 Turn out on to a lightly floured surface
and knead for about 10 minutes, until
smooth and elastic. Place in a lightly
oiled bowl, cover with lightly oiled clear
film (plastic wrap) and leave to rise in
a warm place for 1$\frac{1}{4}$ hours, or until
doubled in bulk.

4 Turn the dough out on to a floured
surface. Knead for 2–3 minutes, then
roll into a ball. Place on the baking
sheet. Cover with a bowl and leave to
rise in a warm place for 30–45 minutes.

5 Preheat the oven to 230°C/450°F/
Gas 8 towards the end of the rising
time. Mix 30ml/2 tbsp water with
the remaining salt and brush evenly
over the bread. Sprinkle the loaf with
wheat flakes, cracked wheat or a
handful of rolled oats.

6 Bake the bread for 15 minutes,
then reduce the oven temperature
to 200°C/400°F/Gas 6 and bake for
a further 20 minutes, or until the
loaf is firm to the touch and sounds
hollow when tapped on the base.
Cool on a wire rack.

Per loaf Energy 1395kcal/5931kJ; Protein 57.1g; Carbohydrate 287.6g, of which sugars 9.4g; Fat 9.9g, of which saturates 1.4g; Cholesterol 0mg; Calcium 172mg; Fibre 40.5g; Sodium 4926mg.

Onion, olive and Parmesan bread

Versatile and delicious, this tasty bread is made with olive oil and cornmeal. Try it cut into chunks and dipped into olive oil. It is also wonderful as a base for bruschetta or filled with mozzarella and prosciutto, and makes delicious croûtons for tossing into a salad.

Makes 1 large loaf

350g/12oz/3 cups unbleached strong plain (all-purpose) flour, plus a little extra

115g/4oz/1 cup yellow cornmeal, plus a little extra

rounded 5ml/1 tsp salt

15g/¹⁄₂oz fresh yeast or 10ml/2 tsp active dried yeast

5ml/1 tsp muscovado (molasses) sugar

270ml/9fl oz/generous 1 cup warm water

5ml/1 tsp chopped fresh thyme

30ml/2 tbsp olive oil, plus a little extra for greasing

1 onion, finely chopped

75g/3oz/1 cup freshly grated Parmesan cheese

90g/3¹⁄₂oz/scant 1 cup pitted black olives, halved

1 Mix the flour, cornmeal and salt in a warmed bowl. If using fresh yeast, cream it with the sugar and gradually stir in 120ml/4fl oz/¹⁄₂ cup of the warm water. If using dried yeast, stir the sugar into the water and then sprinkle the dried yeast over the surface. Leave in a warm place for 10 minutes, until frothy.

2 Make a well in the centre of the dry ingredients and pour in the yeast liquid and a further 150ml/¹⁄₄ pint/²⁄₃ cup of the remaining warm water.

3 Add the chopped fresh thyme and 15ml/1 tbsp of the olive oil and mix thoroughly with a wooden spoon, gradually drawing in the dry ingredients until they are fully incorporated. Add a dash more warm water, if necessary, to make a soft, but not sticky, dough.

4 Knead the dough on a lightly floured work surface for 5 minutes, until smooth and elastic. Place in a clean, lightly oiled bowl and place in a polythene bag or cover with oiled clear film (plastic wrap). Set aside to rise in a warm, not hot place for 1–2 hours or until well risen.

5 Meanwhile, heat the remaining olive oil in a heavy frying pan. Add the onion and cook gently for 8 minutes, until softened. Set aside to cool.

6 Brush a baking sheet with olive oil. Turn out the dough on to a floured work surface. Knead in the onions, followed by the Parmesan and olives.

7 Shape the dough into a rough oval loaf. Sprinkle a little cornmeal on the work surface and roll the bread in it, then place on the prepared baking sheet. Make several slits across the top.

8 Slip the baking sheet into the polythene bag or cover with oiled clear film and leave to rise in a warm place for about 1 hour, or until well risen.

9 Preheat the oven to 200°C/400°F/ Gas 6. Bake for 30–35 minutes, or until the bread sounds hollow when tapped on the base. Cool on a wire rack.

Variation Alternatively, shape the dough into a loaf, roll in cornmeal and place in an oiled loaf tin (pan). Leave to rise in the tin, then bake as in step 8.

Per loaf Energy 1142kcal/4803kJ; Protein 37.4g; Carbohydrate 182.5g, of which sugars 6.4g; Fat 32.5g, of which saturates 10.4g; Cholesterol 38mg; Calcium 733mg; Fibre 8.4g; Sodium 1428mg.

Walnut and caramelized onion scones

These savoury scones are delicious served warm with butter, artisan cheese and fruit chutney. They can be made as small scones for a party, topped with cheese or cold meat.

Makes 10–12

90g/3½oz/7 tbsp butter or non-hydrogenated margarine

15ml/1 tbsp olive oil

1 Spanish (Bermuda) onion, chopped

5ml/1 tsp cumin seeds, lightly crushed

200g/7oz/1¾ cups self-raising (self-rising) flour

5ml/1 tsp baking powder

25g/1oz/¼ cup fine oatmeal

5ml/1 tsp light unrefined muscovado (brown) sugar

90g/3½oz/scant 1 cup chopped walnuts

5ml/1 tsp chopped fresh thyme

120–150ml/4–5fl oz/½–⅔ cup buttermilk

a little milk or soya milk

sea salt and ground black pepper

1 Melt 15g/½oz/1 tbsp of the butter with the oil in a small pan and cook the onion gently, covered, for 10–12 minutes. Uncover, then continue to cook gently until it begins to brown.

2 Add half the cumin seeds and increase the heat slightly. Continue to cook, stirring occasionally, until the onion begins to caramelize. Cool. Preheat the oven to 200°C/400°F/Gas 6.

3 Sift the flour and baking powder into a large bowl and add the oatmeal, sugar, 2.5ml/½ tsp salt and black pepper. Add the remaining butter or margarine and rub in until the mixture resembles fine breadcrumbs.

4 Add the cooked onion and cumin mixture, chopped walnuts and chopped fresh thyme, then bind to make a soft, but not sticky, dough with the buttermilk.

5 Roll or pat out the mixture to an even thickness of just over 1cm/½ in. Stamp out 10–12 scones using a 5–6cm/ 2–2½ in plain round cutter.

6 Place the scones on a floured baking tray, glaze with the milk or soya milk and scatter with a little salt and the remaining cumin seeds. Bake the scones for 12–15 minutes until well-risen and golden brown. Allow to cool for a few minutes on a wire rack and serve warm spread with butter, non-hydrogenated margarine or goat's cheese.

Per portion Energy 131kcal/543kJ; Protein 1.8g; Carbohydrate 3g, of which sugars 1.3g; Fat 12.6g, of which saturates 4.6g; Cholesterol 17mg; Calcium 23mg; Fibre 0.5g; Sodium 51mg.

Bara brith fruited teabread

The name for this traditional Welsh loaf means 'speckled bread'. For a hint of citrus, add grated lemon or orange rind to the batter before baking. Spread with butter and honey.

Makes 1 large loaf

225g/8oz/1⅓ cups mixed dried fruit and chopped mixed (candied) peel

225ml/8fl oz/1 cup hot strong tea, strained

225g/8oz/2 cups self-raising (self-rising) flour

5ml/1 tsp mixed (apple pie) spice

25g/1oz/2 tbsp butter

100g/3½oz/8 tbsp soft brown sugar

1 egg, lightly beaten

Cook's tip The flavour of the loaf can be varied subtly by using a variety of teas – try the distinctive perfume of Earl Grey.

1 Put the fruit into a heatproof bowl and pour the hot tea over it. Cover and leave to stand at room temperature for several hours or overnight.

2 Preheat the oven to 180°C/350°F/ Gas 4. Grease a 900g/2lb loaf tin (pan) and line it with baking parchment.

3 Sift the flour and the mixed spice into a large mixing bowl. Add the butter and, with your fingertips, rub it into the flour until the mixture starts to resemble fine breadcrumbs.

4 Stir the soft brown sugar into the flour and spice mixture, then add the dried fruit and its liquid along with the beaten egg. Stir well with a wooden spoon to make a mixture with a soft consistency.

5 Transfer the mixture to the prepared loaf tin and level the surface. Put into the hot oven and cook for about 1 hour or until a skewer inserted in the centre comes out clean. Turn out on a wire rack and leave to cool completely.

Per loaf Energy 2024kcal/8588kJ; Protein 33.2g; Carbohydrate 432.7g, of which sugars 261.3g; Fat 29.9g, of which saturates 15g; Cholesterol 244mg; Calcium 565mg; Fibre 11.9g; Sodium 342mg.

Teatime crumpets

Toasting English crumpets on an open fire is a country tradition. These are made with a yeast batter and cooked in metal rings on a griddle. They are equally tasty with either savoury or sweet toppings – try golden syrup, honey or preserves, or sliced ham or cheese.

Makes about 10

225g/8oz/2 cups plain (all-purpose) flour

2.5ml/½ tsp salt

2.5ml/½ tsp bicarbonate of soda (baking soda)

5ml/1 tsp fast-action yeast granules

150ml/¼ pint/⅔ cup milk

oil, for greasing

1 Sift the flour, salt and bicarbonate of soda into a bowl and stir in the yeast. Make a well in the centre. Heat the milk with 200ml/7fl oz/scant 1 cup water until lukewarm and tip into the well.

2 Mix well with a whisk or wooden spoon, beating vigorously to make a thick smooth batter. Cover and leave in a warm place for about 1 hour until the mixture has a spongy texture. Re-whisk the batter before cooking.

3 Heat a griddle or heavy frying pan. Lightly oil the hot surface and the inside of three or four metal rings, each measuring about 8cm/3½in in diameter. Place the oiled rings on the hot surface and leave for 1–2 minutes until hot.

4 Spoon the batter into the rings to a depth of about 1cm/½in. Cook over a medium-high heat for about 6 minutes until the top surface is set and bubbles have burst open to make holes.

5 When set, carefully lift off the metal rings and flip the crumpets over, cooking the second side for just 1 minute until lightly browned.

6 Lift off and leave to cool completely on a wire rack. Repeat with the remaining crumpet mixture. Just before serving, toast the crumpets on both sides and butter generously.

Per portion Energy 93kcal/393kJ; Protein 3g; Carbohydrate 16.5g, of which sugars 1g; Fat 2.1g, of which saturates 1g; Cholesterol 21mg; Calcium 48mg; Fibre 0.6g; Sodium 21mg.

Scones with jam and cream

For many people, English afternoon tea without a plate of scones would be unthinkable. Quick and easy to make, these are best served fresh and warm from the oven. Top with cream and jam or soft fruits in the summer, and bottled or preserved fruits in the winter.

Makes about 12

450g/1lb/4 cups self-raising (self-rising) flour, or 450g/1lb/ 4 cups plain (all-purpose) flour and 10ml/2 tsp baking powder

5ml/1 tsp salt

55g/2oz/¼ cup butter, chilled and cut into small cubes

15ml/1 tbsp lemon juice

about 400ml/14fl oz/1⅔ cups milk, plus extra to glaze

butter, jam and cream, to serve

1 Preheat the oven to 230°C/450°F/ Gas 8. Sift the flour, baking powder (if using) and salt into a mixing bowl, and stir to mix through. Add the butter and rub it lightly into the flour with your fingertips until the mixture resembles fine, even-textured breadcrumbs.

2 Whisk the lemon juice into the milk and leave for about 1 minute to thicken slightly, then pour into the flour mixture and mix quickly to make a soft but pliable dough. The softer the mixture, the lighter the resulting scones will be, but if it is too sticky they will spread during baking and lose their shape.

3 Knead the dough briefly, then roll it out on a lightly floured surface to a thickness of at least 2.5cm/1in. Using a 5cm/2in biscuit (cookie) cutter, and dipping it into flour each time, stamp out 12 rounds. Place the dough rounds on a well-floured baking sheet. Re-roll the trimmings and cut out more scones.

4 Brush the tops with a little milk, then put into the hot oven and cook for about 20 minutes, or until risen.

5 Remove from the oven and wrap the scones in a clean dish towel to keep them warm and soft until ready to eat. Eat the scones with butter, plenty of jam and a generous dollop of clotted or whipped double (heavy) cream.

Variation To make savoury cheese scones, add 115g/4oz/1 cup of grated cheese, such as mature (sharp) Cheddar, to the dough and knead it in thoroughly before rolling out and cutting into shapes.

Per portion Energy 177kcal/749kJ; Protein 4.7g; Carbohydrate 30.7g, of which sugars 2.2g; Fat 4.8g, of which saturates 2.8g; Cholesterol 12mg; Calcium 93mg; Fibre 1.2g; Sodium 43mg.

Sugar shortbread rounds

Shortbread should always be in the biscuit tin or cookie jar – it is so moreish. Serve these melting buttery biscuits with a cup of tea or with fruit fools or junket. A traditional Scottish favourite, they can also be half-dipped into melted chocolate and left to set.

Makes about 24

450g/1lb/2 cups salted butter

225g/8oz/1 heaped cup caster (superfine) sugar

450g/1lb/4 cups plain (all-purpose) flour

225g/8oz/scant 1½ cups ground rice or rice flour

5ml/1 tsp salt

demerara (raw) sugar, to decorate

golden caster (superfine) sugar, for dusting

Cook's tip Rice flour adds a grittiness to the dough, distinguishing home-made shortbread from bought varieties.

1 Preheat the oven to 190°C/375°F/ Gas 5. Make sure all the ingredients are at room temperature. Salted butter has more flavour than unsalted (sweet), but if you only have unsalted, then use it – don't make a special trip to the shops to buy some.

2 In a food processor or bowl, cream the butter and sugar together until light, pale and fluffy. If you used a food processor, scrape the mixture out into a mixing bowl.

3 Sift together the flour, ground rice or rice flour and salt and stir into the butter and sugar with a wooden spoon, until the mixture resembles fine breadcrumbs.

4 Working quickly, gather the dough together with your hand, then put it on a clean work surface. Knead lightly together until it forms a ball but take care not to over-knead or the shortbread will be tough and greasy. Lightly roll into a sausage shape, about 7.5cm/3in thick. Wrap in clear film (plastic wrap) and chill until firm.

5 Pour the demerara sugar on to a sheet of baking parchment. Unwrap the dough and roll in the sugar until evenly coated. Slice the roll into discs about 1cm/½in thick.

6 Place the discs on to two baking sheets lined with baking parchment, spacing well apart. Bake for 20–25 minutes until very pale gold (but not dark).

7 Remove from the oven and sprinkle with golden caster sugar. Allow to cool for 10 minutes before transferring to a wire rack to cool completely.

Per portion Energy 275kcal/1147kJ; Protein 2.5g; Carbohydrate 32g, of which sugars 10.2g; Fat 15.7g, of which saturates 9.8g; Cholesterol 40mg; Calcium 37mg; Fibre 0.8g; Sodium 197mg.

Cherry melting moments

As the name suggests, these crisp biscuits really do melt in the mouth. They have a texture like shortbread but are covered in rolled oats to give a crunchy surface and extra flavour. They are traditionally topped with a toothsome nugget of red glacé cherry.

Makes about 16–20

40g/1½oz/3 tbsp soft butter

65g/2½oz/5 tbsp lard

75g/3oz/6 tbsp caster (superfine) sugar

1 egg yolk, beaten

few drops of vanilla or almond extract

150g/5oz/1¼ cups self-raising (self-rising) flour

rolled oats, for coating

4–5 glacé (candied) cherries

3 Spread rolled oats on a sheet of baking parchment and toss the balls in them until evenly coated.

4 Place the balls, spaced slightly apart, on two baking (cookie) sheets. Flatten each ball a little with your thumb. Cut the cherries into quarters and place a piece of cherry on top of each biscuit (cookie). Put into the hot oven and cook for 15–20 minutes, until they are lightly browned.

5 Allow the biscuits to cool for a few minutes on the baking sheets before transferring them to a wire rack to cool completely.

1 Preheat the oven to 180°C/350°F/ Gas 4. Beat together the butter, lard and sugar, then gradually beat in the egg yolk and vanilla or almond extract.

2 Sift the flour over and stir to make a soft dough. Roll into 16–20 small balls.

Per portion Energy 88kcal/370kJ; Protein 0.7g; Carbohydrate 10.9g, of which sugars 5.4g; Fat 5g, of which saturates 2.4g; Cholesterol 7mg; Calcium 30mg; Fibre 0.3g; Sodium 40mg.

Ginger biscuits

These crisp little biscuits are very versatile. You can cut them into any shape – but stars and hearts are the traditional forms – and they can also be decorated with icing. They are good served with ice cream or as part of a selection of biscuits for cheese.

Makes about 50

150g/5½oz/½ cup plus 3 tbsp butter

400g/14oz/2 cups sugar

50ml/2fl oz/¼ cup golden (light corn) syrup

15ml/1 tbsp treacle (molasses)

15ml/1 tbsp ground ginger

30ml/2 tbsp ground cinnamon

15ml/1 tbsp ground cloves

5ml/1 tsp ground cardamom

5ml/1 tsp bicarbonate of soda (baking soda)

250ml/8fl oz/1 cup water

150g/5oz/1¼ cups plain (all-purpose) flour

1 Put the butter, sugar, syrup, treacle, ginger, cinnamon, cloves and cardamom in a heavy pan and heat gently until the butter has melted.

2 Put the bicarbonate of soda and water in a large heatproof bowl. Pour in the warm spice mixture and mix well together, then add the flour and stir until well blended. Wrap in clear film (plastic wrap) and put in the refrigerator overnight to rest.

3 Preheat the oven to 220°C/425°F/ Gas 7. Line several baking sheets with baking parchment. Knead the dough, then roll out on a lightly floured surface as thinly as possible. Cut the dough into shapes of your choice and place on the baking sheets.

4 Bake the biscuits (cookies) in the oven for about 5 minutes until golden brown, adding them in batches until all the biscuits are cooked. Leave to cool on the baking sheet. Make sure the biscuits are completely cold before icing or decorating them.

Per portion Energy 31kcal/130kJ; Protein 0.2g; Carbohydrate 5.8g, of which sugars 4.2g; Fat 0.8g, of which saturates 0.5g; Cholesterol 2mg; Calcium 5mg; Fibre 0.1g; Sodium13mg.

Porridge biscuits

Nutritious, delicious and chewy, oats are a major ingredient in these traditional country biscuits. They are store-cupboard standbys, and you can embellish the recipe by adding whichever varieties of chopped nuts, dried fruits or seeds you have to hand.

Makes about 18

115g/4oz/½ cup butter

115g/4oz/½ cup soft brown sugar

115g/4oz/½ cup golden (light corn) syrup

150g/5oz/1¼ cups self-raising (self-rising) flour

150g/5oz rolled porridge oats

1 Preheat the oven to 180°C/350°F/Gas 4. Line two baking (cookie) sheets with baking parchment, or grease with butter.

2 Gently heat the butter, sugar and golden syrup until the butter has melted and the sugar has dissolved. Remove from the heat and leave to cool slightly.

3 Sift the flour and stir into the mixture in the pan, together with the oats, to make a soft dough.

4 Roll the dough into small balls and arrange them on the prepared baking sheets, leaving plenty of room for them to spread. Flatten each ball slightly with a palette knife or a metal spatula.

5 Put one tray into the hot oven and cook for 12–15 minutes until golden brown and cooked through.

6 Leave to cool on the baking sheet for 1–2 minutes, then carefully transfer to a wire rack to crisp up and cool completely, while you cook the remaining batches.

Variation Add 25g/1oz/¼ cup chopped toasted almonds or walnuts, or a small handful of dried fruit, such as raisins, sultanas (golden raisins), chopped dried figs, dates or apricots, in step 3.

Per portion Energy 151kcal/637kJ; Protein 1.8g; Carbohydrate 23.9g, of which sugars 11.9g; Fat 6g, of which saturates 3.3g; Cholesterol 14mg; Calcium 22mg; Fibre 0.8g; Sodium 59mg.

Honey cake

The type of honey you choose affects the flavour of this cake. Use a darker honey in the recipe, then drizzle over a flower honey such as orange blossom while the cake is still warm.

Makes 16 squares

175g/6oz/³⁄₄ cup butter

175g/6oz/³⁄₄ cup clear honey

115g/4oz/¹⁄₂ cup soft brown sugar

2 eggs, lightly beaten

15–30ml/1–2 tbsp milk

225g/8oz/2 cups self-raising (self-rising) flour

3 Beat the eggs and milk into the cooled mixture. Sift the flour over the top, stir in and beat well until smooth.

4 Place the mixture into the prepared tin, levelling the surface. Put into the hot oven and cook for about 30 minutes until well risen, golden brown and firm to the touch.

5 Leave the cake to cool in the tin for 20 minutes, then turn out, leaving the lining paper in place, on to a wire rack and leave to cool completely.

6 Peel off the paper and cut the cake into 16 squares. Serve with drizzled honey.

1 Grease and line a 23cm/9in square cake tin (pan) with baking parchment. Preheat the oven to 180°C/350°F/Gas 4.

2 Gently heat the butter, honey and sugar, stirring frequently until well amalgamated. Set aside and leave to cool slightly.

Variation Add 5ml/1 tsp ground cinnamon or grated nutmeg to the flour in step 3.

Per portion Energy 152kcal/639kJ; Protein 1.9g; Carbohydrate 23.5g, of which sugars 13g; Fat 6.3g, of which saturates 3.8g; Cholesterol 26mg; Calcium 30mg; Fibre 0.4g; Sodium 49mg

Blueberry muffins

Light and fluffy, muffins are best eaten fresh for breakfast or brunch. Add some chopped pecans or walnuts for extra crunch, or replace the blueberries with fresh cranberries.

Makes 12

180g/6¼oz/generous 1½ cups plain (all-purpose) flour

60g/2¼oz/generous ¼ cup sugar

10ml/2 tsp baking powder

1.5ml/¼ tsp salt

2 eggs

50g/2oz/4 tbsp butter, melted

175ml/6fl oz/¾ cup milk

5ml/1 tsp vanilla extract

5ml/1 tsp grated lemon rind

175g/6oz/1½ cups fresh blueberries

1 Preheat the oven to 200°C/400°F/ Gas 6. Grease a 12-cup muffin tin (pan) or arrange 12 paper muffin cases on a baking tray.

2 Sift the flour, sugar, baking powder and salt into a large mixing bowl. In another bowl, whisk the eggs until blended. Add the melted butter, milk, vanilla and lemon rind to the eggs, and stir thoroughly to combine.

3 Make a well in the dry ingredients and pour in the egg mixture. With a large metal spoon, stir until the flour is just moistened, but not smooth.

4 Add the blueberries to the muffin mixture and gently fold in, being careful not to crush any of the berries while you stir them.

5 Spoon the batter into the muffin tin or paper cases, leaving enough room for the muffins to rise.

6 Bake for 20–25 minutes, until the tops spring back when touched lightly. Leave the muffins in the tin, if using, for 5 minutes before turning out on to a wire rack to cool a little before serving.

Cook's tip If you want to serve these muffins for breakfast, prepare the dry ingredients the night before to save time.

Per portion Energy 236kcal/992kJ; Protein 4.9g; Carbohydrate 34.7g, of which sugars 12.4g; Fat 9.6g, of which saturates 5.6g; Cholesterol 54mg; Calcium 88mg; Fibre 1.4g; Sodium 82mg.

Dark and sticky gingerbread

This is a really special gingerbread. The secret of its dark, rich stickiness lies in the huge amount of treacle used. It is very tactile and literally sticks to the roof of your mouth when you eat it. Slice and serve with butter or cream cheese, or spread with vanilla butter icing.

Makes an 18cm/7in square cake

225g/8oz/2 cups plain (all-purpose) flour

10ml/2 tsp ground ginger

5ml/1 tsp mixed (apple pie) spice

a pinch of salt

2 pieces stem (preserved) ginger, drained and chopped

115g/4oz/½ cup butter, softened

115g/4oz/¾ cup dark muscovado (molasses) sugar, sifted

275g/10oz/scant 1 cup black treacle (molasses), at room temperature

2 eggs, beaten

2.5ml/½ tsp bicarbonate of soda (baking soda)

30ml/2 tbsp milk, warmed

butter or cream cheese, to serve

1 Preheat the oven to 160°C/325°F/ Gas 3. Grease and line the base of an 18cm/7in square cake tin (pan) that measures about 7.5cm/3in deep.

2 Sift the flour, ground ginger, mixed spice and salt into a bowl. Add the ginger and toss it in the flour to coat.

3 Cream the butter and sugar together until fluffy, then gradually stir in the treacle. Gradually beat in the eggs, then the flour mixture.

4 Dissolve the bicarbonate of soda in the milk and gradually beat this into the mixture. Pour the mixture into the prepared tin and bake for 45 minutes.

5 Reduce the oven temperature to 150°C/300°F/Gas 2 and bake for a further 30 minutes. The gingerbread should look very dark and slightly risen. Remove the tray from the oven and check the cake is cooked by inserting a metal skewer into the middle. If it comes out clean, the cake is done. Don't worry if the gingerbread sinks slightly in the middle – it always does.

6 Cool the gingerbread for 5 minutes in the tin, then turn out and cool on a wire rack. At this stage, the gingerbread will be dark, but not sticky at all. Keep it for 2–3 days in an airtight container and the outside will become sticky and moist. Slice when ready, then spread with butter or cream cheese.

Per cake Energy 2274kcal/9594kJ; Protein 36.7g; Carbohydrate 399g, of which sugars 252.9g; Fat 70g, of which saturates 28.3g; Cholesterol 11mg; Calcium 589mg; Fibre 21.1g; Sodium 928mg.

Old-fashioned treacle cake

Quick to make and very moreish, this fruit-studded, crumbly cake hails from Wales and would have originally been baked on a tin plate. The black treacle gives the cake both a rich colour and deep flavour, and a generous wedge would be a welcome treat at any lunch.

Makes a 20cm/8in cake

250g/9oz/2 cups self-raising (self-rising) flour

2.5ml/½ tsp mixed (apple pie) spice

75g/3oz/6 tbsp butter, cut into cubes

35g/1oz/2 tbsp caster (superfine) sugar

150g/5oz/1 cup mixed dried fruit

1 egg

15ml/1 tbsp black treacle (molasses)

100ml/3½fl oz/scant ½ cup milk

3 Beat the egg and, with a small whisk or a fork, stir in the treacle and then the milk. Stir the liquid into the flour to make a fairly stiff but moist consistency, adding a little extra milk if necessary.

4 Transfer the cake mixture to the prepared dish or tin with a spoon and level out the surface.

5 Bake the cake in the hot oven and cook for about 1 hour until it has risen, is firm to the touch and fully cooked through. To check if the cake is cooked, insert a small skewer in the centre – it should come out free of sticky mixture.

6 Leave the cooked treacle cake to cool completely. Serve it straight from the dish, cut into wedges.

1 Preheat the oven to 180°C/350°F/ Gas 5. Butter a shallow 20–23cm/ 8–9in ovenproof flan dish or baking tin (pan).

2 Sift the flour and spice into a large mixing bowl. Add the butter and, with your fingertips, rub it into the flour until the mixture resembles fine crumbs. Alternatively, you could do this in a food processor. Stir in the sugar and mixed dried fruit.

Variation Try varying the fruit in this recipe. Experiment with chopped ready-to-eat dried apricots and stem ginger, or a packet of luxury dried fruit. Chopped dates or figs work well too, and make the cake more substantial.

Per cake Energy 2089kcal/8805kJ; Protein 37.4g; Carbohydrate 343g, of which sugars 152.4g; Fat 72.8g, of which saturates 42.2g; Cholesterol 356mg; Calcium 720mg; Fibre 11.1g; Sodium 676mg.

Lemon-frosted whiskey cake

This light, moist cake has the subtle flavours of lemon and cloves. Thickly frosted with a zesty lemon icing, it makes a great winter cake using mostly store-cupboard ingredients.

Makes an 18cm/7in round cake

225g/8oz/1⅓ cups sultanas (golden raisins)

grated rind of 1 lemon

150ml/¼ pint/⅔ cup Irish whiskey

175g/6oz/¾ cup butter, softened

175g/6oz/¾ cup soft light brown sugar

175g/6oz/1½ cups plain (all-purpose) flour

pinch of salt

1.5ml/¼ tsp ground cloves

5ml/1 tsp baking powder

3 large (US extra large) eggs, separated

For the icing

juice of 1 lemon

225g/8oz/2 cups icing (confectioners') sugar

crystallized lemon slices, to decorate (optional)

1 Put the sultanas and grated lemon rind into a bowl with the whiskey and leave overnight to soak.

2 Preheat the oven to 180°C/350°F/ Gas 4 and grease and base line a loose-based 18cm/7in deep cake tin (pan).

3 Cream the butter and sugar until light and fluffy. Sift the flour, salt, cloves and baking powder together into a bowl.

4 Beat the yolks into the butter and sugar one at a time, adding a little of the flour with each egg and beating well after each addition. Gradually blend in the sultana and whiskey mixture, alternating with the remaining flour. Do not overbeat at this stage.

5 Whisk the egg whites until stiff, then fold them into the mixture with a metal spoon. Turn the mixture into the prepared tin and bake in the preheated oven for 1½ hours, or until well risen and springy to the touch. Turn out and cool on a rack.

6 Meanwhile, make the icing: mix the lemon juice with the sieved (sifted) icing sugar and enough warm water to make a pouring consistency. Lay a plate under the cake rack to catch the drips and pour the icing over the cake a spoonful at a time, letting it dribble down the sides. Any icing dripping on to the plate may be scooped and put on top again. When the icing has set, it can be decorated with lemon slices, if you like.

Per cake Energy 4691kcal/19,730kJ; Protein 48.1g; Carbohydrate 711.2g, of which sugars 577.8g; Fat 167g, of which saturates 97.1g; Cholesterol 1.06g; Calcium 735mg; Fibre 9.9g; Sodium 1.38g.

Irish apple cake

If available, you should choose heritage apple varieties when making this lovely cake. It has a crunchy top and can be served cold at teatime, or warm with double cream as a dessert.

Makes 1 cake

225g/8oz/2 cups self-raising (self-rising) flour

good pinch of salt

pinch of ground cloves

115g/4oz/½ cup butter, at room temperature

3 or 4 cooking apples

115g/4oz/generous ½ cup caster (superfine) sugar

2 eggs, beaten

a little milk, to mix

granulated (white) sugar, to sprinkle over

1 Preheat the oven to 190°C/375°F/Gas 5 and butter a 20cm/8in cake tin (pan).

2 Sieve (sift) the flour, salt and ground cloves into a bowl. Cut in the butter and rub in until the mixture is like fine breadcrumbs. Peel and core the apples. Slice them thinly and add to the rubbed-in mixture with the sugar.

3 Mix in the eggs and enough milk to make a fairly stiff dough, then turn the mixture into the prepared tin and sprinkle with granulated sugar.

4 Bake in the preheated oven for 30–40 minutes, or until springy to the touch. Cool on a wire rack. When cold store in an airtight tin until ready to serve.

Per cake Energy 2315kcal/9717kJ; Protein 37g; Carbohydrate 312.5g, of which sugars 145.3g; Fat 110.9g, of which saturates 64.1g; Cholesterol 702mg; Calcium 948mg; Fibre 10.7g; Sodium 1.68g.

Plum and almond sponge cake

Seasonal country cooking is an obvious necessity in cold areas that have fierce extremes of climate. Traditionally, people ate what they could grow and stored food carefully to survive until the next harvest. Orchards have always been especially prized, and apple, pear and plum trees thrive in many cold countries. These fruits add sweetness, texture and variety to cakes. This sponge is best served warm and is equally good made with apricots or nectarines. The cardamom gives a hint of spice, which complements the fruit perfectly.

Serves 10

450g/1lb pitted fresh plums, coarsely chopped, plus 9 extra plums, stoned and halved, to decorate

300ml/½ pint/1¼ cups water

115g/4oz/½ cup unsalted (sweet) butter, softened

200g/7oz/1 cup caster (superfine) sugar

3 eggs

90g/3½oz/¾ cup toasted, finely chopped almonds

5ml/1 tsp bicarbonate of soda (baking soda)

7.5ml/1½ tsp baking powder

5ml/1 tsp ground cardamom

1.5ml/¼ tsp salt

250g/9oz/2¼ cups plain (all-purpose) flour

15ml/1 tbsp pearl sugar, to decorate

250ml/8fl oz/1 cup double (heavy) cream

10ml/2 tsp vanilla sugar

10ml/2 tsp icing (confectioners') sugar

Variation Pearl sugar – large crystals with a pearly sheen – is commonly used in Scandinavia to decorate pastries, buns and cakes. If you can't find it, use coarsely crushed white sugar cubes.

1 Place the chopped plums in a pan and add the water. Bring to the boil over a medium heat and cook for 10–15 minutes, until soft. Set aside to cool. You will need 350ml/12fl oz/1½ cups stewed plums for the cake.

2 Preheat the oven to 180°C/350°F/ Gas 4. Grease and flour a 24cm/9½in springform cake tin (pan).

3 Cream the butter with the sugar in a mixing bowl until light and fluffy. Beat in the eggs, one at a time.

4 Stir in the stewed plums and the almonds. Add the baking soda, baking powder, cardamom and salt, and stir the mixture well together to distribute the fruit.

5 Gradually stir in the flour, a few spoons at a time, and mix until blended.

6 Pour the mixture into the prepared tin. Place 15 plum halves around the circumference of the cake and the remaining three halves in the centre, cut sides down. Sprinkle the pearl sugar over the cake.

7 Bake for 1 hour, or until the top springs back when lightly touched. Cool in the tin for 15 minutes before unfastening the ring.

8 Beat the double cream until soft peaks form. Stir in the vanilla sugar and the icing sugar and beat until thick. Serve the cake, still slightly warm, or at room temperature, in slices topped with a dollop of whipped cream.

Per portion Energy 311kcal/1308kJ; Protein 6.4g; Carbohydrate 44.5g, of which sugars 15.9g; Fat 13.2g, of which saturates 7.4g; Cholesterol 89mg; Calcium 86mg; Fibre 2.4g; Sodium 102mg.

Rich chocolate cake with chocolate icing

Chocolate cake is a staple of every self-respecting country tea table. A luxurious afternoon treat, this impressive cake with chocolate buttercream would look even more tempting topped with toasted half walnuts, pecans or hazelnuts. Serve with tea or coffee.

Serves 10–12

225g/8oz/2 cups plain (all-purpose) flour

5ml/1 tsp bicarbonate of soda (baking soda)

50g/2oz/$\frac{1}{2}$ cup (unsweetened) cocoa powder

125g/4$\frac{1}{2}$oz/9 tbsp soft butter

250g/9oz/1$\frac{1}{4}$ cups caster (superfine) sugar

3 eggs, beaten

250ml/8fl oz/1 cup buttermilk

For the chocolate buttercream

175g/6oz/1$\frac{1}{2}$ cups icing (confectioners') sugar

115g/4oz/$\frac{1}{2}$ cup soft unsalted (sweet) butter

few drops of vanilla extract

50g/2oz dark (bittersweet) chocolate

1 Butter two 20cm/8in sandwich tins (layer pans) and line the bases with baking parchment. Preheat the oven to 180°C/350°F/Gas 4. Sift the flour with the bicarbonate of soda and cocoa and stir together.

2 Beat the butter and sugar until light and fluffy. Gradually beat in the eggs. Add the flour and buttermilk; mix well.

3 Spoon into the prepared tins. Place into the hot oven and cook for 30–35 minutes until firm to the touch. Turn out of the tins, peel off the paper and leave on a wire rack to cool completely.

4 To make the chocolate buttercream, sift the icing sugar into a bowl. In a separate bowl, beat the butter until very soft and creamy.

5 Beat in half the sifted icing sugar until smooth and light. Gradually beat in the remaining sugar and the vanilla extract. Break the chocolate into squares. Melt in a bowl over a pan of hot water or in a microwave oven on low.

6 Mix the melted chocolate into the buttercream. Use half to sandwich the cakes together, and the rest on the top.

Per portion Energy 430kcal/1790kJ; Protein 7.8g; Carbohydrate 29.5g, of which sugars 28.8g; Fat 32.1g, of which saturates 13.6g; Cholesterol 96mg; Calcium 92mg; Fibre 1.9g; Sodium 125mg.

Victoria sponge

This light cake was named in honour of England's Queen Victoria, and is a favourite at baking competitions. It is based on equal quantities of fat, sugar, eggs and flour. Fill with jam or preserves of your choice, or soft summer fruits such as strawberries or raspberries.

Serves 6–8

3 large eggs

few drops of vanilla extract

175g/6oz/¾ cup soft butter

175g/6oz/¾ cup caster (superfine) sugar

175g/6oz/1½ cups self-raising (self-rising) flour

about 60ml/4 tbsp jam

icing (confectioners') sugar, to dust

1 Preheat the oven to 180°C/350°F/ Gas 4. Butter two 20cm/8in sandwich tins (layer pans) and line the bases of each with baking parchment.

2 Lightly beat the eggs with the vanilla extract. In a large mixing bowl, whisk the butter with the sugar until the mixture is pale, light and fluffy.

3 Gradually add the eggs, beating well after each addition. Sift the flour over the top and, using a metal spoon, fold in lightly until the mixture is smooth.

4 Divide the mixture between the prepared tins. Cook for 20 minutes until golden and firm to the touch.

5 Leave the cakes to cool in the tins for a few minutes then carefully turn out on to a wire rack. Remove the paper and leave to cool completely.

6 When the cakes are cold, sandwich the two halves together with plenty of jam. Finally, sift a little icing sugar over the top to cover the surface of the cake.

Variations
• Instead of vanilla extract, beat a little finely grated lemon rind into the butter and sugar mixture in step 2. Sandwich the cakes together with lemon curd.
• For a cream cake, sandwich with a thin layer of strawberry jam and a thick layer of whipped cream, topped with sliced fresh strawberries. Decorate the top of the cake with whipped cream and extra strawberries.

Per portion Energy 368kcal/1543kJ; Protein 4.6g; Carbohydrate 44.7g, of which sugars 28.5g; Fat 20.3g, of which saturates 12g; Cholesterol 118mg; Calcium 104mg; Fibre 0.7g; Sodium 241mg.

Preserves, relishes and sauces

As well as preserving the taste of summer fruits and vegetables, it is immensely satisfying to make your own jams, jellies and relishes. Country-style home-made ones always taste better than store-bought varieties, and also make lovely gifts. Spicy and fruity relishes enliven the simplest of rustic dishes, and stirring a bubbling pot of preserves is a highly pleasurable rural pastime – both easy and rewarding.

Blackcurrant jam

Dark, jewelled blackcurrants look and taste fabulous in this classic fruity jam. Serve on hot buttered toast, crumpets or croissants, or use as a filling for cakes.

Makes about 1.3kg/3lb

1.3kg/3lb/12 cups blackcurrants

grated rind and juice of 1 orange

475ml/16fl oz/2 cups water

1.3kg/3lb/6½ cups granulated (white) sugar, warmed

30ml/2 tbsp cassis (optional)

1 Place the blackcurrants, orange rind and juice and water in a large heavy pan. Bring to the boil, reduce the heat and simmer for 30 minutes.

2 Add the warmed sugar to the pan and stir over a low heat until the sugar has dissolved.

3 Bring the mixture to the boil and cook for about 8 minutes, or until the jam reaches setting point (105°C/220°F).

4 Remove the pan from the heat and skim off any scum from the surface using a slotted spoon.

5 Leave to cool for 5 minutes, then stir in the cassis, if using.

6 Pour the jam into warmed sterilized jars and seal. Leave the jars to cool completely, then label and store in a cool, dark place. The jam will keep for up to 6 months.

Per portion Energy 5504kcal/23,503kJ; Protein 18.4g; Carbohydrate 1448.7g, of which sugars 1448.7g; Fat 0.1g, of which saturates 0g; Cholesterol 0mg; Calcium 1474mg; Fibre 46.9g; Sodium 122mg.

Cherry berry conserve

Tart cranberries add an extra dimension to this delicious berry conserve. It is perfect for adding to sweet sauces, serving with roast duck, or for simply spreading on hot crumpets.

1 Put the cranberries in a food processor and process until coarsely chopped. Scrape into a pan and add the cherries, fruit syrup and lemon juice.

2 Add the water to the pan. Cover and bring to the boil, then simmer for 20–30 minutes, or until the cranberries are very tender.

3 Add the sugar to the pan and heat gently, stirring, until the sugar has dissolved. Bring to the boil, then cook for 10 minutes, or to setting point (105°C/220°F).

Makes about 1.3kg/3lb

350g/12oz/3 cups fresh cranberries

1kg/2¼lb/5½ cups cherries, pitted

120ml/4fl oz/½ cup blackcurrant or raspberry syrup

juice of 2 lemons

250ml/8fl oz/1 cup water

1.3kg/3lb/6½ cups preserving or granulated (white) sugar, warmed

4 Remove the pan from the heat and skim off and discard any scum using a slotted spoon. Leave to cool for 10 minutes, then stir gently and pour into warmed sterilized jars. Seal, label and store in a cool, dark place.

Cook's tip The cranberries must be cooked until very tender before the sugar is added, otherwise they will become tough.

Per portion Energy 5859kcal/24,986kJ; Protein 16.7g; Carbohydrate 1540.4g, of which sugars 1540.4g; Fat 1.4g, of which saturates 0g; Cholesterol 0mg; Calcium 844mg; Fibre 14.6g; Sodium 105mg.

Hedgerow jelly

In the autumn, foraged hedgerow fruits such as damsons, blackberries and elderberries are wonderful for this delightful country jelly. Serve with cold meats or cheese.

Makes about 1.3kg/3lb

450g/1lb damsons, washed

450g/1lb/4 cups blackberries, washed

225g/8oz/2 cups raspberries

225g/8oz/2 cups elderberries, washed

juice and pips (seeds) of 2 large lemons

about 1.3kg/3lb/6½ cups preserving or granulated (white) sugar, warmed

1 Put the fruit, lemon juice and pips in a large pan. Add water to just below the level of the fruit. Cover and simmer for 1 hour. Mash the fruit, then leave to cool slightly.

2 Pour into a scalded jelly bag suspended over a non-metallic bowl and leave to drain overnight. Don't squeeze the bag as this will cloud the jelly.

3 Measure the strained juice into a preserving pan. Add 450g/1lb/ 2¼ cups sugar for every 600ml/ 1 pint/2½ cups strained fruit juice.

4 Heat the mixture, stirring, over a low heat until the sugar has dissolved.

5 Increase the heat and boil rapidly without stirring for 10–15 minutes, or until the jelly reaches setting point (105°C/220°F).

6 Remove the pan from the heat and skim off any scum using a slotted spoon.

7 Ladle into warmed, sterilized jars and seal. Leave to cool, then label and store for up to 6 months.

Per portion Energy 5229kcal/22,306kJ; Protein 9.3g; Carbohydrate 1382.8g, of which sugars 1382.8g; Fat 0.4g, of which saturates 0g; Cholesterol 0mg; Calcium 799mg; Fibre 8.6g; Sodium 86mg.

Spiced cider jelly

This wonderfully spicy jelly goes well with cheese and crackers, or can simply be spread on to warm toast. It is also good spooned into rice pudding or added to apple pie filling.

Makes about 1.3kg/3lb

900g/2lb tart cooking apples, washed and coarsely chopped, with skins and cores intact

900ml/1¼ pints/3¾ cups sweet cider

juice and pips (seeds) of 2 oranges

1 cinnamon stick

6 whole cloves

150ml/½ pint/⅔ cup water

about 900g/2lb/4½ cups preserving or granulated (white) sugar, warmed

1 Put the apples, cider, juice and pips, cinnamon, cloves and water in a large pan. Bring to the boil, cover and simmer for about 1 hour.

2 Leave to cool slightly, then pour the fruit into a scalded jelly bag suspended over a non-metallic bowl and leave to drain overnight.

3 Measure the strained juice into a preserving pan. Add 450g/1lb/2¼ cups warmed sugar for every 600ml/1 pint/2½ cups juice.

4 Heat, stirring, over a low heat until the sugar has dissolved. Increase the heat and boil, without stirring, for 10 minutes, or until the jelly reaches setting point (105°C/220°F).

5 Remove from the heat and skim off any scum. Ladle into warmed sterilized jars. Leave to cool, then cover, seal and label the jars. Store in a dark cupboard for up to 6 months.

Per portion Energy 3975kcal/16,950kJ; Protein 5.4g; Carbohydrate 990.6g, of which sugars 990.6g; Fat 0.3g, of which saturates 0g; Cholesterol 0mg; Calcium 561mg; Fibre 4.8g; Sodium 123mg.

Pickled spiced red cabbage

This delicately spiced and vibrant-coloured pickle is an old-fashioned favourite to serve with bread and cheese for an informal lunch, or to accompany pies, terrines or cold cuts.

Makes about 1–1.6kg/2¼–3½lb

675g/1½lb/6 cups red cabbage, shredded

1 large Spanish (Bermuda) onion, sliced

30ml/2 tbsp sea salt

600ml/1 pint/2½ cups red wine vinegar

75g/3oz/6 tbsp light muscovado (brown) sugar

15ml/1 tbsp coriander seeds

3 cloves

2.5cm/1in piece fresh root ginger

1 whole star anise

2 bay leaves

4 eating apples

1 Put the cabbage and onion in a bowl, add the salt and mix well until thoroughly combined.

2 Transfer the mixture into a colander over a bowl and leave to drain overnight.

3 The next day, rinse the salted vegetables, drain well and pat dry using kitchen paper. Transfer them to a colander.

4 Pour the vinegar into a pan, add the sugar, spices and bay leaves and boil. Remove from the heat and leave to cool.

5 Core and chop the apples, then layer with the cabbage and onions in sterilized preserving jars. Pour over the cooled spiced vinegar. Seal the jars and store for 1 week before eating. Eat within 2 months. Once opened, store in the refrigerator.

Per portion Energy 674kcal/2868kJ; Protein 12g; Carbohydrate 161.4g, of which sugars 159.3g; Fat 2g, of which saturates 0g; Cholesterol 0mg; Calcium 405mg; Fibre 23g; Sodium 64mg.

Traditional pickled onions

Essential for a ploughman's lunch, pickled onions should be crunchy and pungent, and stored for at least six weeks for the flavours to develop. Try making some for Christmas.

Makes about 4 jars

1kg/2¼lb pickling (pearl) onions

115g/4oz/½ cup salt

750ml/1¼ pints/3 cups malt vinegar

15ml/1 tbsp sugar

2–3 dried red chillies

5ml/1 tsp brown mustard seeds

15ml/1 tbsp coriander seeds

5ml/1 tsp allspice berries

5ml/1 tsp black peppercorns

5cm/2in piece fresh root ginger, sliced

2–3 blades mace

2–3 fresh bay leaves

1 To peel the onions, trim off the root ends, but leave the onion layers attached. Cut a thin slice off the top (neck) end of the onion. Place the onions in a bowl, then cover with boiling water. Leave to stand for about 4 minutes, then drain. The skin should then be easy to peel using a small, sharp knife.

2 Place the peeled onions in a bowl and cover with cold water, then drain the water into a large pan. Add the salt and heat slightly to dissolve it, then cool before pouring the brine over the onions.

3 Place a plate inside the top of the bowl and weigh it down slightly so that it keeps all the onions submerged in the brine. Leave to stand for 24 hours.

4 Meanwhile, place the vinegar in a large pan. Wrap all the remaining ingredients, except the bay leaves, in a piece of muslin (cheesecloth). Bring to the boil, simmer for about 5 minutes, then remove the pan from the heat. Set aside, cover and leave in a cool place overnight to infuse.

5 The next day, drain the onions, rinse and pat dry. Pack them into sterilized 450g/1lb jars. Add some or all of the spice from the vinegar, except the ginger slices. The pickle will become hotter if you add the chillies. Pour the vinegar over to cover and add the bay leaves. (Store leftover vinegar in a bottle for another batch of pickles.)

6 Seal the jars with non-metallic lids and store in a cool, dark place for at least 6 weeks before eating.

Per portion Energy 109kcal/454kJ; Protein 3.1g; Carbohydrate 24.5g, of which sugars 18.6g; Fat 0.5g, of which saturates 0g; Cholesterol 0mg; Calcium 67mg; Fibre 3.6g; Sodium 8mg.

Sweet piccalilli

Undoubtedly one of the most popular relishes, piccalilli can be eaten with grilled sausages, ham, chops or cold meats, or a strong, well-flavoured cheese such as Cheddar. It should contain a good selection of fresh, crunchy vegetables in a smooth mustard sauce.

Makes about 1.8kg/4lb

1 large cauliflower

450g/1lb pickling (pearl) onions

900g/2lb mixed vegetables, such as marrow (large zucchini), cucumber, French (green) beans

225g/8oz/1 cup salt

2.4 litres/4 pints/10 cups cold water

200g/7oz/1 cup granulated (white) sugar

2 garlic cloves, peeled and crushed

10ml/2 tsp mustard powder

5ml/1 tsp ground ginger

1 litre/1¾ pints/4 cups distilled (white) vinegar

25g/1oz/¼ cup plain (all-purpose) flour

15ml/1 tbsp turmeric

Cook's tip Traditional preserving pans are copper, but if you don't have a preserving pan, any stainless steel, shallow and wide-topped pan will be suitable – this will aid evaporation and give a good result.

1 Prepare the vegetables. Divide the cauliflower into small florets; peel and quarter the pickling onions; seed and finely dice the marrow and cucumber; top and tail the French beans, then cut them into 2.5cm/1in lengths.

2 Layer the vegetables in a large glass or stainless steel bowl, generously sprinkling each layer with salt. Pour over the water, cover the bowl with clear film (plastic wrap) and leave to soak for about 24 hours.

3 Drain the soaked vegetables and discard the brine. Rinse well in several changes of cold water to remove as much salt as possible, then drain them thoroughly.

4 Put the sugar, garlic, mustard, ginger and 900ml/1½ pints/3¾ cups of the vinegar in a preserving pan. Heat gently, stirring occasionally, until the sugar has dissolved.

5 Add the vegetables to the pan, bring to the boil, reduce the heat and simmer for 10–15 minutes, or until they are almost tender.

6 Mix the flour and turmeric with the remaining vinegar and stir into the vegetables. Bring to the boil, stirring, and simmer for 5 minutes, until the piccalilli is thick.

7 Spoon the piccalilli into warmed sterilized jars, cover and seal. Store in a cool, dark place for at least 2 weeks. Use within 1 year.

Per portion Energy 1358kcal/5757kJ; Protein 34.1g; Carbohydrate 300.8g, of which sugars 266g; Fat 12g, of which saturates 1.2g; Cholesterol 0mg; Calcium 555mg; Fibre 20.6g; Sodium 4011mg.

Green tomato chutney

This is a classic chutney for using the last tomatoes of summer that just never seem to ripen. Apples and onions contribute essential flavour, which is enhanced by the addition of spice. This zesty chutney is good in sandwiches, for barbecues and with burgers.

Makes about 2.5kg/5½lb

1.8kg/4lb green tomatoes, chopped

450g/1lb cooking apples, peeled, cored and chopped

450g/1lb onions, chopped

2 large garlic cloves, crushed

15ml/1 tbsp salt

45ml/3 tbsp pickling spice

600ml/1 pint/2½ cups cider vinegar

450g/1lb/2¼ cups granulated (white) sugar

1 Place the tomatoes, apples, onions and garlic in a large pan and add the salt.

2 Tie the pickling spice in a piece of muslin (cheesecloth) and add to the ingredients in the pan.

3 Add half the vinegar to the pan and bring to the boil. Reduce the heat, then simmer for 1 hour, or until the chutney is reduced and thick, stirring frequently.

4 Put the sugar and remaining vinegar in a pan and heat gently until the sugar has dissolved, then add to the chutney. Simmer for 1½ hours until thick, stirring the mixture occasionally.

5 Remove the muslin bag from the chutney, then spoon the hot chutney into warmed sterilized jars. Cover and seal immediately. Allow the chutney to mature for at least 1 month before using.

Per portion Energy 2398kcal/10,233kJ; Protein 21.6g; Carbohydrate 601.7g, of which sugars 591.3g; Fat 6.8g, of which saturates 1.8g; Cholesterol 0mg; Calcium 495mg; Fibre 31.5g; Sodium 2177mg.

Plum and cherry relish

This simple sweet-and-sour fruit relish complements rich poultry, game or meat, such as roast duck or grilled duck breasts. You can sieve a few spoonfuls into a sauce or gravy to give fruity zest and flavour, as well as adding an appetizing splash of bright red colour.

1 Halve and pit the plums, then roughly chop the flesh. Pit all the cherries and cut them in half.

2 Cook the shallots gently in the oil for 5 minutes, or until soft. Add the fruit, sherry, vinegars, bay leaf and sugar.

3 Slowly bring the mixture to the boil, stirring until the sugar has dissolved completely. Increase the heat and cook briskly for about 15 minutes, or until the relish is very thick and the fruit tender.

4 Remove the bay leaf and spoon the relish into warmed sterilized jars. Cover and seal. Store the relish in the refrigerator and use within 3 months.

Makes about 350g/12oz

350g/12oz dark-skinned red plums

350g/12oz/2 cups cherries

2 shallots, finely chopped

15ml/1 tbsp olive oil

30ml/2 tbsp dry sherry

60ml/4 tbsp red wine vinegar

15ml/1 tbsp balsamic vinegar

1 bay leaf

90g/3½oz/scant ½ cup demerara (raw) sugar

Cook's tip Use a large preserving pan in which the mixture comes only half-way up the side. Always use just-ripe or slightly under-ripe fruits, as the pectin levels reduce when the fruit ripens. Pectin is essential to achieve a good set.

Per portion Energy 804kcal/3407kJ; Protein 6.5g; Carbohydrate 170.3g, of which sugars 168.9g; Fat 11.8g, of which saturates 1.6g; Cholesterol 0mg; Calcium 156mg; Fibre 9.6g; Sodium 21mg.

Mint sauce

In England, mint sauce is the traditional and inseparable accompaniment to roast lamb. Its fresh tart and astringent flavour is the perfect foil to rich, strongly flavoured lamb. As well as being extremely simple to make, it is infinitely superior to the store-bought varieties.

Makes about 250ml/8fl oz/1cup

1 large bunch mint

105ml/7 tbsp boiling water

150ml/¼ pint/⅔ cup wine vinegar

30ml/2 tbsp granulated (white) sugar

Cook's tip To make a quick and speedy Indian raita for serving with crispy poppadums, simply stir a little mint sauce into a small bowl of natural (plain) yogurt. Serve the raita alongside a bowl of tangy mango chutney.

1 Using a sharp knife, chop the mint very finely and place it in a 600ml/ 1 pint/2½ cup jug (pitcher). Pour the boiling water over the mint and leave to infuse for about 10 minutes.

2 When the mint infusion has cooled and is lukewarm, stir in the wine vinegar and sugar. Continue stirring (but do not mash up the mint leaves) until the sugar has dissolved completely.

3 Pour the mint sauce into a warmed sterilized bottle or jar. Seal the jar, label it with the date and store in the refrigerator or a cool, dark place.

Cook's tip This mint sauce can keep for up to 6 months when stored in the refrigerator, but is best when used within 3 weeks.

Per portion Energy 161kcal/685kJ; Protein 3.9g; Carbohydrate 36.6g, of which sugars 31.3g; Fat 0.7g, of which saturates 0g; Cholesterol 0mg; Calcium 226mg; Fibre 0g; Sodium 17mg.

Real horseradish sauce

Fiery, peppery horseradish sauce is without doubt the essential accompaniment to roast beef, and is also delicious served with smoked salmon. Horseradish, like chilli, is a powerful ingredient, so take care when handling it, and always wash your hands afterwards.

Makes about 200ml/7fl oz/scant 1 cup

45ml/3 tbsp freshly grated horseradish root

15ml/1 tbsp white wine vinegar

5ml/1 tsp granulated (white) sugar

pinch of salt

150ml/¼ pint/⅔ cup thick double (heavy) cream, for serving

Cook's tip To counteract the potent fumes of the horseradish, keep the root submerged in water while you chop and peel it. Use a food processor to do the fine chopping or grating, and avert your head when removing the lid.

1 Place the grated horseradish in a bowl, then add the white wine vinegar, granulated sugar and just a pinch of salt.

2 Stir the ingredients together, mixing them well until they are thoroughly combined and smooth.

3 Pour the mixture into a sterilized jar. It will keep in the refrigerator for up to 6 months.

4 A few hours before you intend to serve the sauce, stir the cream into the horseradish and leave to infuse. Stir once again before serving.

Per portion Energy 774kcal/3190kJ; Protein 2.8g; Carbohydrate 9.9g, of which sugars 9.8g; Fat 80.7g, of which saturates 50.1g; Cholesterol 206mg; Calcium 98mg; Fibre 1.1g; Sodium 40mg.

Moutarde aux fines herbes

This fragrant, hot mustard may be used either as a delicious condiment or for coating meats such as chicken and pork, or oily fish such as mackerel, before cooking. It is also fabulous when smeared thinly on cheese on toast, for an added bite.

Makes about 300ml/½ pint/1¼ cups

75g/3oz/scant ½ cup white mustard seeds

50g/2oz/¼ cup soft light brown sugar

5ml/1 tsp salt

5ml/1 tsp whole peppercorns

2.5ml/½ tsp ground turmeric

200ml/7fl oz/scant 1 cup distilled malt vinegar

60ml/4 tbsp chopped fresh mixed herbs, such as parsley, sage, thyme and rosemary

1 Put the mustard seeds, sugar, salt, whole peppercorns and ground turmeric into a food processor or blender and process for about 1 minute, or until the peppercorns are coarsely chopped.

2 Gradually add the vinegar to the mustard mixture, 15ml/1 tbsp at a time, processing well between each addition, then continue processing until a coarse paste forms.

3 Add the chopped fresh herbs to the mustard and mix well, then leave to stand for 10–15 minutes until the mustard thickens slightly.

4 Spoon the mustard into a 300ml/½ pint/1¼ cup sterilized jar. Cover the surface of the mustard with a baking parchment disc, then seal with a screw-top lid or a cork, and label. Store in a cool, dark place for up to 3 months.

Per portion Energy 553kcal/2324kJ; Protein 23.4g; Carbohydrate 69.1g, of which sugars 53.4g; Fat 34.5g, of which saturates 1.1g; Cholesterol 3mg; Calcium 374mg; Fibre 2.5g; Sodium 23mg.

Honey mustard

Delicious home-made mustards mature to make the most aromatic of condiments. This honey mustard is richly flavoured and is wonderful served with meats and cheeses, or stirred into sauces and salad dressings to give an extra peppery bite. The addition of honey gives a sweet counterbalance to the hot mustard seeds.

Makes about 500g/1¼b

225g/8oz/1 cup mustard seeds

15ml/1 tbsp ground cinnamon

2.5ml/½ tsp ground ginger

300ml/½ pint/1½ cups white wine vinegar

90ml/6 tbsp dark clear honey

Cook's tip Use well-flavoured clear honey for this recipe. Set (crystallized) honey does not have the right consistency and will not work well.

1 Put the mustard seeds in a bowl with the cinnamon and ginger, and pour over the white wine vinegar. Stir well to mix, then cover and leave to soak overnight in a cool place.

2 The next day, put the mustard mixture in a mortar and pound with a pestle, adding the honey very gradually.

3 Continue pounding and mixing until the mustard resembles a stiff paste. If the mixture becomes too stiff, add a little extra vinegar to achieve the desired consistency.

4 Spoon the mustard into four warmed sterilized jars. Seal and label the jars, then store in a cool, dark place or in the refrigerator. Keep refrigerated after opening, and use within 4 weeks.

Per portion Energy 1276kcal/5345kJ; Protein 65.4g; Carbohydrate 115.3g, of which sugars 68.8g; Fat 101.5g, of which saturates 3.4g; Cholesterol 9mg; Calcium 747mg; Fibre 0g; Sodium 21mg.

Index

Figures in *italics* indicate captions.

Picture acknowledgements

t=top, b=bottom, l=left, r=right
iStockphoto: 11t, 27b, 28t, 29tl, 29tr, 32bl.